CW00644370

Windows® CE Programming: Developing Applications for the Handheld PC

Jeff Baker

MACMILLAN
TECHNICAL
PUBLISHING
U·S·A

Macmillan Technical Publishing, Indianapolis, Indiana

Windows® CE Programming: Developing Applications for the Handheld PC

By Jeff Baker

Published by:
Macmillan Technical Publishing
201 West 103rd Street
Indianapolis, IN 46290 USA

All rights reserved. No part of this book may be reproduced or transmitted in any form or by any means, electronic or mechanical, including photocopying, recording, or by any information storage and retrieval system, without written permission from the publisher, except for the inclusion of brief quotations in a review.

Copyright© 1997 by Macmillan Technical Publishing

Printed in the United States of America 1 2 3 4 5 6 7 8 9 0

Library of Congress Cataloging-in-Publication Number 96-79358

ISBN: 1-57870-005-1

Warning and Disclaimer

This book is designed to provide information about Windows CE programming. Every effort has been made to make this book as complete and as accurate as possible, but no warranty or fitness is implied.

The information is provided on an "as is" basis. The author and Macmillan Technical Publishing shall have neither liability nor responsibility to any person or entity with respect to any loss or damages arising from the information contained in this book or from the use of the discs or programs that may accompany it.

Editor-In-Chief *Jim LeValley*

Marketing Manager *Kourtnaye Sturgeon*

Managing Editor *Sarah Kearns*

Director of Development *Kezia Endsley*

Acquisitions Coordinator
Amy Lewis

Senior Editor
Suzanne Snyder

Development Editor
Brad M. Miser

Project Editors
Noelle Gasco
Matt Litten
Brian Sweany

Copy Editors
Wendy Garrison
Krista Hansing

Software Product Specialist
Steve Flatt

Assistant Marketing Manager
Gretchen Schlesinger

Editorial Assistant
Karen Opal

Manufacturing Coordinator
Brook Farling

Cover Designer
Nathan Clement

Cover Production
Nathan Clement

Book Designer
Glenn Larsen

Director of Production
Larry Klein

Production Team Supervisor
Beth Lewis

Graphics Image Specialists
Steve Adams
Sadie Crawford
Will Cruz

Production Analysts
Erich J. Richter
Dan Harris

Production Team
Jenny Earhart
Laura A. Knox
Heather Stephenson
Donna Wright

Indexer
Kevin Fulcher

About the Author

Jeff Baker received his Bachelors of Science degree in Computer Science from Indiana University. Jeff is a Lead Software Engineer for Software Artistry, a leading developer of help desk software. He is currently working on a multi-platform graphical user interface class library. Jeff has previously worked on one of the largest distributed computing applications in commercial use, as well as one of the leading document managment applications. Jeff lives with his wife, Melanie, in Indianapolis, Indiana.

Trademark Acknowledgments

All terms mentioned in this book that are known to be trademarks or service marks have been appropriately capitalized. Macmillan Technical Publishing cannot attest to the accuracy of this information. Use of a term in this book should not be regarded as affecting the validity of any trademark or service mark.

Dedication

For Anita, and for Monica and Elizabeth, with love.

Acknowledgments

First, I would like to thank all the folks at Macmillan Technical Publishing, especially Jim LeValley and Amy Lewis, for their assistance, guidance, and patience in this project.

I would also like to thank Carl who got me started in this project in the first place.

And thanks to Bryan at Software Artistry for understanding the impact this project has had on my "day job."

To all my family and friends who urged me on by the repeated, "Is the book done yet?"—I'm glad I can finally say "yes."

Finally, I can't forget to thank the most important person on this project, my wife Melanie. She kept me going, prodded me on, and generally put up with all late nights and lonely weekends that I spent in front of the computer. It looks like my eight-month project will finish just slightly ahead of her nine-month project.

I wish to express my heartfelt gratitude to my friends and mentors at PSW Technologies, whose inspiration, support, and patience made this book possible. Especially Brian Baisley, for his friendship and loyalty, and Frank King, for his remarkable perspicacity and that mysterious cachet.

Thanks also to Wayne Mock and Venki Iyer for their important contributions and deep thoughts. Thanks to Chris Brown and Douglas Miller of Softway, Mark Knecht of Datafocus, and Sayan Chakraborty of Cygnus Support, each for their kind support and encouragement.

Much of the software on the CD is the product of the Free Software Foundation. Over many years, thousands of programmers around the world have made these programs widely portable and robust. Many widely used commercial and free software applications would not exist without them—more perhaps than many of us realize. We wish to thank all of these programmers for all of their efforts, especially Richard Stallman, founder of the Free Software Foundation for his vision and encouragement to make our humble contributions free software.

Thanks to Tom Dickey for his kind permission to redistribute c_count. Thanks also to the intrepid programmers who blazed trails before us, porting Unix applications to Windows NT, especially Jerry Frain, Geoff Voelker, Bram Moolenaar, and the many contributors to the gnu-win32 project hosted by Cygnus.

I am also indebted to my friends and colleagues over the years whose invaluable and sometimes unintentional contributions are all over this book, especially Scott Guthrie, Ed Dolph, and Larry Leblanc.

And finally thanks to my Mom and Dad, with love and respect.

—Jeff Baker

June 10, 1997

Contents at a Glance

Table of Contents

1

Introduction to Windows CE

I n the fall of 1996, Microsoft introduced the newest member of the Windows family of operating systems: Windows CE. Windows CE is a small, 32-bit, platform-independent operating system positioned for a wide range of hardware applications.

The initial focus of the Windows CE operating system is on a new set of devices for the hand-held computer market. Microsoft has given the new category of computers the name Handheld PC. This new terminology reflects the desire by Microsoft and its partners to set the Handheld PC apart from the current generation of Personal Digital Assistant (PDA) devices or personal organizers.

A Handheld PC running Windows CE is designed to be a mobile companion to the desktop PC (running Microsoft Windows 95, of course). Windows CE provides users with a familiar interface, and supports many forms of data synchronization between the Handheld PC and the desktop PC.

So what does the CE stand for? Compact Edition? Consumer Electronics? Committee Endorsed? Can't Explain? Well, officially, it doesn't stand for anything, just like NT doesn't (currently) stand for anything. Apparently, many suffixes were considered and CE won out. Microsoft officials say that the CE suffix is a lot like the LX or ES that is used with many automobile models in that it doesn't really stand for anything although it sounds like it should.

Windows CE History

Although branded a 1.0 release, Microsoft has been working to develop hand-held computing technology for at least five years. The WinPad and Pulsar projects were the ancestors of Windows CE, but those projects never made it to market.

WinPad

In 1992, Microsoft began work on a stripped-down version of Windows 3.1 that would be used to produce a Windows-based handheld computer. Like Apple's Newton, WinPad did not have a keyboard, but did employ handwriting recognition technology as its means of input.

WinPad was intended to be a mobile companion to the desktop PC. WinPad could be connected to the desktop PC through a serial connection. Once connected, data would be automatically synchronized between the WinPad device and the desktop PC. Applications for Win-Pad were written in Visual Basic.

Many factors influenced the ultimate demise of the WinPad project. The estimated consumer price of building a WinPad device was around $900, probably more than buyers would be willing to pay. The Apple Newton had failed to live up to its hype and consequently negatively affected the entire PDA market. Finally, the handwriting recognition technology of the time was slow and error-prone, making data entry difficult.

Pulsar

In the fall of 1993, another project, named Pulsar, was started by the Advanced Technology group at Microsoft. The goal of the Pulsar project was to create a new "super-pager" that allowed individuals to communicate with each other and with services over two-way wireless networks.

Pulsar was positioned as a consumer device, not a desktop companion tool like WinPad. Aimed primarily at noncomputer users, Pulsar used a "social-interface" like General Magic's Magic Cap, or the more recent Microsoft Bob.

The Pulsar device was roughly the size of a large pager and therefore (obviously) contained no keyboard. Input to the device was done through an on-screen keyboard. Programming on the Pulsar device was also largely done with Visual Basic.

Early consumer testing of the Pulsar revealed that the small size of the device and lack of a keyboard were serious drawbacks. In addition, most people felt that this was not a device they needed or would be willing to pay a monthly fee to use.

Pegasus

In late 1994, Microsoft decided to combine the two handheld device efforts into one group, under the code name, Pegasus. Like the WinPad project, the overall goal was to create a mobile device that would be a companion to the desktop PC (running a Windows operating system).

Other goals of the Pegasus project included to deliver a device with a price-point near $500, create a platform suitable for communication, and to provide an open development environment for building Pegasus applications. Overall, the goal was to create a useful PC companion tool, not a super-PDA.

None of the WinPad code was carried over into the Pegasus project. The Pulsar team, however, had developed a lightweight Win32-subset kernel that evolved into the Windows CE operating system.

The Pegasus project continued through 1995, eventually adopting the Windows 95 interface and becoming Windows CE. By early 1996, hardware developers became partners on the project and were creating prototype devices. A beta program was also launched so developers could start building applications for this new operating system.

At Comdex in the fall of 1996, Microsoft officially announced the Pegasus project, now christened "Windows CE." A few manufacturers released their Handheld PCs at that time while other Handheld PCs were not released until the spring and early summer of 1997. At the time of this writing, seven manufacturers produce Handheld PCs. Chapter 3, "Handheld PC Hardware," lists information on each of the devices.

Future of Windows CE

Not only has Windows CE surpassed its WinPad and Pulsar ancestors by actually making it to market, it also appears to have a bright future.

There are currently over 3,000 independent software vendors building applications for Windows CE. The applications range from PIM applications that perform simple tasks such as managing a grocery list, to complex applications for retail sales clerks and healthcare professionals. Many new companies have been created to focus on Windows CE and the new markets that have emerged around it.

At the time of this writing, Microsoft is well underway with the next major version of the Windows CE operating system. Windows CE 2.0 is scheduled to include new platform support, new technology support (ActiveX and Java), LAN connectivity, and color display support.

In addition to adding features to the operating system, Windows CE will likely be used in other types of devices. The devices might include something simple such as a phone or pager, or something complex such as an onboard navigation and control system in an automobile. The current generation of Handheld PCs could also be adapted to larger devices (bigger keyboards and color screens), or smaller devices such as a wallet-sized device.

Windows CE is designed to be suitable for many different systems. Anything with a display interface is a likely target: cash register, gasoline pump, ATM, and so on. The possibilities are nearly endless—although it will likely be quite some time before Windows CE is controlling your toaster...

Windows CE References

There is a lot of information currently available about Windows CE, and the volume of that information is certainly going to increase. There are many great Web sites devoted to Windows CE, as well as newsgroups, mailing lists, books, and magazines.

Handheld PC Manufacturers

Currently there are seven manufacturers with Windows CE-based Handheld PCs. All of the manufacturers have web sites, which are listed in the following table.

Site Name	URL
Casio Cassiopeia	http://www.casiohpc.com
Compaq PC Companion	http://www.compaq.com/us/ common/prodinfo/handhelds
Hewlett-Packard 300LX, 320LX	http://www.hp.com/handheld
Hitachi Handheld PC	http://www.hitachi.com
LG Handheld PC	http://www.lgeus.com/hpc
NEC MobilePro	http://www.nec.com
Philips Velo 1	http://www.velo1.com

Microsoft Windows CE Site

As the developer of Windows CE, Microsoft maintains a Web site full of information, upgrades, and software. The site can be found at `http://www.microsoft.com/windowsce`. One area of this site, which is devoted to developers, contains information relevant to developing applications for Windows CE. A direct link to the developer section is `http://www.microsoft.com/windowsce/developer`.

Other WWW Sites

There are many great Web sites that contain Windows CE and Hand-held PC information. Unfortunately, great sites today could be average or even gone tomorrow. The following table lists some of the best Web sites at the time of this writing.

Site Name	URL
HPC.net	http://www.windowsce.com
Craig Peacock's WinCE Page	http://homepages. enterprise.net/craig/ windowsce.html
HotPocket PDA	http://hotpocket.com
HPCPage	http://www.hpcpage.com
Worldwide Windows CE	http://www.ziplink.net/ ~maxm/windowsce/index.html
Chris DeHerrera's Windows CE Website	http://members.aol.com/ pcdchrisd/wce/wce.htm
Windows CE Hardware Compatibility List	http://www.microsoft.com/ isapi/hwtest/hsearchce.idc
Windows CE On-Line	http://www.arcos.org/worlds/

Newsgroups

Newsgroups, or Usenet newsgroups, are electronic bulletin boards where people can share information. Access to a news server is required to read information from or post questions to a newsgroup.

Microsoft provides a news server (msnews.microsoft.com) that has multiple newsgroups relevant to Windows CE. The microsoft.public.windowsce newsgroup contains general Windows CE information, microsoft.vc.vcce covers Visual C++ for Windows CE, and `microsoft.programmer.win32.wince` offers information on programming with Windows CE.

Currently, no Usenet newsgroups are dedicated to Windows CE, although occasionally some contain content on Windows CE. The `comp.sys.palmtops` and `comp.sys.handhelds` newsgroups cover a broad range of devices that include Windows CE.

FAQs

FAQs, or Frequently Asked Questions, have become a common source of information with the popularity of the Internet. A FAQ for a particular subject or product can be created and maintained by the official source of that product, or by someone interested in spreading information about that technology. The following table lists some of the FAQ lists that have recently appeared for Windows CE.

Site Name	URL
Microsoft Windows CE FAQ	http://www.microsoft.com/ windowsce/hpc/home/faq.htm
Craig Peacock's Windows CE FAQ	http://homepages. enterprise.net/craig/hpc/ cefaq.html
Chris DeHerrera's Windows CE FAQ	http://members.aol.com/ pdcchrisd/wce/wcefaq.htm

Mailing Lists

Mailing lists are similar to newsgroups, except that when you post a message, it is sent as an e-mail message to everyone on the mailing list. Currently, two mailing lists cover Windows CE. Use the `http://www.dillernet.com/wince.html` Web site to join Andy Diller's Windows CE mailing list and `http://cgi.skyweyr.comwindowscetalk.home` to subscribe to WindowsCE.com's Windows CE Talk mailing list.

Magazines

Although nearly every magazine that covers the Windows operating system has done articles on Windows CE, some magazines cover Windows CE regularly. The following table lists the current magazines (print and electronic) that cover Windows CE along with their Web sites.

Magazine	URL
Mobile Worker Magazine	http://www.microsoft.com/windowsce/hpc/mobile
Mobilis Magazine	http://www.volksware.com/mobilis
Handheld PC Magazine	http://www.thaddeus.com/wince/hpc.htm
Handheld Systems Journal	http://www.cdpubs.com/hhsj.html
Pen Computing Magazine	http://www.pencomputing.com
Mobile Computing	http://www.mobilecomputing.com
PMN Publications	http://www.pmn.co.uk

About This Book

The purpose of this book is to provide as much information as possible about developing applications for the Windows CE operating system. The intent is to cover the entire process of developing an application for Windows CE, from installing the Windows CE SDK, to writing and testing the application, to building the install program and providing help files.

The audience for this book is anyone who is interested in creating applications for Windows CE and Handheld PCs. Although Chapter 5,

"Hello Windows CE," describes some of the very basic fundamentals of Windows (and Windows CE) programming, this book is not an introduction to Windows programming. Instead, this book focuses on the issues and details specific or unique to programming for Windows CE. Therefore, a familiarity with Windows programming is assumed.

One item that will greatly benefit both beginning and advanced Windows CE programmers is the sample code provided in each chapter. While reference listings and textual information can describe a feature or function, sample code demonstrates its practical application and use. The book also has an accompanying CD-ROM that contains the code samples that are discussed and listed in every chapter, which you can use or adapt for your own Windows CE applications.

This book takes a somewhat unique approach in that most of the example code developed throughout the book is used to build a real application. Rather than create disparate examples for different programming elements, the goal of the book is to build a "real application"; you will likely use a similar method to create your own applications later. As new elements or aspects to programming Windows CE are covered, they are added to the example application.

The application created in this book is called TravelManager. The TravelManager application is a PIM type application that can be used to manage information during a trip, such as airline flights, hotel and automobile reservations, expenses, and notes related to the trip. The main window for the TravelManager application is shown in Figure 1.1.

Figure 1.1

TravelManager's main window.

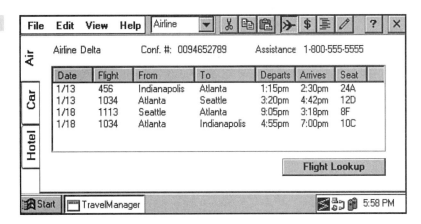

The TravelManager application is started in Chapter 5, "Hello Windows CE," and is enhanced through each subsequent chapter. The CD-ROM contains directories for each chapter and also includes the TravelManager application with the features added in that chapter. Another directory on the CD-ROM contains the completed TravelManager application. The disc install page (Appendix A, "Getting Started with the CD-ROM") at the end of this book details the contents of the CD-ROM and provides directions for accessing the samples.

This book is organized in chapters that represent different functional areas of Windows CE programming. The chapters do not necessarily have to be read in order, however, some chapters build upon information from previous chapters. The following list provides an overview of the areas covered in the ensuing chapters of this book:

- Chapter 2, "Windows CE Operating System," identifies the components of the Windows CE operating system and discusses the differences between Windows CE and other versions of Windows.

- Chapter 3, "Handheld PC Hardware," details the specific hardware components that make up the Handheld PC and describes the specifications and features of each of the current Handheld PC models.

- Chapter 4, "Visual C++ for Windows CE," covers each of the components and tools used in building Windows CE applications.

- Chapter 5, "Hello Windows CE," implements a simple Windows CE application in both C and C++ and describes the main components in nearly all Windows CE applications.

- Chapter 6, "User Interface Basics," explores the basic elements of user interfaces in Windows CE applications, including command bars.

- Chapter 7, "Controls," defines the common controls supported in Windows CE that give a Windows CE application the same look and feel as a Windows 95 application.

- Chapter 8, "Input and Output," explores input and output mechanisms for interacting with the user, including keyboard, stylus, timers, graphics, and notifications.

- Chapter 9, "Registry and File System," details the registry and file system support in Windows CE and the differences of those same components in other versions of Windows.

- Chapter 10, "Windows CE Databases," describes the database functionality that is built into Windows CE and that can be utilized in Windows CE applications.

- Chapter 11, "Windows CE Help Files," details the new help engine present in Windows CE.

- Chapter 12, "Windows CE Application Loader," describes the process of installing a Windows CE application onto the Handheld PC device.

- Chapter 13, "File Filters," examines the construction and operation of file filters, which allow data files to be converted when transferred from the desktop PC to the Handheld PC or vice versa.

- Chapter 14, "Remote API Functions," describes the functions available to a Windows 95 application on the desktop PC that can directly manipulate data on a connected Handheld PC.

- Appendix A, "Getting Started with the CD-ROM," details how to access the sample source code and executable files contained on the CD-ROM.

CHAPTER 2

Windows CE Operating System

Windows CE is a fully 32-bit, super lightweight, multitasking, multithreaded, platform-independent, new operating system from Microsoft that is intended to become the operating system for a variety of computing devices.

Visually, Windows CE looks very much like Windows 95. This will appeal to users who are familiar with the Windows 95 interface because their knowledge of Windows 95 will be directly transferable to the Windows CE operating system. Likewise, developers who have experience programming for Windows 95 will easily be able to apply that experience to create Windows CE applications.

Programmatically, Windows CE is also very much like Windows 95. In other words, developers who are familiar with the Windows programming model and Win32 API will be very comfortable with the Windows CE API, which is essentially a subset of the Win32 API. Although many API function groups are absent from the Windows CE API, it adds a few API groups that are unique to Windows CE.

The architectural structure of Windows CE, on the other hand, differs from that in Windows 95. Like any operating system, Windows CE has the major components such as memory management, file system, graphical display, and so on. On the other hand, because Windows CE is constrained by the hardware on which it is designed to run, many of these standard components differ from those in other versions of Windows.

The first section of this chapter details the specific components in the Windows CE operating system. Later chapters cover specific programming examples in much greater detail.

The second section of this chapter explores porting existing Windows applications to Windows CE. Specifically, it presents the major list of changes between the Windows CE API and the Win32 API.

Windows CE Components

Windows CE can be broken down into many different components, including the kernel and user interface. This section details the major components of Windows CE.

Note that the descriptions presented here relate to Windows CE as used on Handheld PCs (currently the only available devices that use Windows CE).

The major functions of Windows CE are separated into components so that device manufacturers can essentially pick and choose the parts that they need for their particular device that may or may not be an HPC (obviously, it is not quite that simple). Future devices using Windows CE, for instance, may have substantially different interfaces than the interface used on Handheld PCs.

Shell

When you first turn on the Handheld PC, Windows CE starts, displaying the Windows CE desktop. The desktop looks almost identical to a shrunken version of the Windows 95 or Windows NT 4.0 desktop, as shown in Figure 2.1.

The shell contains the familiar Start button in the lower-left corner. The Windows CE Start button offers the same functionality as it does under Windows 95. Clicking the Start button displays a menu of options for accessing help, running a program, exploring the file system, launching the Control Panel, and shutting down the device.

Figure 2.1

The Windows CE desktop.

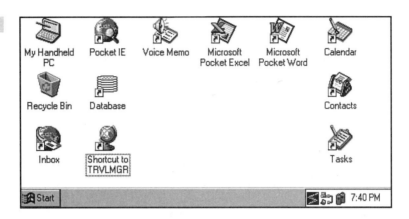

There is a difference, however, in the presentation of the options under the Start menu. Because Windows CE does not support cascading menus, menu options that would normally lead to a submenu containing more choices now open another window to display the next level of choices. Choosing the Programs menu option, for instance, opens an Explorer window that displays the contents of the Programs folder.

The Start button is part of the taskbar that is displayed across the bottom of the screen. As with Windows 95 and Windows NT, the taskbar is always visible. The taskbar displays a "button" for each of the currently running applications. Clicking a button brings the corresponding application to the front, just like it does in Windows 95. A new feature in the Windows CE taskbar is the ability to minimize the currently active window by clicking its corresponding button on the taskbar.

The right side of the taskbar displays a clock and an area for notification icons. The small icons display status information (such as if your device is using A/C power or if the batteries are low) or notify the user of various events (such as if you are connected to a desktop PC or you set the alarm). Applications can add icons to this area as needed.

The remainder of the desktop above the taskbar is an area for shortcuts to applications or folders as well as special icons for the Recycle Bin and My Handheld PC. The My Handheld PC icon launches the Windows CE Explorer, which you use to navigate files and folders on the Handheld PC.

Control Panel

Like in Windows 95, you adjust settings for Windows CE using applets found in the Control Panel folder. To access the Control Panel, choose the Settings menu option on the Start menu.

The following applets are standard in Windows CE:

- **Backlight**. Changes screen backlighting options (only present on devices with backlighting).

- **Communications**. Changes device name and dial-out settings.

- **Display**. Changes background wallpaper and contrast settings.

- **Keyboard**. Changes delay and repeat rates.

- **Owner**. Changes owner profile.

- **Password**. Changes owner password and security settings.

- **Power**. Changes power management options.

- **Remove Programs**. Uninstalls programs from the device.

- **Stylus**. Calibrates touch screen and sets double tap rate.

- **System**. Changes memory settings and displays system information.

- **Volume and Sounds**. Changes volume and event sounds.

- **World Clock**. Changes date, time, and alarm options.

Windows CE also supports the ability to create user-defined Control Panel applets. Applications can install their own Control Panel applets (with the .cpl extension) in the \Windows directory.

The Control Panel applet has the same structure under Windows CE as it does under Windows 95. The Control Panel and the applet communicate through messages sent to the CPlApplet function of the applet. Windows CE uses the same messages as Windows 95, except for CPL_SELECT.

Although the Control Panel applet has the same structure under Windows CE and Windows 95, an applet compiled for Windows 95 will not directly run under Windows CE.

Applications

Windows CE includes many applications that make the Handheld PC very functional right out of the box. The standard Windows CE applications include the following:

- **Microsoft Pocket Word**. A subset of the Microsoft Word word processor application.

- **Microsoft Pocket Excel**. A subset of the Microsoft Excel spreadsheet application.

- **Pocket Internet Explorer**. Windows CE's Web browser.

- **Inbox**. An application for sending and receiving e-mail.

- **Calendar**. A scheduler for managing appointments and events.

- **Contacts**. An electronic address book.

- **Tasks**. Electronic "to-do" lists.

- **Calculator**. A simple on-screen calculator.

- **Terminal**. A simple terminal emulation program.

- **World Clock**. Displays date and time for multiple cities.

- **Solitaire**. Windows' standard game.

Kernel

The fact that Windows CE is small and lightweight definitely does not equate to it being a less powerful operating system. The Windows CE kernel, which was rewritten specifically for non-PC devices, implements the Win32 process, thread, and virtual memory model. The system is limited to 32 processes, but the total number of threads is limited only by available memory.

Windows CE supports multitasking by implementing the multithreaded Win32 programming model. Windows CE can manage multiple processes, where each process might contain more than one thread of execution.

Like Windows NT, Windows CE employs a preemptive, priority-based scheduler. Each thread is assigned a priority and CPU time is allocated based on the assigned priorities.

Windows CE has seven priority levels, which are grouped into three classifications. The priority levels of Time Critical and Highest are for Interrupt-class threads. Interrupt-class priorities are normally reserved for operating system routines. The Above Normal, Normal, Below Normal, and Lowest priorities are given to Main-class threads, which encompasses most applications. The Idle priority is used with Idle-class threads and will only run after all other threads have finished.

The Windows CE kernel also supports a variety of synchronization primitives. The initial version of Windows CE supports the Critical Section and Event synchronization objects.

The kernel is also responsible for the allocation and management of memory under Windows CE. Information regarding the memory architecture under Windows CE is presented later in this chapter.

Graphics, Windowing, and Events Subsystem

The functionality present in the Win32 User and GDI libraries has been combined in Windows CE. The Graphics, Windowing, and Events Subsystem (GWES) libraries contain most of the user interface functionality for Windows CE.

Although the Windows CE desktop looks nearly identical to the Windows 95 desktop, the underlying user interface functionality has many limitations.

Most user interface limitations are due to the limited memory and small displays available in the current set of Windows CE Handheld PCs.

GDI

The Graphics Device Interface (GDI) functionality in Windows CE is a subset of the full Win32 GDI functionality. Many GDI functions, such as color support, are not applicable to the type of display devices currently used. Other functions place too much of a burden on limited system resources. Still others are not needed due to redundancy—the same functionality can be achieved using another function or functions.

The following is a list of many limitations of the Windows CE GDI:

- Printing and printer device contexts are not supported.
- TrueType fonts are not supported.
- Metafiles are not supported.
- MM_TEXT is the only mapping mode supported.
- Color and custom palettes are not supported.
- Coordinate space transformation functions are not supported.
- Only limited support exists for bit block transfers.
- The concept of a current point is not supported, so there is only limited line-drawing support.
- Hatch brushes are not supported.
- Geometric pens are not supported.
- Filling a region is not supported.
- Chords and Pies are not supported.

Windowing

As mentioned previously, Windows CE 1.0 does not support cascading menus. If there is a need for a second level of menus, an application must instead create another window to display the next level of options.

Windows CE does not support the creation of owned or topmost windows, except for dialog boxes. Due to the severely limited screen real-estate, it is not feasible to work with multiple overlapped windows. Thus, Multiple Document Interface (MDI) is not supported.

Windows cannot be resized by the user, so most application windows should always be full-screen. It is possible to create nonmaximized windows, like the Help application or one mode of the Windows CE Calculator, but it is not common.

Another difference in Windows CE due to the limited screen size is that windows do not have a nonclient area. Thus, windows do not have title bars, menu bars, or toolbars.

Windows CE defines a new control, called a CommandBar, which takes the place of an application's menu bars and toolbars. Applications can easily add menus, toolbar buttons, and combo boxes to the Command-Bar. The CommandBar can also display system buttons for accessing help and closing a window. Figure 2.2 shows an application with a CommandBar.

Figure 2.2

An application with a CommandBar.

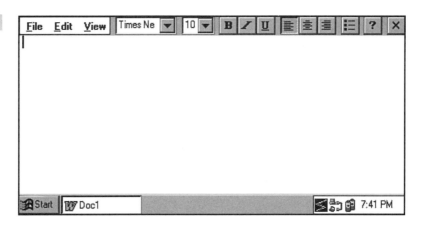

Another beneficial feature is that Windows CE supports nearly all Win32 common controls.

Common controls that Windows CE does not support include simple combo boxes, owner-draw buttons, static frames, and wizards.

In addition, Windows CE supports two common dialog boxes: File Open and File Save As.

Because a Handheld PC does not have a mouse, Windows CE does not have cursor support. Support exists for a special wait cursor, which an application can display to indicate it is busy, but there are no other available cursors.

Events

The event model in Windows CE is identical to that in Windows 95. Windows CE is event-driven and uses the MSG message structure to pass information. One limitation in Windows CE is that hooking messages are not supported.

Memory Architecture

An area in Windows CE that is very different from its Windows 95 and Windows NT siblings is memory architecture. Windows CE's physical memory is comprised of both ROM and RAM.

The ROM contains most of the Windows CE operating system and standard applications. When running an application found in ROM, the Windows CE kernel is able to reference the code directly in ROM without having to load the code into RAM first. This execute-in-place allows for faster execution and reduces system overhead placed on the RAM.

The RAM, which is divided into two sections, is used for the storage of information (data, programs, and so on) and runtime memory. The section used for the storage of data and programs is called the object store (see the "Object Store" section of this chapter for more information). The other section is for system storage. You can configure the amount of RAM allocated to each section, but the default is 1 MB per section (on a device with 2 MB of RAM).

The system storage section of the RAM is the runtime memory used by applications and the operating system. Memory is allocated from the system storage section for heaps, stacks, global and static variables, application code, and so on.

Windows CE initializes the system storage into a single 4 GB virtual address space that is shared by all processes. The kernel then maps these addresses onto physical memory.

The address space is divided into thirty-three 32 MB "slots." If an application attempts to read from or write to any address above these slots, an access violation occurs. Each process is assigned its own slot, with slot zero (the lowermost 32 MB) reserved for the currently running process.

A Handheld PC is a low memory device, so RAM is always at a premium. When Windows CE detects a low-memory condition, the system "filters" the request by limiting the amount actually allocated. This prevents a single application from using one large allocation, thereby stealing all available memory. It is very important, therefore, to verify the success of memory allocations in Windows CE applications.

In addition to limiting the amount of memory that an application can have, Windows CE can also request memory back from previous allocations. The system sends a WM_HIBERNATE message to each application asking the application to free any memory possible.

Object Store

The *object store* on a Windows CE device is analogous to the hard drive on a desktop PC. The object store consists of three distinct components: the file system, the registry, and databases. The operating system automatically compresses all data in the object store at a compression ratio of about 2 to 1.

Windows CE File System

The Windows CE file system is manipulated by the common Win32 file functions. The directory structure of the Windows CE file system is similar to Windows 95, except that in Windows CE, drive letters are not used because the RAM is considered to be a single volume.

All of the files from the ROM chip appear in the \Windows directory, but you can also put user (RAM) files in the \Windows directory. A user file in \Windows hides any ROM file of the same name.

The Windows CE file system does not support the concept of a working directory. The \Windows directory is the only location Windows CE checks when loading DLLs, so applications should install their DLLs in the \Windows directory.

See Chapter 9, "Registry and File System," for more information on the Windows CE File System.

Windows CE Registry

The Windows CE system registry is nearly identical to the Windows 95 registry. Windows CE supports the Win32 registry functions for accessing the registry.

See Chapter 9 for more information on the Windows CE Registry.

Windows CE Databases

Built-in database support is a unique function of Windows CE. Windows CE databases consist of any number of records, each containing one or more properties. Windows CE adds a rich set of API functions for manipulating Windows CE databases.

See Chapter 10, "Windows CE Databases," for more information on Windows CE Databases.

Power Management

Most Windows CE devices will be battery operated and have a very limited energy supply. (The current generation of Handheld PCs runs on two AA batteries, for instance.) Windows CE constantly monitors the state of the system to determine how best to conserve power.

One technique Windows CE uses to conserve power is to shut off the processor whenever possible, even when the device is on. When all threads are waiting for events and the user is not typing, the processor can be powered down.

When the device is turned off, all hardware devices—including the processor, the display, the keyboard decoder, and attached PCMCIA cards—are powered down.

In the off state, however, Windows CE still uses some power to maintain its clock and the applications and persistent data stored in RAM.

Applications are not notified before the power is shut off. However, device drivers are notified when the system is being suspended and have the capability to stop the power from being shut off (if they are receiving data, for instance).

Notifications

Notifications are the mechanism Windows CE uses to communicate with the user and Windows CE-based applications. A *notification* is a signal from the operating system that an event has occurred. Windows CE includes a new set of API functions to work with notifications. An application registers a notification for an event, and Windows CE generates a notification when the event occurs.

Windows CE supports two types of notifications: user and application. A user notification alerts the user about a timed event, such as an appointment. Based on user preferences, the system notifies the user by flashing an external LED, displaying a dialog box, or playing a sound. An application notification alerts an application of system events, such as AC power state, PCMCIA card insertion, and communication connections.

See Chapter 8, "Input and Output," for more information on Windows CE Notifications.

Communications

As a remote device, communication is an important issue with Handheld PCs. Windows CE supports a variety of communication protocols for communicating with other devices.

Windows CE supported communication application programming interfaces consist of a subset of WinSock (version 1.1), Remote Access Service (RAS) connection and management functions, Win32 serial functions, and a subset of the Telephony API (TAPI).

Windows CE supports most of the common WinSock functions. It exposes TCP/IP and IrDA through the WinSock API.

Most of the procedures and issues with communications programming are no different under Window CE than under other Windows versions. Because the supported communication mechanisms in Windows CE are a very large subject, it is not included in this general Windows CE programming book.

Desktop Connectivity

One of the key features of Windows CE and the Handheld PC is simple and seamless synchronization with the desktop PC. Users access this feature by using the Handheld PC Explorer application on the desktop PC to transfer files and synchronize their PIM data.

Applications can be programmed such that they have access to the desktop connectivity functionality. Windows CE has added new API functionality for synchronizing data between machines, converting files, and installing applications.

See Chapter 12, "Windows CE Application Loader," and Chapter 13, "File Filters," for more information on desktop connectivity.

Remote API

Another new set of functionality in Windows CE is the set of Remote API (RAPI) functions. This API is a set of functions that can be called from an application running on the desktop PC, but which is actually executed on the remote Windows CE device.

Windows CE supports RAPI functions for performing file management, database management, registry functions, and some miscellaneous system management functions.

The RAPI functions are implemented as a thin layer on the top of the actual Windows CE API calls. In most cases, the RAPI calls take the same arguments and have the same behavior as the local Windows CE functions.

See Chapter 14, "Remote API Functions," for more information on the Windows CE Remote API.

Help System

Windows CE is the first operating system of the Windows family to abandon WinHelp as the help system. The extreme space limitations on Windows CE devices make the Windows WinHelp mechanism impractical.

Windows CE introduces a new help system in which the help files are authored in the HyperText Markup Language (HTML). The Windows CE help system, Pocket Help, supports basic formatting such as jumps, bitmaps, and tables.

See Chapter 11, "Windows CE Help Files," for more information on Windows CE help files.

Unicode

A very important aspect that affects many of the Windows CE components mentioned previously as well as the programming of applications is Windows CE full support of only Unicode. This is in contrast to Windows 95, which supports only 8-bit characters, and Windows NT, which natively supports Unicode, but also works with 8-bit characters.

Some important guidelines for using Unicode in applications are as follows:

- Use the Windows CE API string functions (`lstrlen`, for instance) rather than those from the C runtime library.

- Use TCHAR, LPTSTR, and so on for declarations. The code can then be compiled for either ASCII or Unicode.

- Use the TEXT macro for string literals (for example, `TEXT("Your Text")`).

- Remember that a character is longer than one byte in length, and strings end with two zeros rather than one.

- When incrementing an array pointer or character count, use sizeof(TCHAR) to ensure that it is valid for either ASCII or Unicode.

- When converting ASCII strings, include `tchar.h`—it has all the necessary conversions.

Windows CE API

Although Windows CE was designed and written from scratch, Microsoft chose to make the Application Programming Interface (API) for Windows CE a subset of Microsoft's Win32 API. Win32API is used to build applications for Windows 95 and Windows NT. This choice greatly benefits the thousands of experienced Windows programmers who are already working with the Win32 API.

However, because Windows CE requires only 105 KB of ROM and about 400 KB of RAM to run, numerous Win32 pieces had to be excluded to create an operating system that small; Windows CE only supports about 500 of the 2000 or so Win32 APIs.

Although supporting only 1/4 of Win32 APIs seems like a very small portion, most of the missing functions are contained in technology that Windows CE does not support. Some of the areas that Windows CE does not support include the following:

- OLE
- COM
- ActiveX
- MAPI
- ODBC
- DDE
- Printing
- Multimedia
- DirectX
- Console applications
- Security
- Help
- Named events
- Interapplication synchronization
- APIs for 16-bit compatibility

In addition to supporting 500 existing Win32 functions, the Windows CE API provides APIs to support the capabilities of Windows CE that are not present in other versions of Windows or to support functions of Windows CE that are simplified versions of full Win32 functions. Areas of Windows CE-specific APIs include the following:

- Windows CE databases

- Windows CE notifications

- CommandBars

- The Help system

- The address book

Porting Applications to Windows CE

Given that the programming model under Windows CE is nearly identical to that required to build other Windows programs, and because the Windows CE API implements the vast majority of the core Win32 APIs, it is possible to port an existing Windows application to Windows CE. However, because Windows CE and the Handheld PC have some unique constraints, it may be more difficult to port an existing application rather than just create a new Windows CE-specific application.

For instance, the memory on a Handheld PC is extremely limited. An entry-level Handheld PC has 1 MB of "disk space" and 1 MB of runtime memory. Most modern applications were created when memory and disk space were not much of an issue; most of today's applications install tens or even hundreds of megabytes worth of files and usually take many megabytes worth of memory just to start up. Obviously, large complex applications like this are not likely to be ported to Windows CE.

Another issue is processing power. Although the Handheld PCs have very powerful processors for their class, they are definitely not on the same level as most developers' machines. Handheld PCs simply are not suited for complex calculations or computations.

The nature of the Handheld PC suggests that users demand very quick response times to any action. Applications need to be structured, therefore, to provide the desired level of responsiveness while still achieving the desired results (perhaps by using background threads to perform processing).

You should also consider the form factor of the Handheld PC when creating a Windows CE application. Both the screen and the keyboard are very small. Displaying too much information on the screen affects readability, and forcing the user to enter too much data via the keyboard might frustrate him.

All of these issues are not meant to discourage you from creating a Windows CE application. Windows CE is a very capable operating system that has a rich set of development tools and functionality. Just keep in mind that many of the limitations of Windows CE need to be addressed early on when you design your application, not while trying to port an existing Windows 95 or Windows NT application to Windows CE.

3

Handheld PC Hardware

The first device to use the Windows CE operating system is the Handheld PC; in fact, the Handheld PC was specifically designed to run Windows CE.

The Handheld PC is a new category of computer—a mobile companion as well as a device that brings Windows to the palm of your hand. The Handheld PC is more powerful than other electronic organizers, yet seems easy to use because of the similarity between the Windows CE interface and the Windows 95 or Windows NT 4.0 interfaces.

Rather than building the hardware for Handheld PCs itself, Microsoft partnered with seven well-known hardware manufacturers who developed the first Handheld PCs. Microsoft defined a reference platform on which the manufacturers created their own versions of the Handheld PCs.

Using an approach it has taken in other markets, Microsoft defined a minimal hardware specification for the Handheld PC, but allowed each manufacturer to add other capabilities and features. The key requirements for Handheld PC hardware are:

- A pocket form factor; size should not exceed 7"×4"×1"

- Power is supplied by two AA batteries

- Lightweight; Handheld PCs should weigh less than 1 pound

- A QWERTY keyboard containing standard keys (including Ctrl, Alt, Shift)

- An LCD touch screen display of at least 480×240 pixels with 4 grayscales and 2 bits per pixel

- A stylus to use like a mouse on the touch screen

- A minimum of 4 MB of ROM and 2 MB of RAM

- An infrared port

- A serial port

- A PCMCIA slot

- A built-in audio output device

The first section of this chapter details the specific hardware components that make up the Handheld PC. The second section describes the specifications and features of each of the current Handheld PC models.

Handheld PC Components

As the name implies, a Handheld PC is a personal computer. As such, the Handheld PC has most of the same components as a traditional personal computer. These components are detailed in the following sections.

Microprocessor

To achieve the goal of making Windows CE a suitable operating system for a wide range of devices, Windows CE supports a variety of microprocessors.

The microprocessor architectures currently supported are the Hitachi SH3, the MIPS (R3000/R4000), and Intel x86 series (for the emulation environment). The specific chip sets used in the initial generation of Handheld PCs are the Hitachi SH3, the NEC MIPS VR4101, and the Philips TwoChipPIC (MIPS processor). All the current chip sets are based on RISC architecture.

Given the design of Windows CE, other 32-bit processors can be readily supported by porting the Windows CE kernel and building the cross-compilers. Microsoft, for example, has recently announced Windows CE support for the Arm, StrongArm, and PowerPC processors.

An important factor in Handheld PC devices is the balance between processor speed and power consumption. Windows CE is constantly looking for power savings by switching the CPU operating mode.

Handheld PC microprocessors have three different modes of operation designed to minimize power consumption: The Full Speed mode is used when applications are executing; The Standby mode is used during brief idle periods and uses less than one-tenth the power of full-speed mode; The Suspend mode is used during long idle periods and uses less than one-thousandth the power of Full Speed mode.

Because the processor is such a significant consumer of power when running, applications should return control to the operating system whenever possible. Unnecessarily running the CPU (for example, in a PeekMessage loop) will consume power and can usually be handled differently.

Because each of the supported processors for Windows CE uses different instruction sets, application developers must produce a binary image of their application for each processor. Luckily, the Windows CE development environment does most of the work by allowing the creation of multiple binary images from one set of source code.

Related to the microprocessor, Handheld PCs have two hardware timers. The first hardware timer is a high-resolution timer that provides scheduling interrupts and timer events. The second hardware timer is a low-resolution real-time clock that maintains the current data and time for the Handheld PC.

Memory

Memory for the Handheld PC is a combination of ROM and RAM. Handheld PCs have a minimum of 4 MB of ROM, which contains the operating system and bundled applications. By placing the operating system and applications in ROM, upgrading to a new version may be as simple as replacing the ROM.

Handheld PCs also contain at least 2 MB of battery-backed RAM. This RAM is used for both runtime memory and data storage, as described in Chapter 2, "Windows CE Operating System," under the "Memory Architecture" section.

Some Handheld PC manufacturers allow the device to use additional RAM by providing expansion slots. Windows CE automatically detects the presence of additional RAM and adds it to the pool with the base RAM for the device.

Even when turned off, power is still being used to maintain the state of the RAM. This is necessary to maintain the state of the object store (saved files, programs, and so on), and to maintain the state of the runtime memory so that when powered on, the device is in the exact same state as when powered off (for example, when all the same applications are still running).

Because RAM is not cleared when the Handheld PC is powered down, another mechanism was created to clear the RAM in the event the system stops responding or becomes unstable. A hardware reset button provided on each device produces a nonmaskable reset interrupt that resets the runtime (system storage) portion of RAM. Note that removing all batteries would reset the entire RAM, resulting in the loss of any data or programs stored in the object store.

The Handheld PC's memory limitations are a very big challenge to application developers. Multi-megabyte applications, which are common on desktop PCs, will not fit in the object store of the Handheld PC. Some have compared programming Windows CE applications to the "old days" of programming, when file size and memory usage were extremely important considerations.

Screen

The reference design for the Handheld PC specifies a 480×240 pixel liquid crystal display type. Windows CE currently only supports a monochrome display with 2 bits per pixel. This allows for four colors: black, white, light gray, and dark gray.

The Handheld PC screen is a continuous resistive touch panel that gives the user the ability to select items on the screen without using a mouse. Handheld PCs all come with a stylus, although any pointing device (such as your finger) works with the touch screen.

The display contrast can be changed by the user to accommodate different lighting conditions. The contrast is adjusted either by a dial on the side of the case, or by using the Alt+< and Alt+> key combinations.

Another feature of the screen is backlighting. Many manufacturers add backlighting support to the Handheld PC display. Backlighting enhances the ability to read the screen in low-light or no-light situations. Of course, the negative aspect of backlighting is that it increases power consumption and will therefore drain the batteries faster.

Some manufacturers have also enhanced the Handheld PC screen as a point of differentiation. The Hewlett-Packard device uses a 640×240 pixel display, which is wider than all the other Handheld PCs. The Hitachi and LG Electronics Handheld PCs use a .26mm dot-pitch as opposed to other companies which opt for a .24mm dot-pitch. This larger dot-pitch supposedly makes the screen more readable.

Note

> The optimal solution bases the presentation of information on the screen size. An application can call GetSystemMetrics (with SM_CXSCREEN and SM_CYSCREEN) to get information on the size of the screen and adjust its output accordingly.

Dealing with the limited screen real estate, varying screen sizes, and other display limitations of Windows CE devices are some of the biggest challenges in developing Windows CE applications.

Keyboard

Because Windows CE does not currently include built-in handwriting recognition, all Handheld PCs include a QWERTY-style keyboard. The keyboard includes the standard extra keys such as Ctrl, Alt, and two Shift keys. Most also include the new "Windows" key.

The specific shape and feel of the keyboard is one of the features that most differentiates the various Handheld PC devices: Some devices use square keys while others use oval keys; some devices use hard-plastic keys while others use softer rubbery keys.

Enhancing the keyboard for additional functionality is a common theme among manufacturers. The Hewlett-Packard device, for example, added a keyboard sequence for generating the British pound symbol while the Philips device features keyboard accelerators (Alt+1, Alt+2, and so on) for quickly launching most built-in applications (Pocket Word, Calendar, and so on).

Programmatically, the keyboard functions the same under Windows CE as under Windows 95. Keyboard events are sent to applications through familiar Windows 95 messages such as the following:

```
WM_KEYUP, WM_KEYDOWN, WM_CHAR,
```

See Chapter 8, "Input and Output," for more information on keyboard processing.

Stylus

All Handheld PCs are equipped with a stylus for use with the touch-sensitive display (although the touch screen does not require the stylus to operate). The stylus replaces a mouse for use as a point-and-select device.

Although the method for generating the mouse and stylus events is quite different between Windows CE and other versions of Windows, the way applications interpret those events is quite similar. Windows CE uses the same WM_LBUTTONDOWN, WM_LBUTTONUP, and

WM_LBUTTONDBLCLK as Win32. These messages signal when the user has pressed on the touch screen, let up from the touch screen, or double-tapped on the screen, respectively.

There is no direct equivalent to the right button on a mouse. The customary way to get right-button functionality is to have the user press the Alt key while tapping.

Tip

> Alt+tap does not generate right-button messages (WM_RBUTTONDOWN or WM_RBUTTONDBLCLK, for instance). To use Alt+tap, check to see if the Alt key (VK_MENU) is depressed when handling WM_LBUTTONDOWN messages.

See Chapter 8 for more information on stylus processing.

Audio

All the current Handheld PC devices have built-in audio-output hardware, and Windows CE has support for playing wave (.wav) files. Applications can programmatically play a sound or associate sounds with notification events.

See Chapter 8 for more information on audio support.

Serial Port

All current Handheld PCs have a built-in serial interface for connecting to RS-232 devices. The primary use of the serial port is to connect the Handheld PC to the desktop PC. The serial interface between the desktop PC and Handheld PC is used to synchronize PIM data, copy files, install applications, back up and restore data, and debug Windows CE applications.

Windows CE provides support for standard Win32 serial API functions. It exposes file-handling capabilities for creating, reading, and writing files, as well as serial communication functions. The supported Win32 serial API functions include the following:

- CreateFile

- ReadFile

- WriteFile

- CloseHandle

- GetCommState

- SetCommState

- EscapeCommFunction

- GetCommTimeouts

- SetCommTimeouts

- SetCommMask

- WaitCommEvent

- GetCommModemStatus

Infrared Port

All of the current Handheld PC devices include an infrared communications port. Windows CE supports infrared communications hardware that conforms to the industry standard—Infrared Data Association's (IrDA) specifications.

The initial version of Windows CE supports infrared connectivity from Handheld PC to Handheld PC only—connectivity to infrared-enabled desktop PCs is not currently supported. However, the Hewlett-Packard Handheld PC does support printing to a Hewlett-Packard printer through the infrared port.

Programmatically, Windows CE supports the IrDA standard via the WinSock API. The specification for Infrared Sockets (IrSock) provides extensions to WinSock for infrared link communication channel. The following functions are supported for IrSock. Some of those functions include the following modifications incorporated for IrDA:

- Accept

- Bind

- Closesocket

- Connect

- Getsockopt

- Listen

- Recv

- Send

- Setsockopt

- Socket

LED

Some Handheld PCs include an externally visible LED of which the primary function is to notify the user of an event. The LED flashes until the user handles or fixes the notification. Windows CE provides API functions for setting notifications, which includes flashing the LED.

Refer to Chapter 8 for information on programmatically creating notifications that include flashing the LED.

PCMCIA Slot

Each of the current Handheld PCs incorporates a PCMCIA slot that can be used to add devices to the system, such as modems or flash-RAM cards, while Windows CE includes built-in support for many PCMCIA devices. In addition, Windows CE supports installable device drivers, so PCMCIA manufacturers can create client drives for their devices. Taking it a step further, Visual C++ for Windows CE currently includes the Device Driver Kit (DDK) necessary for creating device drivers for Windows CE.

Windows CE commonly uses PCMCIA to increase the storage capacity of the Handheld PC. Windows CE can work with ATA type II flash memory cards and SRAM cards. Windows CE automatically recognizes these memory cards and creates the \PC Card directory that maps to the device. This essentially increases the object store space on the Handheld PC. Files can then be saved in the PC Card folder (and consequently on the memory card). Windows CE databases cannot be saved to a PC Card.

Power use is an important consideration while using PCMCIA devices in a Handheld PC because many PCMCIA devices use a significant amount of power and therefore decrease battery life. For example, some 28.8 and 33.6 PCMCIA modems used in a Handheld PC will completely drain a pair of fresh batteries in just a couple of minutes. Manufacturers are now starting to produce low-power PCMCIA devices that are more suitable for use in a Handheld PC.

Handheld PC Manufacturers

This section lists the specifications and features of all currently available Handheld PCs.

Note that some details common to all the Handheld PCs are not re-listed for each Handheld PC model. For example, all the current Handheld PCs come with a stylus, so it is not included in these lists.

Casio Cassiopeia

Casio was the first manufacturer to begin working with Microsoft on the Windows CE project and the first to reach the new Handheld PC market with its Cassiopeia device. Casio provides three models of the Cassiopeia. The major differences between the models lie in the amount of RAM included, not to mention the fact that one model includes a docking cradle and AC power adapter. Table 3.1 lists the Cassiopeia hardware specifications.

Table 3.1

Cassiopeia Hardware Specifications

Category	Description
Models:	A-10, A-11, A-11Plus
Size:	6.9"×3.6"×1"
Weight:	13.4 ounces
CPU:	Hitachi SH3
CPU Speed:	40 MHz
Screen (pixels):	480×240
Screen (diagonal):	5.1 inches
Screen dot pitch:	.24 mm
Backlight:	Yes
Power Supply:	Two AA alkaline or NiMH batteries
ROM:	4 MB
RAM:	2 MB (A-10), 4 MB (A-11), 6 MB (A-11Plus)
PCMCIA:	One built-in slot
Interfaces:	Serial port, Infrared port
Audio:	Built-in speaker
Indicator LED:	Yes, for alarms
Additional features:	CD-ROM of additional applications

The following is a list of optional accessories available with the Casio Cassiopeia:

- Docking Station

- Docking station set (includes docking station, AC adapter, rechargeable battery pack, and charger)

- MiniDock

- MiniDock Set (includes MiniDock and AC adapter)

- Rechargeable battery pack

- Charger for rechargeable battery pack

- Data Communications Cable (to connect Casio digital camera)

NEC MobilePro

The NEC MobilePro Handheld PC is the only device to use the NEC Vr4101 MIPS processor. NEC claims this processor has the best performance per watt ratio of all the current Handheld PC devices. Another way in which it contrasts with the current Handheld PCs is the MobilePro's softer rubbery keyboard keys, which is a small feature that some users might appreciate. Table 3.2 lists the hardware specifications of the MobilPro.

Table 3.2

NEC MobilePro Hardware Specifications

Category	Description
Models:	200, 400
Size:	6.89"×3.74"×1.03"
Weight:	12.8 ounces
CPU:	NEC Vr4101
CPU Speed:	33 MHz
Screen (pixels):	480×240
Screen (diagonal):	5.1 inches
Screen dot pitch:	.24 mm
Backlight:	No
Power Supply:	Two AA alkaline or NiMH batteries
ROM:	8 MB
RAM:	2 MB (200), 4 MB (400)

Catergory	Description
PCMCIA:	One built-in slot
Interfaces:	Serial port, Infrared port
Audio:	Built-in speaker
Indicator LED:	Yes, for alarms

The following is a list of optional accessories available for the MobilPro:

- Docking cradle
- Direct connection cable
- AC power adapter
- NiMH rechargeable battery pack
- NiMH battery charger
- Stylus pack
- Carrying case

Compaq PC Companion

The Compaq PC Companion Handheld PCs are manufactured by Casio and differ from the Cassiopeia only in colors and labeling. Compaq provides three models: C120 with 2 MB RAM; C140 with 4 MB; and C120+ with 2 MB RAM, 14.4 PCMCIA modem, AC adapter, and Quick Connect cradle. Table 3.3 lists more hardware specifications for the Companion.

Table 3.3

Companion Hardware Specifications

Category	Description
Models:	C120, C140, C120+
Size:	6.9"×3.6"×1"

continues

Table 3.3

Companion Hardware Specifications, continued

Category	Description
Weight:	13.4 ounces
CPU:	Hitachi SH3
CPU Speed:	40 MHz
Screen (pixels):	480×240
Screen (diagonal):	5.1 inches
Screen dot pitch:	.24 mm
Backlight:	Yes
Power Supply:	Two AA alkaline or NiMH batteries
ROM:	4 MB
RAM:	2 MB (C120, C120+), 4 MB (C140)
PCMCIA:	One built-in slot
Interfaces:	Serial port, Infrared port
Audio:	Built-in speaker
Indicator LED:	Yes, for alarms

The following optional accessories are available for the Compaq Companion:

- 2 MB memory expansion
- 10 MB Flash RAM
- 14.4 LP PC card modem
- Combo Pack (includes AC adapter and Quick Connect cradle)
- Power Pack (includes AC adapter, Quick Connect cradle, NiMH battery pack, and battery charger)
- Convenience cradle

- Stylus 3-Pack

- Carrying Case

- Slipcase

LG Electronics

LG Electronics enters the Handheld PC market with its GP40M device. The differentiating features of the GP40M include a larger dot-pitch in the screen, a built-in microphone, and an optional built-in 14.4 modem. Table 3.4 lists available hardware specifications for the GP40M.

Table 3.4

GP40M Hardware Specifications

Category	Description
Model:	GP40M
Size:	6.45"×3.76"×1"
Weight:	11.4 ounces
CPU:	Hitachi SH3
CPU Speed:	40 MHz
Screen (pixels):	480×240
Screen (diagonal):	5.6 inches
Screen dot pitch:	.26 mm
Backlight:	No
Power Supply:	Two AA alkaline or NiMH batteries
ROM:	4 MB
RAM:	2 MB, 4 MB
PCMCIA:	One built-in slot
Interfaces:	Serial port, Infrared port

continues

Table 3.4

GP40M Hardware Specifications, continued

Category	Description
Audio:	Built-in speaker and microphone
Indicator LED:	Yes, for alarms
Additional Features:	CD-ROM of additional applications

The GP40M Handheld PC has the option of a 14.4 modem; however, it does not occupy PCMCIA slot.

Hitachi

Although Hitachi manufactures the microprocessor for all but two of the devices, it does not build its own Handheld PC. The Hitachi Handheld PC is manufactured by LG Electronics and differs from the GP40M only in color and labeling. Table 3.5 lists the available hardware specifications.

Table 3.5

Hitachi Handheld PC Hardware Specifications

Category	Description
Models:	HPW10E2, HPW10E4
Size:	6.45"×3.76"×1"
Weight:	11.4 ounces
CPU:	Hitachi SH3
CPU Speed:	40 MHz
Screen (pixels):	480×240
Screen (diagonal):	5.6 inches
Screen dot pitch:	.26 mm
Backlight:	No

Category	Description
Power Supply:	Two AA alkaline or NiMH batteries
ROM:	4 MB
RAM:	2 MB (HPW10E2), 4 MB (HPW10E4)
PCMCIA:	One built-in slot
Interfaces:	Serial port, Infrared port
Audio:	Built-in speaker and microphone
Indicator LED:	Yes, for alarms
Additional Features:	CD-ROM of additional applications

Similar to LG Technologies' GP40M, the optional accessory available is a 14.4 modem; however, it does not occupy PCMCIA slot.

HP 300LX, 320LX

The Hewlett-Packard Handheld PC is the most unique among the current set of devices because it uses a bigger screen. The screen is considerably wider—640 pixels instead of 480. The HP device also includes limited printing support and additional applications in the ROM chip (see Table 3.6).

Table 3.6

HP Handheld PC Hardware Specifications

Category	Description
Models:	300LX, 320LX
Size:	7.2"×3.67"×1.1"
Weight:	15.6 ounces
CPU:	Hitachi SH3
CPU Speed:	44 MHz
Screen (pixels):	640×240

continues

Table 3.6

HP Handheld PC Hardware Specifications, continued

Category	Description
Screen (diagonal):	6.5 inches
Screen dot pitch:	.24 mm
Backlight:	Yes (in 320LX only)
Power Supply:	Two AA alkaline or NiMH batteries
ROM:	5 MB
RAM:	2 MB (300LX), 4 MB (320LX)
PCMCIA:	One built-in slot
Interfaces:	Serial port, Infrared port
Audio:	Built-in speaker
Indicator LED:	No
Additional Features:	CD-ROM of additional applications; Printing support; Data backup to PC card; Additional applications in ROM; Embedded numeric keypad (uses M, J, K, L, U, I, O, 7, 8, 9 keys); CompactFlash slot in 320LX

The following optional accessories are available for the HP Handheld PC:

- HP docking cradle (included with 320LX)

- HP AC adapter

- HP CompactFlash memory

- HP leather case

- Spare styluses

Philips Velo 1

Philips differentiates its Velo 1 in the Handheld PC market by providing a unique design and additional features. The exterior of the case is a very sleek dark blue and metallic combination with a rubbery feel. The interior features a stylish keyboard with rounded keys that are both attractive and functional (see Table 3.7).

The additional features of the Velo 1 include a microphone that can be used to record speech even when the device is closed, and a built-in 19.2 modem with an angled phone jack on the left side of the display screen.

Table 3.7

Velo 1 Hardware Specifications

Category	Description
Models:	4 MB, 4 MB Rechargeable
Size:	6.75"×3.75"×1.25"
Weight:	13.8 ounces
CPU:	MIPS R3910
CPU Speed:	36.864 MHz
Screen (pixels):	480×240
Screen (diagonal):	5.1 inches
Screen dot pitch:	.24 mm
Backlight:	Yes
Power Supply:	Two AA alkaline or NiMH batteries
ROM:	8 MB
RAM:	4 MB
PCMCIA:	Requires optional V-Module that attaches to Velo 1
Interfaces:	Serial port, Infrared port

continues

Table 3.7

Velo 1 Hardware Specifications, continued

Category	Description
Audio:	Built-in speaker and microphone
Indicator LED:	3 LEDs: alarm, battery charging, communication
Additional Features:	Built-in 19.2 modem; Two expansion slots for DRAM, FLASH, or ROM; 10 Quick Start keys; Omni-directional microphone; Voice recording; Additional application in ROM; CD-ROM of additional applications

The following lists optional accessories available for the Phillips Velo 1:

- Velo Dock

- Traveling AC adapter

- Flash memory

- Type II PC card V-Module

- NiMH rechargeable battery pack

- Velo carrying case

CHAPTER 4

Visual C++ for Windows CE

In much the same way that the Handheld PC user interface should be very familiar to a Windows user, the Windows CE development environment should be very familiar to a Windows developer. All this familiarity is no coincidence. A familiar interface on the Handheld PC means users are less intimidated when using this new tool; a familiar development environment means developers can more easily build applications for Windows CE. Both of these factors give Windows CE and the Handheld PC the opportunity to succeed where many other handheld devices have failed.

The Application Programming Interface (API) to Windows CE is essentially a subset of the Win32 APIs that are the fundamental building blocks for all Windows 95 and NT applications. This means an experienced Win32 developer has a great deal of knowledge that can be applied directly to building Windows CE applications.

This familiarity is even greater because Windows CE applications are actually created on "regular" PCs. Windows CE application development is performed in a cross-platform environment where the `edit`, `compile`, `link`, `resource edit`, and `debug` functions occur on a Windows-based desktop computer.

The tools necessary for Windows CE application development are packaged as an extension to the Microsoft Visual C++ development environment.

The Windows CE development environment is packaged as an add-on extension to the Microsoft Visual C++ product and includes everything needed for writing applications for Windows CE. This includes cross-compilers, the SDK and DDK, remote tools, remote debugging capabilities, and even an emulation environment.

It is important to note that because Windows CE applications are built on a desktop PC and Visual C++ for Windows CE includes an emulation environment, it is completely possible to create Windows CE applications without having a Handheld PC. Of course, at some point the application should be tested on an actual Handheld PC.

This chapter will cover each of the components and tools used in building Windows CE applications.

Development Environment

Currently the only way to get the SDK and tools needed for creating Windows CE applications is with the Microsoft Visual C++ for Windows CE product. This section provides information about what is included with the Visual C++ for Windows CE product, what is needed to use it, and how it is installed.

Note

The information in this chapter applies to version 1.0 of Microsoft Visual C++ for Windows CE. Subsequent versions of Visual C++ for Windows CE or Windows CE support for other development environments differ somewhat from the information provided here.

Installing Visual C++ for Windows CE

The installation of Visual C++ for Windows CE is very straightforward. The major prerequisite is that Visual C++ 5.0 must first be installed on the system. Other requirements for Visual C++ for Windows CE include:

- A PC with a 486/66 MHz or higher processor

- Microsoft Windows NT Workstation 4.0

- Microsoft Visual C++ 5.0, Professional or Enterprise edition

- 24 MB of RAM; 32 MB recommended

- 100 MB of free disk space

Because Visual C++ for Windows CE integrates directly into the Visual C++ development environment, it is very version specific. Visual C++ for Windows CE version 1.0 will only work with Visual C++ 5.0, Professional or Enterprise edition.

Although Microsoft strongly recommends Windows NT 4.0 as the operating system platform, Visual C++ for Windows CE can be installed on Windows 95 with a few limitations. Some of the drawbacks of using Windows 95 are that emulation, remote debugging, and remote tools will not work with Windows 95.

In addition to the Windows CE add-on for Visual C++, the Visual C++ for Windows CE CD-ROM also contains version 1.1 of the Handheld PC Explorer. The installation procedure is:

1. Insert the CD-ROM.

2. Run setup.exe from the \wcedev directory on the CD-ROM.

3. Either choose Yes to install Handheld PC Explorer when prompted, or run setup.exe from the \hpxexpl directory on the CD-ROM.

Remote Connection and RAS settings

The remote connection between the desktop and remote tools requires the Remote Access Service (RAS) to be installed. If the RAS is not currently installed, the following section details the procedure for configuring RAS on the desktop PC for Windows CE development.

Installing/Configuring Remote Access Service (RAS)

To install and configure RAS, perform the following procedure:

1. Choose Start, Settings, Control Panel.

2. Double-click Network.

3. Select the Services tab.

4. If Remote Access Service is not listed, click Add and then select Remote Access Service and click OK. After being prompted, insert your NT CD-ROM.

5. In the Network Services list box, select Remote Access Service and click Properties.

6. If the COM port you want to use is displayed in the list box, you will need to remove it. Select the COM port, click Remove, and then Yes to confirm.

7. In the Remote Access Setup dialog box, click Add.

8. Click Install Modem, set the "don't detect my modem; I will select it from a list" check box to TRUE, and click Next. Be prepared to wait a while as a list of all supported modems is loaded.

9. In the Manufacturers list, select Standard modem types. In the Models list, select Dial-Up Networking Serial Cable between 2 PCs, and click Next.

10. Select the Selected ports radio button, select the COM port you will use to connect to the device, and then click Next.

11. Take note of any warning or informational messages that may pop up.

12. If a Location information dialog box pops up, type any 3-digit number in the area code box and click Next.

13. Continue by clicking Finish, and then affirmatively exiting all the dialog boxes until you reach the Add RAS Device dialog box.

14. The drop-down list should now contain the port that you have just configured. Select the port, and click OK. On some builds of NT, the drop-down list may not display the port that was just added. If it does not, repeat steps 8-14. Eventually, NT will detect the modem.

15. In the Remote Access Setup dialog box, select the port that you have just configured, and click Configure.

16. Select the Receive calls only radio button, and click OK.

17. In the Remote Access Setup dialog box, click Network.

18. In the Server Settings group, set the TCP/IP check box to TRUE. If you have no other modem previously installed, make sure you clear the other check boxes. Otherwise, leave the other check boxes as they are.

19. Click the Configure button for TCP/IP.

20. Select the This computer only radio button.

21. Select the Use static address pool radio button. For Begin, enter **192.168.55.100;** for End, enter **192.168.55.112**.

22. Make sure you clear the Allow remote clients to request a predetermined IP address check box.

23. Continue by affirmatively exiting all the dialog boxes, clicking Close when you reach the Network dialog box.

24. If a Microsoft TCP/IP Properties dialog box pops up, click OK.

25. Restart your computer when prompted.

Setting Permissions for a Guest Account

In order for Handheld PCs to connect to Windows NT, the guest user should be enabled. When first connecting, the User Logon dialog box will appear on the Handheld PC. Enter **guest** for User with no password or domain entries. The following directions detail the steps for enabling the guest account:

1. In Programs, Administrative Tools, start User Manager.

2. In the top box, double-click Guest.

3. Make sure that the Account Disabled check box is FALSE.

4. Click OK and close the User Manager dialog box.

5. In Programs, Administrative Tools, start Remote Access Admin.

6. Choose Users, Permissions.

7. In the Users list box, select Guest, and set the Grant dialing permission to user check box to TRUE.

8. Click OK.

9. Select Server, Select Domain or Server.

10. In the Domain entry field, type your machine name (for example, **MYACCOUNT1**).

11. Click OK.

Components of Visual C++ for Windows CE

Installing Visual C++ for Windows CE produces almost no visual difference in the Visual C++ integrated development environment (IDE). This keeps with Microsoft's goal of maintaining a familiar environment for building Windows CE applications. About the only interface change is the addition of new menu options specific to developing Windows CE applications.

Although there are only minor interface changes, Visual C++ for Windows CE includes many components. The components include:

- Windows CE API (essentially a subset of the Win32 API set)

- Windows CE C Runtime library (essentially a subset of the standard C Runtime library)

- SHCL cross-compiler for SH3 devices

- CLMIPS cross-compiler for MIPS devices

- App Wizard support for creating Windows CE applications

- Enhancements to Resource Editor to handle Windows CE four-color bitmaps

- MFC for Windows CE (a subset of the MFC classes for Win32)

- Remote versions of common development tools such as Spy, MemView, Zoomin, and Regedit (These tools are discussed later in this chapter in the section, "Windows CE Remote Tools.")

- Windows CE SDK documentation

- Windows CE DDK documentation

Windows CE Targets

Visual C++ for Windows CE uses the Visual C++ IDE's existing support for multiple targets. Previous targets in the IDS included the Win32 Release and Win32 Debug. Visual C++ for Windows CE enables the following new targets:

- Win32 (WCE MIPS) Release

- Win32 (WCE MIPS) Debug

- Win32 (WCE SH) Release

- Win32 (WCE SH) Debug

- Win32 (WCE x86em) Release

- Win32 (WCE x86em) Debug

MFC

Although not part of the early beta releases of the Windows CE SDK, Microsoft Foundation Classes (MFC) support was added by the time the SDK was officially released. The MFC support in Windows CE is a subset of the full MFC support for the Win32 API.

The addition of MFC greatly benefits the thousands of developers who have experience in MFC programming. There are some drawbacks however. One important issue is that the initial set of Handheld PCs do not have the MFC runtime DLLs in ROM. This means that applications that need the MFC runtime library must install the DLL as part of their installation.

Another related issue is the size of the MFC DLL. The debug MFC DLL has over 700K for the SH3 processor and over 1 MB for the MIPS processor. This makes debugging MFC applications next to impossible on a 2 MB Handheld PC. The release of MFC DLL has 300K for the SH3 processor and 400K for the MIPS processor. While they certainly fit on the Handheld PC, the DLL would take up a significant portion of the object store on a 2 MB machine.

Note

> The programs and sample application developed throughout the course of this book were done using the straight Windows CE API and not MFC. The major reason for this is that most of the book was completed before MFC for Windows CE was available. In addition, the straight Windows CE API is the lowest common denominator, so the information should benefit both MFC and non-MFC programmers.

MFC for Windows CE incorporates a large subset of MFC for Win32. The following table lists the supported MFC for Windows CE classes.

CArchive	CEditView	CMapWordToPtr	CSize
CArchive-Exception	CEvent	CMemoryException	CSliderCtrl
CArray	CException	CMenu	CSpinButtonCtrl
CBitmap	CFile	CNotSupported-Exception	CSplitterWnd
CBitmap-Button	CFileDialog	CObArray	CStatic

CBrush	CFile-Exception	CObject	CString
CButton	CFileStatus	CObList	CStringArray
CByteArray	CFindReplace-Dialog	CPaintDC	CStringList
CClientDC	CFont	CPen	CSyncObject
CCmdTarget	CFormView	CPoint	CTabCtrl
CCmdUI	CFrameWnd	CProgressCtrl	CTime
CComboBox	CGdiObject	CPropertyPage	CTimeSpan
CCommand-LineInfo	CHeaderCtrl	CProperty-Sheet	CTreeCtrl
CCommonDialog	CImageList	CPtrArray	CTreeView
CCreate-Context	CList (template)	CPtrList	CTypedPtrArray
CCritical-Section	CListBox	CRecentFileList	CTypedPtrLis
CCtrlView	CListCtrl	CRect	CTypePtrMap
CData-Exchange	CListView	CRectTracker	CUIntArray
CDC	CMap (template)	CResource-Exception	CUserException
CDialog	CMapPtrToPtr	CRgn	CView
CDocTemplate	CMapPtrToWord	CRuntimeClass	CWaitCursor
CDocument	CMapString-ToOb	CScrollBar	CWinApp

CDumpContext	CMapString- ToPtr	CScrollView	CWindowDC
CDWordArray	CMapString- ToString	CSingleDoc- Template	CWinThread
CEdit CWordArray	CMapWordToOb	CSingleLock	CWnd

Creating Windows CE Applications

By integrating the development tools for Windows CE into the Visual C++ environment, the process and procedures for creating Windows CE applications are immediately familiar to existing Visual C++ users. Visual C++ for Windows CE enables developers to edit code and resources and compile, link, and run or debug Windows CE applications from within the Visual Studio, just as they can with other Windows applications.

This section will not finely detail every step necessary in building applications using Visual C++. Instead, specific areas that are unique or different for building Windows CE applications will be covered.

Building Applications

The general process for creating Windows CE applications is as follows:

1. Create a new project. Valid project types for Windows CE development are Application, MFC, AppWizards, Dynamic-Link Library, Static Library, and Makefile.

2. When creating the project, include the target platforms for the project. Windows CE applications would likely always include Win32 (x86EM) for emulation on an x86 host, Winn32 (WCE-MIPS) for a MIPS target device (VR4100 or PR3910), and Win32 (WCESH) for an SH3 target device.

3. Write the application. Make sure to only use API functions that are supported on Windows CE.

4. Build the application. Note that Visual C++ will build only one target platform at a time. The Build, Set Active Configuration menu option sets the target platform that will be built.

5. Execute and debug the application in Emulation mode. It is most convenient to do most of the testing and debugging using the built-in emulation environment. Choosing the x86EM target enables the application to work in the emulation environment.

6. Execute and debug the application on the Handheld PC. Testing on the Handheld PC ensures the proper end-user functionality.

Debugging Applications

One of the nicest features of Visual C++ for Windows CE is the ability to debug a Windows CE application. Debugging an application is nothing unusual. The remarkable part is that the application is running on both the Handheld PC and the debugger; meanwhile, its output is on the desktop PC. This enables a developer to take advantage of the features and functionality of the Visual C++ debugger.

Remote debugging is accomplished using the serial connection between the Handheld PC and the desktop PC. The serial connection is shared between the RAS connection (for copying files, applications, and so on to the device) and the remote debugging service. The RAS connection is configured through the Control Panel, as described previously in this chapter. The Remote Debugging connection is configured from within Visual C++ with the Build, Debugger Remote Connection menu option.

The Debugger Remote Connection dialog box enables the debugging connection setting to be specified for each target platform. Debugging Windows CE applications requires configuring the Win32 (WCE MIPS) and Win32 (WCE SH) targets. Choose the Serial connection method and then use the Settings dialog box to specify the connector port, baud rate, and so on.

Once properly configured, follow this procedure for debugging a remote Windows CE application:

1. If you are not connected to the device with Handheld PC Explorer, start the Remote Connection Server.

2. Build the project. This step will automatically download the application to the Handheld PC.

3. Start the debugging session by choosing Step Into or Go if a breakpoint has been set.

4. The IDE will download and initialize the debug subsystem on the device. After debugging is initialized on the device, the IDE will run through a series of loads until it hits the breakpoint. The IDE debugger is then connected to the device and can control the debug session.

5. Debug the application (as if it were a regular Windows application).

6. Use the Stop Debugging option to cleanly exit the debugging session (this must be done while stopped in the debugger).

Visual C++ identifies the following differences between native (local) debugging and remote debugging:

- All exceptions from any process on the target machine are caught by the debugger and the default handling is to always stop.

- The order for remote symbol mappings starts with the project directory and any project subdirectories.

- Debug\Stop debugging behavior is continue on exit.

- There is no asynchronous communications with the target (no asynchronous stop, breakpoints, memory updates, and so on).

- There is no support for single button stepping out of routines. An alternative is to set a breakpoint or run to cursor on the call stack routine calling the current routine.

Shell Emulation

A unique feature of Visual C++ for Windows CE is the capability to run Windows CE applications on the desktop computer. The Windows CE emulation environment makes it possible to build and test Windows CE applications entirely under Windows NT.

The SDK provides a very faithful emulation of the Windows CE operating system. Of course, performance and hardware specific features are not emulated, so at some point testing is required on a physical Windows CE device. According to Microsoft, approximately 90 percent of an application development process can take place entirely in emulation. Figure 4.1 shows an example of an application running under the emulation environment.

Figure 4.1

The Microsoft Windows CE emulation environment.

One component of the emulation environment is the object store. The object store is contained in the file Wceobstr.dat. It contains the registry, databases, and files. The tree structure is identical to the real object store on a Handheld PC device; all semantics are the same. The root is "\", for example, and there is no concept of a current directory. The application FILESYS.EXE is used to manage the object store.

The other major component of the emulation environment is the shell. The application SHELL32.EXE emulates the Handheld PC shell. The emulation shell provides the same screen size and has the same look and feel as the real Handheld PC shell.

The emulation environment is started automatically when running or debugging an application that has a target of x86EM. The emulation environment can also be started directly by running SHELL32.EXE.

The Settings menu option on the Start menu in the emulation shell enables some configuration of the emulation shell. Specifically, the screen size of the emulation shell can be configured as well as the placement of the emulation shell.

As stated in the preceding text, emulation provides an environment that is very close to the actual Windows CE environment. However, there are small interface differences as well as missing functionality from the emulation environment. The visual appearance and size of tab controls, for example, can be slightly different under emulation.

Areas that are not supported under emulation include:

- 2bpp bitmaps

- The WM_HIBERNATE message

- Functionality related to LED support

- Infrared functionality

- PCMCIA functionality

Windows CE Remote Tools

The Windows CE SDK includes many tools and utilities that are useful in creating Windows CE applications. Some of these tools are "remote" versions of familiar Win32 SDK tools; others are tools unique to the Windows CE development environment.

Handheld PC Explorer

The Handheld PC Explorer is an application that comes with Handheld PC devices and is mainly an end-user application. The functionality of this tool is like the normal Windows Explorer with the exception of the file system that is explored on the Handheld PC (see Figure 4.2).

This tool enables the user to copy, move, delete, and rename files and directories that reside on the Handheld PC (when the application is running on the desktop PC). The tool can also be used to copy files between the Handheld PC and the desktop PC.

When the Handheld PC Explorer tool is started, it attempts to create a serial connection between the Handheld PC and the desktop PC. If the connection is successful, the Handheld PC Explorer will attempt to synchronize the PIM data and enable the user to back up the object store. The Explorer interface is then displayed, allowing the user to perform file management on the Handheld PC.

Figure 4.2

The Handheld PC Explorer application.

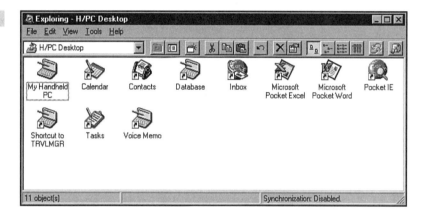

Remote Connection Server

This tool establishes a serial connection between the desktop PC and the Handheld PC. Although the Handheld PC Explorer application contains the same connection functionality, the Remote Connection Server is very useful during application development and testing.

The Remote Connection Server does not assume any relationship between the desktop PC and the Handheld PC, so no synchronization is attempted once the connection is made. This makes the connection process much faster, which is very convenient if the Handheld PC is being frequently connected and disconnected from the serial connection.

Remote Spy

Like the local desktop Spy++ application, Remote Spy is used to view the messages that are being sent to a particular window. The Remote Spy runs on the desktop PC but examines windows on the Handheld PC. Figure 4.3 shows the interface for the Remote Spy tool.

Figure 4.3

The Remote Spy application.

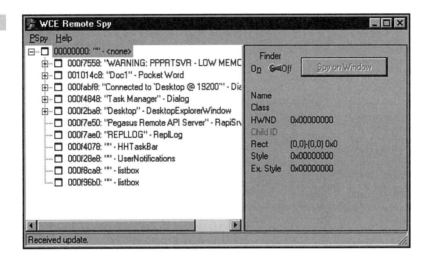

The Remote Spy tool shows the hierarchy of windows that is created on the Handheld PC and displays various window attributes for the window that is selected. Clicking the Spy on Window button brings up another window, which logs the messages that are sent to the selected window. Like the desktop version, the tools can be configured to only display selective messages.

Much like the functionality of the desktop version for interactively finding a window, clicking the Finder switch enables a window to be selected on the Handheld PC using the stylus. Once a window is selected on the Handheld PC, it is highlighted in the Remote Spy interface.

Remote Registry Editor

Although much of the system information for Windows CE is maintained in the Windows CE registry, there is no end-user tool for directly manipulating the registry (such as Regedit). Instead, the

Windows CE SDK include a desktop PC application that can manipulate the contents of a connected Handheld PC. Figure 4.4 shows the Remote Registry Editor.

The Remote Registry Editor has the same functionality as the local desktop Registry Editor. It enables keys and values to be viewed, modified, and deleted. It also has a search mechanism for finding information in the registry.

Figure 4.4

The Remote Registry Editor application.

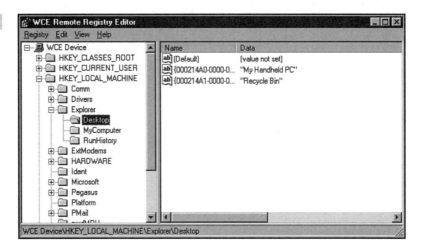

An important difference in the Remote Registry Editor is that updating the registry is a two step process. A change made to the registry is not reflected to the physical Handheld PC registry until it is "exported." Selecting the Export Registry menu option copies any registry changes to the Handheld PC device.

Note that the following characters cannot be used in values that are exported to the Handheld PC device:

0x005e ('^')

0x007e ('~')

0x003d ('=')

0x0022 ('"')

Remote Zoomin

Remote Zoomin is the counterpart to the Win32 SDK Zoomin application. Remote Zoomin captures a portion of the Handheld PC screen. Figure 4.5 shows the Remote Zoomin tool with a full screen captured.

Figure 4.5

The Remote Zoomin application.

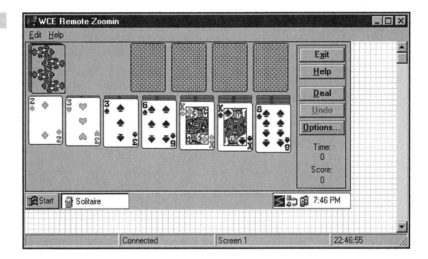

In addition to zooming in to a portion of the Handheld PC screen, the Zoomin tool is also very convenient for doing a screen capture of the entire Handheld PC screen. The Get Full HPC Screen menu option captures the entire Handheld PC screen.

You can capture a smaller portion of the Handheld PC screen by selecting the Define HPC Zoom Area menu option and then drawing a rectangle with the stylus directly on the Handheld PC screen.

The Refresh HPC Zoom Area menu option refreshes the Remote Zoomin window with the current contents of the Handheld PC screen (for the previously set zoom area).

You can increase or decrease the magnification of the image in the Remote Zoomin window by using the scrollbar on the right side of the window.

Remote Object Viewer

The Remote Object Viewer application is a tool that can view and manipulate a Windows CE object store. The object store can be on a remote Handheld PC, or the object store that is created for the emulation environment. Figure 4.6 shows the Remote Object Viewer interface.

Figure 4.6

The Remote Object Viewer application.

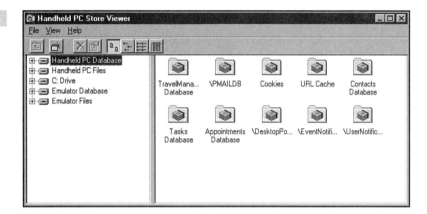

The Remote Object Viewer's tree displays a variety of objects that includes the following:

• **Handheld PC Database**. This node contains all of the databases on the Handheld PC. When a database is selected, the right pane displays that database's records.

• **Handheld PC Files**. This node contains the directories and files in the Handheld PC object store. When a directory is selected, the right pane displays the directory's files and subdirectories.

• **C: Drive**. This is the desktop machine's boot drive. This node is present to allow copying and moving of files between the desktop PC and the Handheld PC.

• **Emulator Database**. This node contains all of the databases in the emulation environment. When a database is selected, the right pane displays that database's records.

• **Emulator Files**. This node contains the directories and files in the emulation environment object store. When a directory is selected, the right pane displays the directory's files and subdirectories.

An important feature of the Remote Object Viewer is the capability to copy information between the Handheld PC object store and the emulation environment object store. This makes it easy to put information in the object store under the emulation environment. This is done in order to debug or test an application under emulation that requires information from the object store.

Another feature of the Remote Object Viewer is the capability to directly edit database records. Double-clicking a record in the right pane displays a properties window that shows the record's properties and values. The values can be changed by double-clicking a particular property.

Remote Memory Viewer

The last and most complex tool included in the Windows CE SDK is the Remote Memory Viewer. Contrary to its name, this tool does a lot more than examine memory on the Handheld PC. Figure 4.7 shows the WCE Remote Memory Viewer.

Figure 4.7

The Remote Memory Viewer application.

WCE Remote Memory Viewer

File   View   Options   Help

Process Name	Proc#	PID	Ptr	Slot	Code	R/W	R/O	Stack	Resv
NK.EXE	8001e720	20	8001c5e0	02	1192(216)...	108KB	168KB	4KB	3756KB
replog.exe	8001e7ac	141	80346000	04	140(0)KB	28KB	44KB	8KB	1164KB
filesys.exe	8001e838	62	803eb000	06	204(0)KB	36KB	24KB	4KB	16072KB
device.exe	8001e8c4	c3	803e0000	08	792(200)KB	88KB	104KB	48KB	1824KB
gwes.exe	8001e950	e4	8038a000	0a	592(0)KB	124KB	240KB	36KB	1580KB
afd.exe	8001e9dc	105	80374000	0c	416(0)KB	96KB	60KB	20KB	2604KB

Thread Handle	Owner Name	Running In..	Priority	Status	SchedFlags
803fe9a8	NK.EXE	NK.EXE	3	00000000	00000003
803fece8	NK.EXE	NK.EXE	1	00000000	00000003
80015044	NK.EXE	NK.EXE	3	00000000	00000003
803f7e5c	replog.exe	gwes.exe	3	00000000	00000003
803fe810	filesys.exe	filesys.exe	3	00000000	00000003
803fb8e4	device.exe	device.exe	3	00000000	00000003

Module Name	In-Use Flags	Handle	Base Ptr	Start IP
pmemtool.dll	00000200	803f6f40	03af0000	01af1660
PEGOBJ.dll	00000002	803f76a0	03ca0000	01ca249c
Unimodem.dll	00000008	803f8240	03ba0000	01ba3a34
TAPI.dll	00000008	803f8358	03bb0000	01bb2bec
commctrl.dll	00000248	803fe9c	03f90000	01f92194
IRDASTK.dll	00000020	803f9460	03c20000	01c22a24

| 55% Free | | Dump 1 | | 22:48:53 |

The Remote Memory Viewer tool can be used to examine many aspects of the Windows CE memory architecture as presented in Chapter 1. Some of the information displayed in the Remote Memory Viewer deals with the low-level Windows CE kernel implementation and is beyond the scope of this book. This section will detail the information presented in the Remote Memory Viewer, but not necessarily attempt to explain exactly what it means.

The Remote Memory Viewer is divided into three panes. The top pane displays information about the processes currently running on the Handheld PC. The following columns of the top pane detail information about the process:

```
Process Name : Name of the process
Proc # : Process handle (HINSTANCE).
PID : Process ID
Ptr : Address of slot containing process.
Slot : Slot in address space containing the process
Code : Number of ROM code pages used. The number of RAM code pages
➥used is displayed in parenthesis.
R/W : The number of read/write data pages.
R/O : The number of read only data pages.
Stack : The number of stack pages.
Resv : The number of pages reserved.
```

The middle pane displays information about all the currently executing threads on the Handheld PC. The information displayed for each thread includes the following:

- **Thread Handle**. The thread ID number. This is the handle returned by CreateThread.

- **Owner Name**. The name of the executable that launched the process.

- **Running In**. The name of the process that owns the thread.

- **Priority**. The thread priority value.

- **Status**. The thread status value.

- **SchedFlags**. The scheduling flag's value.

The following table lists the possible scheduling flags.

Scheduling Flag	Thread State	Description
0	Runable	Thread is either running or will run when time sliced.
1	Sleeping	Thread is waiting for time to pass (e.g.: called Sleep).
2	Critical	Thread Section Block has blocked on a call to EnterCriticalSection.
3	Event Blocked	Thread has blocked on a call to WaitForSingleObject with an event handle.
4	Suspended	Thread is suspended.
5	Terminated	Thread has terminated.

The bottom pane of the Remote Memory Viewer application lists information about the current modules (DLLs) that are loaded. The columns of this pane include the following:

- **Module Name**. The name of the module.

- **In-use flags**. Indicates which processes are using the DLL.

- **Handle**. The handle to the module.

- **Base Ptr**. The DLL's base pointer (starting point in memory).

- **Start IP**. The DLL's entry point (address of DllMain).

Double-clicking a process name in the top pane brings up the Process Memory Map dialog box (see Figure 4.8). The memory map shows the pages that are currently allocated to the process and details each page's type. The possible page types include the following:

S: Stack page

C: Code page in ROM

c: Code page in RAM

W: Read/write data page in RAM

R: Read only data page in ROM

r: Read only data page in RAM

O: Object store page

P: Peripheral mapping page

-: Reserved page available to be committed

Figure 4.8

The Process Memory Map dialog box.

A final set of information that can be retrieved with the Remote Memory Viewer is a summary of the resources currently used by the Windows CE kernel. Figure 4.9 shows the Kernel Summary dialog box that is displayed by choosing the View, Kernel Summary menu option.

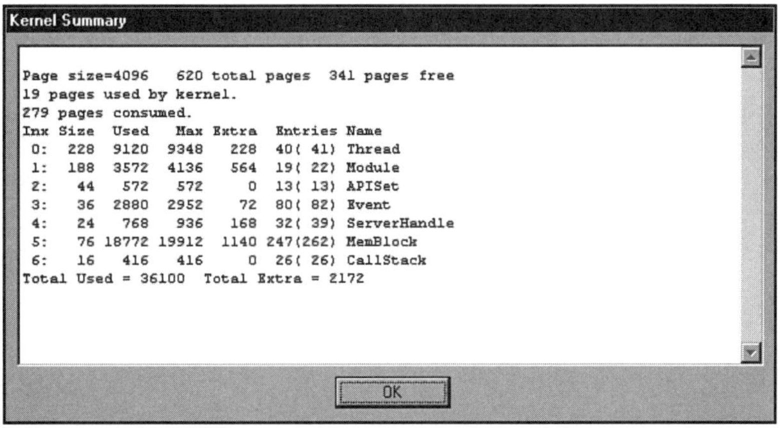

Figure 4.9

The Kernel Summary dialog box.

CHAPTER 5

Hello Windows CE

Carrying on the tradition of a "Hello World" program and a "Hello Windows" program, this chapter presents an analogous program written for Windows CE. This program will show the basic components needed for a Windows CE application.

Because the API for Windows CE is really just a subset of Win32, the "Hello Window CE" program will look very much like a "Hello Windows" program written for Win32. However, there are some obvious—and some subtle—differences. These differences will be explored in detail in this chapter.

Even though much of the code will be identical to a simple Win32 program, these initial steps are examined in detail. Even for the experienced Win32 programmer, some of these steps may be unfamiliar, due to the widespread use of aids like Microsoft Foundation Class (MFC) and Borland's Object Windows Library.

Another benefit of these class libraries is that they implement most of the infrastructure that is needed to use C++ to develop a Windows application. Because the Windows API is primarily designed for C, there are some programming challenges to overcome in order to use C++ to build an application.

Note

During the final stages of this book, MFC support was added for Windows CE development. MFC support for Windows CE is a subset of the full MFC library and has some implications due to the size of the runtime components with the limited storage size available on Handheld PCs.

To begin exploring programming for Windows CE, Hello Windows CE will first be implemented in straight C. This creates a small sample that will make it easier to explore the fundamentals of a Windows CE application.

After examining the components of the application, the sample will be redone in C++. This entails adding the infrastructure described in the preceding text to make building a Windows CE application in C++ easier. Because this infrastructure is easily reusable, the remaining chapters of the book will use C++. Additionally, C++ also makes it simple for you to reuse any of the code presented in this book.

The HELLO Sample

The Hello Windows CE program exhibits all the necessary elements of a Windows CE application. The program, named HELLO, creates a window and displays the text string Hello Windows CE in the center of the window. It also adds a command bar with a close/cancel button so that the window may be closed. Here is the entire listing for the HELLO program:

```
#include <windows.h>

// Class name and window title
WCHAR szClassName[] = TEXT("Hello");
WCHAR szTitle[] = TEXT("Hello Windows CE Application");

// Global Instance handle
HINSTANCE hInst = NULL;

LRESULT CALLBACK WndProc( HWND hWnd,      UINT msg,
                                                          WPARAM
➥wParam
LPARAM lParam )
```

```
{
            HDC hdc;
            PAINTSTRUCT ps;
            RECT rect;
            HWND wndCB;

            switch (msg)
            {

            case WM_CREATE:
                        wndCB = CommandBar_Create(hInst, hWnd, 1);
                        CommandBar_AddAdornments(wndCB, 0, NULL);
                        break;

            case WM_PAINT:
                        hdc = BeginPaint(hWnd, &ps);
                        GetClientRect(hWnd, &rect);
                        DrawText(hdc, TEXT("Hello Windows CE"), -1,
➡&rect,
                                                    DT_SINGLELINE¦DT_CENTER
➡¦DT_VCENTER);
                        EndPaint(hWnd, &ps);
                        break;

            case WM_DESTROY:
                        PostQuitMessage(0);
                        break;

            default:
                        return (DefWindowProc(hWnd, msg, wParam,
➡lParam));
            }

            return (0);
}

BOOL RegisterWindowClass()
{
            WNDCLASSW      wc;

            wc.style                      =    0 ;
            wc.lpfnWndProc        = (WNDPROC) WndProc;
            wc.cbClsExtra          = 0;
            wc.cbWndExtra          = 0;
```

```
                wc.hInstance            = hInst;
                wc.hIcon                   = NULL;
                wc.hCursor               = NULL;
                wc.hbrBackground = (HBRUSH) GetStockObject(WHITE_BRUSH);
                wc.lpszMenuName    = NULL;
                wc.lpszClassName = szClassName;

                return RegisterClass(&wc);
        }

        BOOL CreateMainWindow( int nCmdShow )
        {
                HWND hWnd;

                hWnd = CreateWindowEx(0,
        // extended styles
                                                        szClassName,
        // class name
                                                        szTitle,
        // window title
                                                        WS_VISIBLE,
        // styles
                                                        0,
        // x position
                                                        0,
        // y position
                                                CW_USEDEFAULT,
        // width
                                                CW_USEDEFAULT,
        // height
                                                        NULL,
        // parent
                                                        NULL,
        // menu
                                                        hInst,
        // instance handle
                                                        NULL);
        // user data

                // Did CreateWindow succeed?
                if ( hWnd == 0 )
                {
                        return (FALSE);
                }
```

```
            ShowWindow(hWnd, SW_SHOW);
            UpdateWindow(hWnd);

            return(TRUE);
}

int WINAPI WinMain ( HINSTANCE hInstance,
                                                HINSTANCE
➡hPrevInstance,
                                                LPWSTR
➡lpCmdLine,
                                                int
➡nCmdShow )

{
            MSG msg;

            // Is there another instance already running
            if ( hPrevInstance != 0 )
            {
                        return FALSE;
            }

            // Set the global instance handle
            hInst = hInstance;

            if ( RegisterWindowClass() == FALSE )
            {
                        return(FALSE);
            }

            // API call to initialize common controls
            InitCommonControls();

            if ( CreateMainWindow(nCmdShow) == FALSE )
            {
                        return(FALSE);
            }

            // Main window was created, start the message loop
            while ( GetMessage(&msg, NULL, 0, 0) != FALSE )
            {
```

```
                              TranslateMessage (&msg) ;
                              DispatchMessage(&msg);
               }

               return(msg.wParam);
       }
```

Note

All of the source code presented here can also be found on the accompanying CD-ROM. See Appendix A, "Getting Started with the CD-ROM," for details on the contents of the CD-ROM and for information on accessing the example code.

Once the HELLO sample is built and executed (either in emulation mode, or by downloading it to the Handheld PC and running it), the program creates a normal application window (as shown in Figure 5.1).

Figure 5.1
HELLO application.

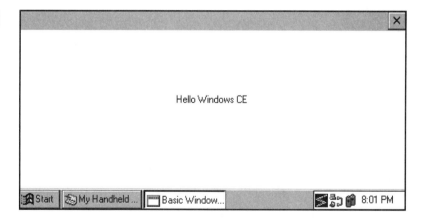

The Windows CE Entry Function

As with other varieties of Windows, WinMain is the entry point into applications written for Windows CE. Except for a few minor deviations, the parameters to the Windows CE WinMain are the same as other platform WinMain functions.

```
int WINAPI WinMain ( HINSTANCE hInstance,
                                                        HINSTANCE
➥hPrevInstance,
                                                        LPWSTR
➥lpCmdLine,
                                                        int
➥nCmdShow )
```

The parameters to WinMain are as follows:

- **hInstance**. This parameter is the handle to the instance of the program. It's identical to the corresponding parameter from the Win32 WinMain.

- **hPrevInstance**. This parameter is obsolete for Windows CE and should always be NULL.

- **lpCmdLine**. This parameter specifies the command line for the application. For Windows CE, this parameter has changed from an LPSTR to an LPWSTR in order to accommodate a UNICODE string.

- **nCmdShow**. This parameter specifies how the window will be shown. Valid values for Windows CE are SW_HIDE, SW_SHOW, SW_SHOWNA, SW_SHOWNOACTIVATE, and SW_SHOWNORMAL.

Registering the Window Class

As in Win32, windows created under Windows CE are based on a window class. Before a window can be created, the window class must be registered with the system using the RegisterClass function.

The window class defines some basic properties of the window, as well as the procedure that processes the messages for the window.

Tip

Windows CE does not support all of the fields in the WNDCLASS structure that are used to define the characteristics of the window. The unsupported fields should be set to NULL.

The following code demonstrates how to register a window class in Windows CE:

```
WNDCLASS     wc;

wc.style                        =    0 ;
wc.lpfnWndProc       = (WNDPROC) WndProc;
wc.cbClsExtra            = 0;
wc.cbWndExtra            = 0;
wc.hInstance             = hInst;
wc.hIcon                        = NULL;
wc.hCursor                    = NULL;
wc.hbrBackground = (HBRUSH) GetStockObject(WHITE_BRUSH);
wc.lpszMenuName      = NULL;
wc.lpszClassName = szClassName;

RegisterClass(&wc);
```

The members of the WNDCLASS structure are as follows:

- **style**. Specifies the class style. Windows CE supports only one style, so this parameter must be NULL.

- **lpfnWndProc**. Points to the window procedure that will process the messages sent to this class of window.

- **cbClsExtra**. Specifies the number of extra bytes to allocate following the window-class structure. The operating system initializes the bytes to zero.

- **cbWndExtra**. Specifies the number of extra bytes to allocate following the window instance. The operating system initializes the bytes to zero.

- **hInstance**. Identifies the instance that the window procedure of this class is within.

- **hIcon**. Identifies the class icon. This member must be a handle of an icon resource. If this member is NULL, an application must draw an icon whenever the user minimizes the application's window.

- **hCursor**. There is no cursor in Windows CE, so this parameter must be NULL.

- **hbrBackground**. Identifies the class background brush.

- **lpszMenuName**. Windows CE does not support default menus, so this parameter must be NULL.

- **lpszClassName**. Points to a null-terminated string that specifies the window class name.

Once all the members of the WNDCLASS structure have been initialized, the structure is passed to the `RegisterClass` function. Each window class only needs registered once, regardless of the number of windows created with that class. That is, the window class defines the general characteristics of a window, thus allowing many different windows to be created under the same window class.

Creating the Main Window

After registering the window class, the actual window can be created with the `CreateWindowEx` function.

```
hWnd = CreateWindowEx(0,
➡// extended styles
                                                szClassName,
// class name
                                                szTitle,
// window title
                                                WS_VISIBLE,
// styles
                                                0,
// x position
                                                0,
// y position
                                                CW_USEDEFAULT,
// width
                                                CW_USEDEFAULT,
// height
                                                NULL,
// parent
                                                NULL,
```

```
                              // menu
                                                               hInst,
                              // instance handle
                                                               NULL);
                              // user data
```

Note

There is also a CreateWindow function with all the same parameters as CreateWindowEx except the first extended style parameter.

The CreateWindowEx function specifies the details of the window's appearance and functionality. The parameters for CreateWindowEx are the same as Win32 with the following exceptions:

- **dwExStyle**. The only supported flags are the following:

  WS_EX_WINDOWEDGE

  WS_EX_CLIENTEDGE

  WS_EX_STATICEDGE

  WS_EX_OVERLAPPEDWINDOW

- **dwStyle**. The only supported flags are the following:

  WS_BORDER

  WS_CAPTION

  WS_CHILD

  WS_CLIPSIBLINGS

  WS_CLIPCHILDREN

  WS_DISABLED

  WS_DLGFRAME

  WS_GROUP

  WS_HSCROLL

WS_OVERLAPPED

WS_TILED

WS_POPUP

WS_TABSTOP

WS_SYSMENU   Windows CE does not have a system menu, but
this flag is used to determine whether the window's title bar
should have accessories such as widgets-buttons, OK, ?, and so
on.

WS_VISIBLE

WS_VSCROLL

The following list includes other facts exclusive to `CreateWindowEx`:

- **WS_CLIPSIBLINGS and WS_CLIPCHILDREN**. All windows are implicitly these two style bits.

- **Owner windows.** These are not supported.

- **LBS_OWNERDRAWFIXED and
  LBS_OWNERDRAWVARIABLE**. These list box styles are not
  supported.

- **CBS_OWNERDRAWFIXED and
  CBS_OWNERDRAWVARIABLE**. These combo box styles are
  not supported.

- `hwndParent`. If this is not NULL, the window is implicitly given
  the WS_CHILD style bit.

- **Menu bars**. These are not supported.

- **SS_SIMPLE**. This is not supported for static controls. You may
  use SS_LEFT or SS_LEFTNOWORDWRAP as a work-around.

- `hMenu`. It must be NULL, unless it is used as a child-window identifier.

- **Owned dialogs**. These are the only dialogs that are supported. They are created via the Dialog Manager API's.

- **MDICLIENT**. This is not supported.

The return value from `CreateWindowEx` is the handle to the newly created window. Once the window is created, it is displayed using the following code:

```
ShowWindow(hWnd, SW_SHOW);
UpdateWindow(hWnd);
```

The `ShowWindow` function sets the specified window's show state. Windows CE only supports the following states:

SW_HIDE

SW_SHOW

SW_SHOWNA

SW_SHOWNOACTIVATE

SW_SHOWNORMAL

The `UpdateWindow` function updates the client area of the specified window by sending a WM_PAINT message to the window procedure of the specified window.

The Message Loop

After the UpdateWindow function call, the window is fully visible. As with all Windows programs, it is now necessary to create a "message loop." This loop will retrieve messages from the message queue and process them. The message loop is demonstrated in the following code:

```
while ( GetMessage(&msg, NULL, 0, 0) != FALSE )
        {
                        TranslateMessage (&msg) ;
                        DispatchMessage(&msg);
        }
```

The `GetMessage`, `TranslateMessage`, and `DispatchMessage` functions have the same syntax and functionality as their counterparts in Win32.

Tip

> Although it's possible in Win32, avoid the use of `PeekMessage` in a while loop in Windows CE. `GetMessage` blocks for a return while `PeekMessage` doesn't. Allowing the system to block the application will allow the operating system to efficiently manage power consumption.

After a message is dispatched from the message loop, the operating system sends the message through the appropriate window procedure for processing. As stated previously, the window class defines the window procedure associated with each class of window. The window procedure has the following format:

```
LRESULT CALLBACK WndProc( HWND hWnd,      UINT msg,
                                                    WPARAM
➥wPara
LPARAM lParam )
```

The syntax and parameters of the window procedure are identical to window procedures under Win32.

Messages

Each message procedure that a window procedure receives is identified by a number that is specified in the msg parameter. The message numbers are defined in header files that are part of the Software Development Kit (SDK).

An application generally uses a switch statement to look for and process the messages it is interested in. The Hello sample handles three messages: WM_CREATE, WM_PAINT, and WM_DESTROY.

The WM_CREATE Message

Once a window has been created but before it is visible, the window receives a WM_CREATE message. This message is identical to the WM_CREATE message under Win32. The LParam parameter points to a CREATESTRUCT that contains information about the window being created. The CREATESTRUCT is defined as follows:

```
typedef struct tagCREATESTRUCT {
        LPVOID          lpCreateParams;
        HINSTANCE hInstance;
        HMENU           hMenu;
        HWND            hwndParent;
        int             cy;
        int             cx;
        int             y;
        int             x;
        LONG            style;
        LPCTSTR         lpszName;
        LPCTSTR         lpszClass;
        DWORD           dwExStyle;
} CREATESTRUCT;
```

The members of the CREATESTRUCT have the same differences in Windows CE that their counterparts have in the CreateWindowEx function's parameter list.

In the handling of the WM_CREATE message, the HELLO program uses the API functions CommandBar_Create and CommandBar_AddAdornments. These functions create a command bar that is a combination of the menu bar, the toolbar, and the title bar. Command bars will be discussed in detail in Chapter 6, "User Interface Basics."

The WM_PAINT Message

The WM_PAINT message informs a program when part or all of the window's client area is "invalid" and needs to be repainted. In the handling of the WM_PAINT message, the HELLO sample program uses the API functions: BeginPaint, GetClientRect, DrawText, and EndPaint.

```
hdc = BeginPaint(hWnd, &ps);
                GetClientRect(hWnd, &rect);
                DrawText(hdc, TEXT("Hello Windows CE"), -1, &rect,
                                        DT_SINGLELINE¦DT_CENTER
➥¦DT_VCENTER);
                EndPaint(hWnd, &ps);
```

The BeginPaint function prepares the specified window for painting, and the EndPaint function marks the end of painting in the specified window. The BeginPaint and EndPaint functions operate the same under Windows CE as they do under Win32.

As in Win32, the GetClientRect function retrieves the dimensions of the client area of the window.

Note

> The GetClientRect does not account for the command bar in the client area. This detail will be covered in the next chapter.

The DrawText function is used to draw text. The parameters tell it what text to draw, where to draw it, and how to draw it. There is no change in this function for Windows CE.

The WM_DESTROY Message

As with other Windows platforms, the WM_DESTROY message indicates that Windows is in the process of destroying a window based on a command from the user. This message could result from the user tapping on the Close button or pressing Alt+F4. The HELLO sample handles the WM_DESTROY message by calling the PostQuitMessage function to end the program.

```
case WM_DESTROY:
            PostQuitMessage(0);
            break;
```

In response to a WM_DESTROY message, the HELLO sample calls the PostQuitMessage function. This function inserts a WM_QUIT message in the program's message queue. The WM_QUIT message is the one message that will cause the GetMessage function in the message loop to return FALSE. This causes WinMain to drop out of the message loop and exit, terminating the program.

Using Unicode Strings

One aspect of Win32 that programmers may or may not be familiar with is Unicode. Windows NT has full support for Unicode, while Windows 95 has very limited support for Unicode. Thus, many Win32 programmers are not accustomed to Unicode because it was not originally used for Windows 3.x and Windows 95 programming.

The good news is that Windows CE fully supports Unicode. The bad news, however, is that you must learn some new techniques for creating and accessing strings. It also means that text stored by a Windows CE program takes up twice as much storage space (16-bit versus 8-bit characters).

The HELLO application uses a macro named TEXT anywhere a string is used. This macro forces the compiler to convert ANSI characters to Unicode characters—it is identical to the TEXT macro under Win32.

Moving to C++

Anyone familiar with MFC or OWL knows that writing a "Hello Windows" program takes a lot less code than the sample has used. That's because MFC and OWL have a lot of their own code to implement some of the basic components the HELLO sample needed. The goal in this instance is not to duplicate those big class libraries, but to do enough to allow you to group some code in C++ classes.

Every Windows application, including Windows CE applications, needs a WinMain. Therefore, WinMain is one C-style function that can't go away. The other big hurdle is the WndProc function. When using MFC, it's rare to use a true WndProc window procedure, but WndProcs already are buried in MFC code. Instead, messages end up in the OnCommand method for the given window class (C++ class, not WNDCLASS class). MFC does the necessary work to get the message from its WndProc to the OnCommand method for the right object.

The following "Hello++ Windows CE" sample implements a simple strategy for using C++ under Windows CE. MFC goes way beyond this strategy; for example, message maps go beyond the scope of this book.

Now that MFC is available for Windows CE development, it may be very useful for some application development. This book uses straight API calls and not MFC, however, in order to focus on the differences between Win32 programming and Windows CE programming.

The HELLO++ Sample

The HELLO++ application has the same functionality as the HELLO application, except that it uses C++ to group some parts together. The sample uses two classes: an application class and a main window class, as shown in the following code.

```
#include <windows.h>

// Class name and window title
WCHAR szClassName[] = TEXT("Helloxx");
WCHAR szTitle[] = TEXT("Hello++ Windows CE Application");

// The application class
class HelloApp
{
public:
        HelloApp();
        ~HelloApp(){}

        BOOL Create(HINSTANCE);
        int Run();
        HINSTANCE m_hInst;
};

// The main window class
class MainWindow
{
public:
        MainWindow() {}
        ~MainWindow() {}

        BOOL Create(HelloApp *);

        void WMCreate(HWND);
        void WMPaint();
```

```cpp
private:
        HWND m_hWnd;
        HelloApp * m_pApp;
};

// Global Window handle
MainWindow * g_pMainWindow = NULL;

// Implementation of MainWindow methods
void MainWindow::WMCreate(HWND hWnd)
{
        HWND wndCB = CommandBar_Create(m_pApp->m_hInst, hWnd, 1);
        CommandBar_AddAdornments(wndCB, 0, NULL);
}


void MainWindow::WMPaint()
{
        HDC hdc;
        PAINTSTRUCT ps;
        RECT rect;

        hdc = BeginPaint(m_hWnd, &ps);
        GetClientRect(m_hWnd, &rect);
        DrawText(hdc, TEXT("Hello Windows CE"), -1, &rect,
                                DT_SINGLELINE|DT_CENTER|DT_VCENTER);
        EndPaint(m_hWnd, &ps);
}

BOOL MainWindow::Create(HelloApp * pHelloApp)
{
        m_pApp = pHelloApp;
        g_pMainWindow = this;

        m_hWnd = CreateWindowEx(0,
➥// extended styles
                                                        szClassName,
// class name
                                                        szTitle,
// window title
                                                        WS_VISIBLE,
// styles
                                                            0,
```

```
// x position
                                                                        0,
// y position
                                                            CW_USEDEFAULT,
// width
                                                            CW_USEDEFAULT,
// height
                                                                     NULL,
// parent
                                                                     NULL,
// menu
                                                                   m_pApp-
>m_hInst,     // instance handle
                                                                    NULL);
// user data

            // Did CreateWindow succeed?
            if ( m_hWnd == 0 )
            {
                        return (FALSE);
            }

            ShowWindow(m_hWnd, SW_SHOW);
            UpdateWindow(m_hWnd);

            return(TRUE);
}


LRESULT CALLBACK WndProc( HWND hWnd,     UINT msg,
                                                            WPARAM
➥wPara
LPARAM lParam )
{
            switch (msg)
            {

            case WM_CREATE:
                        g_pMainWindow->WMCreate(hWnd);
                        break;

            case WM_PAINT:
                        g_pMainWindow->WMPaint();
                        break;
```

```
                case WM_DESTROY:
                            delete g_pMainWindow;
                            PostQuitMessage(0);
                            break;

                default:
                            return (DefWindowProc(hWnd, msg, wParam,
➡lParam));
                }

                return (0);
}

// Implementation of HelloApp methods
HelloApp::HelloApp()
{
                // API call to initialize common controls
                InitCommonControls();
}

BOOL HelloApp::Create(HINSTANCE hInstance)
{
                WNDCLASS        wc;

                m_hInst = hInstance;

                wc.style                       =     0 ;
                wc.lpfnWndProc      = (WNDPROC) WndProc;
                wc.cbClsExtra          = 0;
                wc.cbWndExtra          = 0;
                wc.hInstance           = m_hInst;
                wc.hIcon                       = NULL;
                wc.hCursor                   = NULL;
                wc.hbrBackground = (HBRUSH) GetStockObject(WHITE_BRUSH);
                wc.lpszMenuName     = NULL;
                wc.lpszClassName = szClassName;

                if ( !RegisterClass(&wc) )
                {
                            return FALSE;
                }

                // RegisterClass worked, so create the window
                MainWindow * pMainWindow = new MainWindow();
```

```
            if ( !pMainWindow )
            {
                    return FALSE;
            }

            if ( !pMainWindow->Create(this) )
            {
                    return FALSE;
            }
            return TRUE;
}


int HelloApp::Run()
{
            MSG msg;

            // Main window was created, start the message loop
            while ( GetMessage(&msg, NULL, 0, 0) != FALSE )
            {
                    TranslateMessage (&msg) ;
                    DispatchMessage(&msg);
            }

            return(msg.wParam);
}

int WINAPI WinMain ( HINSTANCE hInstance,
                                                            HINSTANCE
➥hPrevInstance,
                                                            LPWSTR
➥lpCmdLine,
                                                            int
➥nCmdShow )
{
            // Is there another instance already running
            if ( hPrevInstance != 0 )
            {
                    return -1;
            }

            HelloApp * pApp = new HelloApp();

            if ( !pApp )
            {
```

```
                        return -1;
        }

        if ( pApp->Create(hInstance) == FALSE )
        {
                        return -1;
        }

        BOOL exitVal = pApp->Run();

        delete pApp;

        return exitVal;
}
```

The HelloApp Class

The first class in the HELLO++ application is the HelloApp class. This is the application class that comprises most of the functionality that was found in the HELLO application's WinMain.

The first method in the HelloApp class is *Create*. Create is responsible for registering the window class, instantiating a MainWindow object, and invoking the MainWindow's Create method.

The other method in the HelloApp class is *Run*. This method contains the message loop for the application.

The HelloApp class also keeps a member variable for the application's HINSTANCE. Keeping this data in the HelloApp class eliminates the hInst global variable that was used in the HELLO program.

The MainWindow Class

The MainWindow class is the interface to the window. Its methods are Create, WMCreate, and WMPaint.

The Create method is responsible for creating the actual window on the screen. It uses the CreateWindowEx, ShowWindow, and UpdateWindow API functions.

The WMCreate and WMPaint methods handle the WM_CREATE and WM_PAINT messages.

Changes to WinMain and WndProc

Most of the code that makes up the HelloApp and MainWindow classes is just code that is already part of the original HELLO application. The biggest changes in the HELLO++ code are the changes to WinMain and WndProc.

The original WinMain did a lot of disjoint operations: registering a window class, initializing the common controls, creating a window, and entering a message loop. The new WinMain relies on the HelloApp class to do all the necessary work. It does this by instantiating a HelloApp object, calling the Create method for the HelloApp object, and then calling the Run method. It also does some error checking and then deletes the HelloApp object once the Run has returned.

The changes to WndProc are much the same as WinMain. Instead of WndProc handling each message it receives, it now receives the message and calls an appropriate method in the MainWindow class for processing. This allows one object to handle all the functionality for the Main-Window.

An important thing to notice is how the WndProc function knows what object it should use to call the appropriate methods. In this instance, it's using a global variable g_pMainWindow that points to the instance of the MainWindow object. This global pointer is set in the MainWindow::Create method.

Using a global variable to keep track of the MainWindow object may not be the best solution, but it certainly is the easiest to implement. Keeping track of one global variable is fine, but imagine if it was managing ten different windows. A different approach would be to maintain a table that associates a window handle (HWND) with a pointer to the window's C++ class. Another idea would be to store the pointer to the window's C++ object directly in the window structure, using the cbWndExtra parameter of the WNDCLASS structure.

Benefits of C++ over C

Some may consider the changes in HELLO++ to be an extreme amount of extra code for a little organization. In such a simple program, this may be true. However as the projects get bigger, the benefits of C++ become more apparent. C++ also enables code to be more easily reused.

This book does not attempt to preach the benefits of C++ over C. The examples in the book are C++, but because the examples aren't built on top of other C++ class libraries like MFC, it would be fairly easy to turn all of the example's methods into C functions.

6

User Interface Basics

The HELLO and HELLO++ examples covered in Chapter 5, "Hello Windows CE," demonstrated the basic components used to build a Windows CE application. This chapter explores the basic elements of user interfaces in Windows CE applications. Through this interaction, the user will both provide and be provided with information.

As you may recall, the HELLO examples showed a few elements relating to user interface. These examples used the DrawText function to display information on the screen, and enabled the user to close the application by adding a command bar with a close button. These elements of basic user interaction will be explored in more detail later in this chapter.

The TravelManager Application

The remaining chapters of this book do not provide individual little example programs that each display different elements or behaviors—example code of this kind can be useful, but rarely to develop something as simple as the HELLO application. Therefore, the remaining chapters continue examining the programming aspects of Windows CE by developing a "real" application. As new elements of Windows CE are explored, they will be added to the application. Occasionally, a small example program will be created to illustrate some element that doesn't fit well into the continuing application.

Imagine you are going on a trip; it could be either for business or pleasure. What information do you take with you? Most importantly, do you have an itinerary that shows flight information, hotel reservations, and car rental information? You might have some airline data about other flights on the same days you're flying—in case you miss your plane. You also might have various bits of miscellaneous information such as contact names, things to remember, or a list of people to whom you want to send postcards. This information is probably distributed between pieces of paper you carry, data on your laptop, or just in your head. Instead of having this information scattered around, a Handheld PC is the perfect tool for having easy access to all this information!

Rather than describe the application's functionality and interface in complete detail, you'll start simple and build in features as you go. Obviously, to create a Windows CE application, you need the basic components from the previous chapter: WinMain, WndProc, message loop, and so on. In case you need a reference point, the end of this chapter contains the complete code listing for the TravelManager application, including all the features and functionality added in this chapter.

Source code for the TravelManager application can also be found on the accompanying CD-ROM. See Appendix A, "Getting Started with the CD-ROM," for information on installing and building the example code on the CD-ROM.

Working with Command Bars

The first interface component to add to the application is the command bar. Under Windows 95 and Windows NT, the title bar, menu bar, and toolbar are each given a row of space in the window. However, because real estate is such a premium on Windows CE and because applications rarely fill the entire width of the window with menu items or toolbar buttons, Windows CE combines all those elements into a single space known as the command bar. The command bar is located at the top of each window. Four example command bars are shown in Figure 6.1, while the TravelManager's command bar is shown in Figure 6.2.

Figure 6.1

Example command bars.

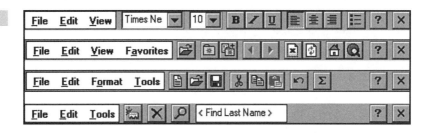

Figure 6.2

The TravelManager application's command bars.

Before examining the code used to create the TravelManager's command bar, the parts of the command bar must be identified. The first box in the command bar is the *menu bar*, consisting of the menus File, Edit, View, and Help. After the menu bar is a *combo box*, which is used by TravelManager as a quick navigation tool. Following the combo box is a number of buttons. The first seven buttons are the TravelManager's buttonbar. The last two buttons, Help and Close, are common to most Windows CE applications.

A command bar can include four different types of elements: menu bars, buttons, combo boxes, and separators. A *separator* divides items into groups by adding space between them.

The position of each element in the command bar is identified by a zero-based index value, with the leftmost item at position zero. This index position is often used to identify where to insert an element into the command bar. The new element is inserted to the left of the specified index position. To insert an element to the right of the current rightmost element, specify an index one greater than the index of that element.

Before adding any control, the command bar must first be created using the CommandBar_Create function. The TravelManager application does this in the new *CreateCommandBar* method of the MainWindow class.

```
HWND hwndCB = CommandBar_Create(m_pApp->m_hInst, m_hWnd,
ID_COMMANDBAR);
```

The CommandBar_Create parameters are as follows:

- **HINSTANCE**. Specifies the application instance in which the command bar is to be created.

- **HWND**. Specifies the parent window for the command bar.

- **int**. Specifies the identifier of the command bar.

Other factors you should consider pertaining to the CommandBar_Create are as follows:

> The return value is a handle to the newly created command bar.

> Windows CE automatically sets the size of the command bar and positions the bar along the top of the parent window's client area.

Because command bars are optional, Windows CE does not automatically account for them when retrieving the client area using the GetClientRect function. To determine the useable portion of the client area, adjust the rect returned from GetClientRect with the height of the command bar. The height of the command bar can be found using the CommandBar_Height function.

Creating Menu Bars

Inserting and formatting menus in Windows CE is similar to inserting and formatting menus in Win32. The `CommandBar_InsertMenubar` function is used to insert a menu bar into a command bar.

```
CommandBar_InsertMenubar(hwndCB, m_pApp->m_hInst, IDM_MAIN_MENU, 0);
```

The `CommandBar_InsertMenubar` parameters are as follows:

- **HWND**. Specifies the handle of the command bar in which to insert the menu bar.

- **HINSTANCE**. Specifies the application instance from which to get the menu resource.

- **WORD**. Specifies the identifier of the menu resource.

- **int**. Specifies the zero-based index of a command bar element. The function inserts the menu bar to the left of this element. Menus are usually started at position zero.

The menu resource format under Windows CE remains unchanged from Win32. The trvlmgr.rc file specifies the menu resource for the TravelManager application:

```
IDM_MAIN_MENU MENU DISCARDABLE
BEGIN
    POPUP "File"
    BEGIN
        MENUITEM "Save",                    ID_FILE_SAVE
        MENUITEM SEPARATOR
        MENUITEM "Exit",                    ID_FILE_EXIT
    END
    POPUP "Edit"
    BEGIN
        MENUITEM "Cut",                     ID_EDIT_CUT
        MENUITEM "Copy",                    ID_EDIT_COPY
        MENUITEM "Paste",                   ID_EDIT_PASTE
    END
    POPUP "View"
```

```
    BEGIN
        MENUITEM "Itinerary",              ID_VIEW_ITINERARY
        MENUITEM "Expenses",               ID_VIEW_EXPENSES
        MENUITEM "Notes",                  ID_VIEW_NOTES
    END
    POPUP "Help"
    BEGIN
        MENUITEM "Contents",               ID_HELP_CONTENTS
        MENUITEM SEPARATOR
        MENUITEM "About",                  ID_HELP_ABOUT
    END
```

The menu resource specifies the structure of the menus, the label for
each menu, and the ID number that Windows CE sends to the application (in a WM_COMMAND message) when the user chooses that
menu item. The ID numbers for the TravelManager are defined in the
resource.h file. The menu resource files and the code can be found on
the accompanying CD-ROM.

After inserting a menu bar into the command bar, the Win32 menu
API functions can be used to manage the menu. To retrieve a handle
to the menu bar, use the CommandBar_GetMenu function. After creating
the menu bar, the TravelManager application adds a check mark to the
Itinerary menu item of the View menu (because this is the default view
that is created). This can be referenced by noticing the following code:

```
HMENU hMenu = CommandBar_GetMenu(hwndCB,0)
CheckMenuItem(hMenu, ID_VIEW_ITINERARY, MF_CHECKED);
```

One difference from Win32 menus is that cascading (sometimes called
hierarchical) menus are not currently supported by Windows CE. As an
alternative to cascading menus, you can increase the number of menu
commands or display further choices in a dialog box.

Creating Combo Boxes

Under Win32, adding a combo box to a toolbar was not an easy task.
Luckily, under Windows CE it is much simpler to add a combo box to
the command bar. By using the CommandBar_InsertComboBox function,
you can easily create a combo box and insert it into a command bar.

```
CommandBar_InsertComboBox(hwndCB, m_pApp->m_hInst, COMBOWIDTH,
                          CBS_DROPDOWNLIST | WS_VSCROLL, ID_COMBO,
                                            COMBOPOSITION);
```

The `CommandBar_InsertComboBox` function parameters are as follows:

- **HWND**. Specifies the handle of the command bar.

- **HINSTANCE**. Specifies the instance of the application.

- **int**. Specifies the width, in pixels, of the combo box.

- **UINT**. Specifies the window styles of the combo box.

Note

Currently, only the CBS_DROPDOWNLIST and WS_VSCROLL styles are supported. The WS_HASSTRINGS, WS_VISIBLE, and WS_CHILD styles are included automatically.

- **WORD**. Specifies the command identifier of the combo box.

- **int**. Specifies the zero-based index of a button. (The new combo box is inserted to the left of this button.)

After creating a combo box in Windows CE, an application can use the Win32 combo box API functions to add items and manage the combo box. The TravelManager application uses a combo box in the command bar to identify the available display options. TravelManager adds the display names to the combo box and selects the first string as demonstrated in the following:

```
if (m_hwndCombo)
{
  SendMessage(m_hwndCombo, CB_ADDSTRING, 0, (LPARAM)L"Airline");
  SendMessage(m_hwndCombo, CB_ADDSTRING, 0, (LPARAM)L"Car Rental");
  SendMessage(m_hwndCombo, CB_ADDSTRING, 0, (LPARAM)L"Hotel");
  SendMessage(m_hwndCombo, CB_ADDSTRING, 0, (LPARAM)L"Expenses");
  SendMessage(m_hwndCombo, CB_ADDSTRING, 0, (LPARAM)L"Notes");

  SendMessage(m_hwndCombo, CB_SETCURSEL, 0, 0);
}
```

Creating Command Bar Buttons

The functionality of a Win32 toolbar is achieved in Windows CE by adding buttons to the command bar. The buttons are added to the command bar by using the CommandBar_AddButtons function.

```
CommandBar_AddButtons(hwndCB, sizeof(tbButton)/sizeof(TBBUTTON),
tbButton);
```

The CommandBar_AddButtons parameters are as follows:

- **HWND**. Specifies the handle of the command bar to which you want to add the buttons.

- **UINT**. Specifies the number of buttons to be added.

- **LPTBBUTTON**. Points to an array of TBBUTTON structures that contains information about the buttons to add. (The same number of elements must be in the array as buttons specified by the second parameter.)

The CommandBar_InsertButton can be used to insert a single button. The parameters to CommandBar_InsertButton are:

- **HWND**. Specifies the handle of the command bar to which to add the button.

- **int**. Specifies the index of a button; the new button is added to the left of it.

- **LPTBBUTTON**. Points to a single TBBUTTON structure that contains information about the button to add.

Button attributes include the image and string displayed in the button, the button state and styles, and the button command identifier. The members of the TBBUTTON structure are as follows:

- **int iBitmap**. Specifies the zero-based index of the image for the button. (When using bitmaps that are provided with the common control library, use the STD_ and VIEW_ constants in this member.)

- **int idCommand**. Specifies the command identifier for the button. This identifier is used in a WM_COMMAND message when the button is chosen. (For separators, this member must be zero.)

- **BYTE fsState**. Specifies the button state flags. This member can be any combination of the following values:

  TBSTATE_CHECKED   The button has the TBSTYLE_CHECKED style and is being pressed.

  TBSTATE_ENABLED   The button accepts user input. A button that does not have this state does not accept user input and is grayed.

  TBSTATE_HIDDEN   The button is not visible and cannot receive user input.

  TBSTATE_PRESSED   The button is being pressed.

  TBSTATE_WRAP   A line break follows the button. The button must also have the TBSTATE_ENABLED state.

  TBSTATE_INDETERMINATE   The button is grayed.

- **BYTE fsStyle**. Specifies the button style. This member can be a combination of the following values:

  TBSTYLE_BUTTON   Creates a standard push button.

  TBSTYLE_CHECK   Creates a button that toggles between the pressed and not pressed states each time the user clicks it. The button has a different background color when it is in the pressed state.

  TBSTYLE_CHECKGROUP   Creates a check button that stays pressed until another button in the group is pressed.

  TBSTYLE_GROUP   Creates a button that stays pressed until another button in the group is pressed.

  TBSTYLE_SEP   Creates a separator, providing a small gap between button groups. (A button that has this style does not receive user input.)

- **DWORD dwData**. Specifies application-defined data.

- **int iString**. Specifies the zero-base index of the string for the button.

The TravelManager application creates a set of buttons using the following TBBUTTON array:

```
static TBBUTTON tbButton[] = {
{0, 0, TBSTATE_ENABLED, TBSTYLE_SEP,     0, 0, 0, -1},
{0, 0, TBSTATE_ENABLED, TBSTYLE_SEP,     0, 0, 0, -1},
{STD_FILESAVE, ID_FILE_SAVE, TBSTATE_ENABLED, TBSTYLE_BUTTON, 0, 0,
➥0, -1},
{0,  0, TBSTATE_ENABLED, TBSTYLE_SEP,    0, 0, 0,  0},
{STD_CUT, ID_EDIT_CUT, TBSTATE_ENABLED, TBSTYLE_BUTTON, 0, 0, 0,  0},
{STD_COPY, ID_EDIT_COPY, TBSTATE_ENABLED, TBSTYLE_BUTTON, 0, 0, 0, -
➥1},
{STD_PASTE, ID_EDIT_PASTE, TBSTATE_ENABLED, TBSTYLE_BUTTON, 0, 0, 0,
➥-1},
{0, 0, TBSTATE_ENABLED, TBSTYLE_SEP,     0, 0, 0,  0},
{15, ID_VIEW_ITINERARY, TBSTATE_ENABLED, TBSTYLE_CHECKGROUP, 0, 0, 0,
➥-1},
{16,ID_VIEW_EXPENSES,TBSTATE_ENABLED, TBSTYLE_CHECKGROUP, 0, 0, 0, -
➥1},
{17,ID_VIEW_NOTES,TBSTATE_ENABLED, TBSTYLE_CHECKGROUP, 0, 0, 0, -1},
{0,0, TBSTATE_ENABLED, TBSTYLE_SEP,      0, 0, 0,  0},
};
```

Button Images

Each button in the command bar can include a bitmapped image. The command bar stores the images for all buttons in an internal image list. Initially, this image list is empty. However, you can add images to the list by using the `CommandBar_AddBitmap` function.

```
CommandBar_AddBitmap(hwndCB, HINST_COMMCTRL, IDB_STD_SMALL_COLOR, 15,
                     0, 0);
CommandBar_AddBitmap(hwndCB, m_pApp->m_hInst, IDB_ITINERAR, 1, 0, 0);
CommandBar_AddBitmap(hwndCB, m_pApp->m_hInst, IDB_EXPENSES, 1, 0, 0);
CommandBar_AddBitmap(hwndCB, m_pApp->m_hInst, IDB_NOTES,    1, 0, 0);
```

The parameters to `CommandBar_AddBitmap` are as follows:

- **HWND**. Specifies the handle of the command bar.

- **HINSTANCE**. Specifies the application instance that contains the bitmap resource. HINST_COMMCTRL can be used to add the system-defined button bitmaps.

- **int**. Specifies the bitmap resource that contains the button images. If HINSTANCE is NULL, this parameter must be a handle to a bitmap that contains the button images.

- **int**. Specifies the number of images in the resource.

- **int**. Reserved. Not used.

- **int**. Reserved. Not used.

A bitmap can consist of more than one image, but the dimensions of each individual image in the bitmap should only be 16×16 pixels. The system assumes all the images in the bitmap are the same size. The first call to the `CommandBar_AddBitmap` function of the previous code sample adds a bitmap that consists of 15 images, therefore the whole bitmap has a height of 16 pixels and a width of 240 pixels (16×15).

Each image has a zero-based index in the list. The first image added to the internal list has an index of zero, the second has an index of one, and so on. `CommandBar_AddBitmap` adds images to the end of the list and returns the index of the first new image that was just added. This index is used to associate the image with a button.

The TravelManager application first adds a set of predefined button images that are part of Windows CE. The HINSTANCE HINST_COMMCTRL is used as the instance handle, and IDB_VIEW_SMALL_COLOR is used as the resource identifier. This resource includes the common images that are associated with buttons such as Fileopen, Cut, Copy, Paste, and so on. Another predefined set of images is the IDB_VIEW_SMALL_COLOR resource, which includes images associated with views (list, detail, large icon, and so on.).

The system header files include constants that define the indices for the predefined images. The constants defined are as follows:

STD_COPY	STD_PROPERTIES	STD_CUT
STD_REDOW	STD_DELETE	STD_REPLACE
STD_FIND	STD_PASTE	STD_FILENEW
STD_PRINT	STD_FILEOPEN	STD_PRINTPRE
STD_FILESAVE	STD_UNDO	STD_HELP
VIEW_DETAILS	VIEW_SORTDATE	VIEW_LARGEICONS
VIEW_LIST	VIEW_SORTNAME	VIEW_SORTSIZE
VIEW_SORTTYPE	VIEW_SMALLICONS	

After adding the set of 15 predefined buttons from the IDB_STD_SMALL_COLOR resource, the TravelManager code adds three more application defined images. These images are the resources IDB_ITINERAR, IDB_EXPENSES, and IDB_NOTES. These identifiers are defined in resource.h and trvlmgr.rc.

```
IDB_ITINERAR    BITMAP  DISCARDABLE    "itinerar.2bp"
IDB_EXPENSES    BITMAP  DISCARDABLE    "expenses.2bp"
IDB_NOTES       BITMAP  DISCARDABLE    "notes.2bp"
```

Tip

As in Win32, these lines associate a resource identifier with a bitmap file. Because these bitmaps hold only one image, the size of each bitmap is 16×16 pixels.

Button Strings

In addition to or instead of an image, a button can also display a text string. As with images, a command bar maintains an internal list that contains all strings available to buttons; these strings are added to the internal list by sending the command bar a TB_ADDSTRING message. The TB_ADDSTRING message specifies the address of the buffer that contains the strings to add. Each string must be null-terminated, and the last string must be terminated with two null characters.

As with images, each string has a zero-based index and that index is used in the TBBUTON structure to specify the position of the string in the list for each button.

Although not used in the TravelManager application, an example of adding strings to the internal command bar list follows:

```
SendMessage(hwndCB, TB_ADDSTRING, (WPARAM)hInst,
            MAKELONG(IDS_NEW, 0));
SendMessage(hwndCB, TB_ADDSTRING, (WPARAM)hInst,
            MAKELONG(IDS_OPEN, 0));
```

After adding strings to the command bar's internal string list, a string can be associated with a button by the iString member of the TBBUT-TON structure. The iString member is set to the desired string's index in the internal list.

Button States and Styles

Each button in a command bar has a current state. The command bar updates the button state to reflect user actions, such as tapping the button. The state indicates whether the button is currently pressed or not pressed, enabled or disabled, or hidden or visible. An application sets the initial button state in the TBBUTTON structure when adding the button to the command bar. The state of a button can be set using the TB_SETSTATE message, and the application can retrieve the state of a button using the TB_GETSTATE message.

The TravelManager application creates a group of three buttons that have the TBSTYLE_CHECKGROUP style. This style creates a set of buttons that toggles between pressed and nonpressed states. Pressing one of the buttons in the group causes the others to be "not-pressed."

The TravelManager uses this button configuration to show which view is currently displayed so that only one of the views can be displayed at one time.

```
SendMessage(hwndCB, TB_SETSTATE, (WPARAM)ID_VIEW_ITINERARY,
            MAKELONG(TBSTATE_ENABLED¦TBSTATE_CHECKED,0));
```

Tooltips

A *tooltip control* is a small window that displays help text. In Win32 applications, the tooltip is displayed when the mouse is positioned over a button on the toolbar. Since there is no mouse in Windows CE, the activation of the tooltip is a bit different. Using the stylus to press and hold down a button on the command bar will display the tooltip.

Warning

> If the stylus is moved off of the button before it is released, no button press event is generated.

Under Win32, when a tooltip becomes activated over a toolbar, the tooltip control sends a request to the application for the text to be displayed. Just as Windows CE has made the displaying of combo boxes much simpler, displaying tooltips is also easier. The tooltip text for the all the command bar buttons can be set when the command bar is created. The CommandBar_AddToolTips function adds tooltips strings to the command bar:

```
static TCHAR * tooltips[] = {
     L"",
     L"",
     L"Cut",
     L"Copy",
     L"Paste",
     L"Itinerary",
     L"Expenses",
     L"Notes",
     L"Help",
     L"Exit"
};

CommandBar_AddToolTips(m_hwndCB, 10, tooltips);
```

The preceding code added the tooltip strings for all command bar buttons for TravelManager's command bar. Although menus and combo boxes cannot display tooltip help, they must be accounted for in the array of tooltip strings. In the TravelManager application, the menu and combo box occupy the first two positions on the command bar. The tooltips array accounts for this by specifying empty strings as the first two strings in the array.

Other Command Bar Functions

Just as Win32 applications usually have minimize, maximize, and close buttons, Windows CE also supports some standard window adornments, such as close and help buttons. These buttons are added with the `CommandBar_AddAdornments` function:

```
CommandBar_AddAdornments(m_hwndCB, CMDBAR_HELP, NULL);
```

The CommandBar_AddAdornments parameters are as follows:

- **HWND**. Specifies the handle of the command bar window.

- **DWORD**. Specifies the optional button flags:

  CMDBAR_HELP   Adds the help button.

  CMDBAR_OK   Adds the OK button.

- **DWORD**. Reserved, must be zero.

By default, the `CommandBar_AddAdornments` adds the close button.

Warning

> The `CommandBar_Destroy` function destroys a command bar window; however, this is not necessary when the command bar's parent window is being destroyed.

There are also functions dealing with command bar visibility. The `CommandBar_Create` function creates a command bar that is initially visible. You can hide and show the command bar by using the `CommandBar_Show` function. Use the `CommandBar_IsVisible` function to determine whether a command bar is currently visible.

Command Bar Messages

Similar to Win32 applications, notifications from command bar elements come in the form of WM_COMMAND messages. Table 6.1 differentiates the messages from the command bar elements.

Table 6.1

Command Bar Message Parameters

Element	LOWORD (wParam)	HIWORD (wParam)	lParam
Menu	menu id	0	0
Button	button id	0	0
Combobox	combo id	notification code	combo window handle

As you can see, messages from menus and command bar buttons look identical. This is quite useful because command bar buttons almost always have a corresponding menu item. Because the message is identical, the same code can be used to perform an action regardless of whether the user presses the command bar button or choose the menu option.

The following snippet of code shows how the TravelManager application responds to command bar messages. See the end of the chapter for the complete code listing.

```
LRESULT MainWindow::WMCommand( HWND hWnd,  UINT msg, WPARAM wParam,
                               LPARAM lParam )
{
  WORD notifyCode = HIWORD(wParam);

  if ( notifyCode == 0)  // from menu?
  {
    switch (LOWORD(wParam))  // which menu item
    {
      case ID_HELP_ABOUT:
        // display About box
        break;
```

```
        case ID_VIEW_ITINERARY:
        case ID_VIEW_EXPENSES:
        case ID_VIEW_NOTES:
            // handle view change
            break;
        }
        return 0;
    }

    if ( notifyCode == CBN_SELCHANGE )
    {
        // selection changed in combo box
    }
```

Windows and Dialog Boxes

As in Win32 applications, Windows CE applications present data to the user and request data from the user through windows and dialog boxes. Nearly every application has at least one main window; however, most applications have many other windows as well.

Dialog boxes are a special type of window that contain various child window controls. The size and placement of these controls are specified in a dialog box template that resides in the application's resource file. From the dialog box template, Windows CE creates the dialog box window and all the child controls, and it also provides a window procedure to process the dialog box messages.

Many of the messages that are processed by the internal dialog box window procedure are also passed to a function within the application called a dialog procedure. This function, which is similar to a normal window procedure (WndProc), generally is used for initializing child window controls, handling child window messages, and ending the dialog box.

Dialog boxes are either modal or modeless. When a dialog box is *modal*, the user cannot switch between the dialog box and another window in the application. The dialog box must be closed by the user before going to any other window in the application. However, with a modal dialog box visible, the user can still switch to other applications. System modal dialog boxes are not supported in Windows CE. Application modal dialog boxes are created with the `DialogBox` function (or one of its variations).

Modeless dialog boxes are basically pop-up windows that can obtain and lose the input focus. The `CreateDialog` function is used to create modeless dialog boxes.

Creating a Dialog Box

The process of creating dialog boxes in Windows CE is the same as the process under Win32. There are functions for creating both modal and modeless dialog boxes from a dialog template resource or template in memory, and using a user-defined data value or not. The following chart summarizes the function and its variations for creating dialog boxes:

- **DialogBox**. The `DialogBox` function creates a modal dialog box from a dialog box template resource. `DialogBox` does not return control until the specified callback function terminates the modal dialog box by calling the `EndDialog` function.

- **DialogBoxParam**. The `DialogBoxParam` function creates a modal dialog box from a dialog box template resource. Before displaying the dialog box, the function passes an application-defined value to the dialog box procedure as the lParam parameter of the WM_INITDIALOG message. An application can use this value to initialize dialog box controls.

- **DialogBoxIndirect**. The `DialogBoxIndirect` function creates a modal dialog box from a dialog box template in memory. The `DialogBoxIndirect` function does not return control until the specified callback function terminates the modal dialog box by calling the `EndDialog` function.

- **DialogBoxIndirectParam**. The `DialogBoxIndirectParam` function creates a modal dialog box from a dialog box template in memory. Before displaying the dialog box, the function passes an application-defined value to the dialog box procedure as the lParam parameter of the WM_INITDIALOG message. An application can use this value to initialize dialog box controls.

- **CreateDialog**. The CreateDialog function creates a modeless dialog box from a dialog box template resource.

- **CreateDialogParam**. The CreateDialogParam function creates a modeless dialog box from a dialog box template resource. Before displaying the dialog box, the function passes an application-defined value to the dialog box procedure as the lParam parameter of the WM_INITDIALOG message. An application can use this value to initialize dialog box controls.

- **CreateDialogIndirect**. The CreateDialogIndirect function creates a modeless dialog box from a dialog box template in memory.

- **CreateDialogIndirectParam**. The CreateDialogIndirectParam function creates a modeless dialog box from a dialog box template in memory. Before displaying the dialog box, the function passes an application-defined value to the dialog box procedure as the lParam parameter of the WM_INITDIALOG message. An application can use this value to initialize dialog box controls.

Even if an application has no other user input, it usually has one specific dialog box. The "About" dialog box is a dialog box displayed by an About menu option. This dialog box displays the name of the application, its copyright notice, and version information, along with any other descriptive or useful information. Some applications even have hidden "Easter egg" screens accessed through the About box.

The first step in adding a dialog box to an application is to create the dialog box template. The dialog box template is a textual specification for the dialog box. It is possible to create the dialog template manually in a text editor; however, tools such as the Visual C++ Developer Studio enable dialog boxes to be created graphically. The dialog box template for the About box in the TravelManager application appears as the following code:

```
ABOUTBOX DIALOG DISCARDABLE  60, 30, 150, 74
STYLE DS_MODALFRAME ¦ DS_CENTER ¦ WS_POPUP ¦ WS_VISIBLE ¦ WS_CAPTION
➥¦
    WS_SYSMENU
CAPTION "About TravelManager"
FONT 8, "MS Shell Dlg"
```

```
BEGIN
    PUSHBUTTON      "OK",IDOK,66,55,40,14
    LTEXT           "TravelManager",-1,42,14,108,28
    ICON            IDI_APPICON,-1,11,10,18,20
END
```

The format of the DIALOG resource is the same under Windows CE as under Win32. The template specifies attributes about the dialog box and the controls that will be displayed on the dialog box. Our ABOUT-BOX dialog box has an icon, static text, and an OK button. (More about controls will be explored further in Chapter 7, "Controls.") The dialog box template also specifies the specific style of a dialog box.

Warning

> Under Windows CE, there are restrictions on the styles that can be specified after the STYLE keyword.

The following includes a list of restricted styles or styles that aren't supported in Windows CE:

- **DS_SETFONT**. You cannot set the font inside dialog boxes.

- **DS_3DLOOK**. Not currently supported.

- **DS_RECURSE**. Not required. Any child dialog box is automatically considered to be a recursive dialog box.

- **DS_CONTROL**. Not required.

- **DS_LOCALEDIT**. Not currently supported.

- **DS_ABSALIGN**. Not currently supported.

- **DS_CENTERMOUSE**. Not currently supported.

- **DS_CONTEXTHELP**. Not currently supported.

- **DS_FIXEDSYS**. Not currently supported.

- **DS_NOFAILCREATE**. Not currently supported.

- **DS_NOIDLEMSG**. Not currently supported.

- **DS_SYSMODAL**. Not currently supported.

- **WS_EX_CONTROLPARENT**. All dialog boxes are automatically assumed to be control parents.

- **WS_POPUP**. This style is assumed if WS_CHILD is not specified.

After the dialog template is defined, displaying a modal dialog box is done with the `DialogBoxParam` function:

```
DialogBoxParam(m_pApp->m_hInst, TEXT("AboutBox"), hWnd,
        (DLGPROC)DlgProc, NULL);
```

The parameters of the `DialogBoxParam` function in Windows CE are the same as under Win32. The parameters to `DialogBoxParam` specify the application instance, the dialog box identifier, the parent window, the dialog procedure, and a user-defined data value.

Dialog and Window Procedures with C++

In the HELLO++ example from the previous chapter, a global variable was used to get from the `WndProc` function to a specific method in the C++ object. Using this technique in the TravelManager application would require many `WndProc` functions and many global variables (one pair for each window created). As a different approach, use just one `WndProc` window procedure and no global variables that are pointers to the C++ objects. To accomplish this, store the pointer to the C++ object in the window itself (actually in the internal structure that Windows CE maintains that describes the window).

Under Win32, data can be stored in the window using the `SetWindowLong` function with the GWL_USERDATA offset. Unfortunately, the GWL_USERDATA is not currently supported in Windows CE. However, you can accomplish the same functionality by allocating extra space in the window class once it is created. The extra space can then be used to store the pointer to the C++ class when a new window is created. As messages are received by the WndProc function, the pointer to the C++ object is retrieved from the window and the appropriate method in the correct C++ object is called. The following excerpts of code from the TravelManager application demonstrate this technique.

Step 1: Allocate space in the window class.

When registering the window class, specify extra space in the cbWndExtra member of the WNDCLASS structure. (Under Windows CE, cbWndExtra must be a multiple of 4.)

```
BOOL TravelManagerApp::Create(HINSTANCE hInstance)
{
    WNDCLASS  wc;

    wc.style         = 0 ;
    wc.lpfnWndProc   = (WNDPROC) WndProc;
    wc.cbClsExtra    = 0;
    wc.cbWndExtra    = 4;        // *** Extra space for C++ ptr ***
    wc.hInstance     = m_hInst;
    wc.hIcon         = NULL;
    wc.hCursor       = NULL;
    wc.hbrBackground = (HBRUSH) GetStockObject(WHITE_BRUSH);
    wc.lpszMenuName  = NULL;
    wc.lpszClassName = szClassName;

    if ( !RegisterClass(&wc) )
    {
        return FALSE;
    }
...
```

Step 2: Pass the pointer to the C++ class in the CreateWindow function.

The last parameter of the CreateWindow function is any user data that will be sent with the WM_CREATE message.

```
BOOL MainWindow::Create()
{
    HWND hWnd = CreateWindow(szClassName,
                            szTitle,
                            WS_VISIBLE,
                            0,
```

```
                              0,
                              CW_USEDEFAULT,
                              CW_USEDEFAULT,
                              NULL,
                              NULL,
                              m_pApp->m_hInst,
                              this);        // *** ptr to 'this' class
***
...
```

Step 3: Set the C++ pointer when processing the WM_CREATE message.

The user data value that was passed in the CreateWindow function is received in the WndProc function in the WM_CREATE message. The lParam value specifies a pointer to a CREATESTRUCT structure, and the lpCreateParams member holds the user data value.

The SetWindowLong function is used to set the user data value in the extra space allocated for the window class. The SetWindowLong function takes a window handle, some user data value, and an offset into the extra window space. Because the TravelManager application uses only one "slot" of extra space, zero is specified as the offset.

```
LRESULT CALLBACK WndProc( HWND hWnd,  UINT msg, WPARAM wParam,
                          LPARAM lParam )
{

    if (msg == WM_CREATE)
    {
        LPCREATESTRUCT lpStruct = (LPCREATESTRUCT) lParam;
        Window * pWindow = (Window *) lpStruct->lpCreateParams;
        SetWindowLong(hWnd, 0, (LONG)pWindow);
        pWindow->WMCreate(hWnd);
        return 0;
    }
...
```

Step 4: Retrieve the C++ pointer when processing other messages.

Using the GetWindowLong function, the user data value is retrieved from the window.

```
LRESULT CALLBACK WndProc( HWND hWnd,  UINT msg, WPARAM wParam,
                             LPARAM lParam )
{

    if (msg == WM_CREATE)
    {
        ...
        return 0;
    }

    Window * pWindow = (Window *)GetWindowLong(hWnd, 0);
 ...
```

Step 5: Call the appropriate method for each message.

Once the pointer to the C++ object for the window is retrieved,
the appropriate method can be called for each message received.
(Obviously, those methods must be defined and coded in the C++
classes.)

```
LRESULT CALLBACK WndProc( HWND hWnd,  UINT msg, WPARAM wParam,
                             LPARAM lParam )
{

    if (msg == WM_CREATE)
    {
        ...
        return 0;
    }

    Window * pWindow = (Window *)GetWindowLong(hWnd, 0);
    switch (msg)
    {
      case WM_COMMAND:
        return( pWindow->WMCommand(hWnd, msg, wParam, lParam) );
        break;

      case WM_NOTIFY:
        return (pWindow->WMNotify(hWnd, msg, wParam, lParam) );
        break;
 ...
```

To make this technique work best, it is necessary to use C++ inheritance in building the C++ window classes. Suppose the application has two C++ "window" classes—for example, ItineraryView and ExpensesView. When creating the Windows window, "this" is passed as the parameter to the CreateWindow function, which is used in the `SetWindowLong` function after the WM_CREATE message is received. So far, so good. But when retrieving the pointer with the `GetWindowLong` function, how can you tell which class type the user data value points to?

By using C++ inheritance, the need to know exactly which class type can be effectively eliminated. If ItineraryView and ExpensesView inherit from the same base class, that class type can be used for the pointer. The TravelManager application uses a base class named Window and derives those view classes from this base class. The following source code demonstrates this:

```
class Window
{
public:
    Window() {}
    ~Window() {}

    virtual BOOL Create() {return FALSE;}

    virtual void WMCreate(HWND) {}
    virtual void WMPaint() {}

    virtual LRESULT WMCommand(HWND, UINT, WPARAM, LPARAM) { return 0;
➥}
    virtual LRESULT WMNotify(HWND, UINT, WPARAM, LPARAM) { return 0;
➥}

    HWND m_hWnd;
};


class ItineraryView : public Window
{
public:
    ItineraryView(MainWindow *);
    ~ItineraryView();
```

```
    BOOL Create();

    LRESULT WMCommand( HWND, UINT, WPARAM, LPARAM ) {return 0;}
  ...
};

class ExpensesView : public Window
{
public:
    ExpensesView(MainWindow *);
    ~ExpensesView();

    BOOL Create();

    LRESULT WMCommand( HWND, UINT, WPARAM, LPARAM ) { return 0;}
  ...
};
```

By using a base class when the C++ pointer is returned with the GetWindowLong function, it is of type Window. Given an object of type Window, the proper method can then be called (for instance, the WM-Command method when a WM_COMMAND message is received). Because the WMCommand is virtual, the WMCommand method that actually gets executed will depend on which type the object really is (for instance, the WMCommand in the ExpensesView if the C++ pointer points to an ExpensesView object). If these concepts are unfamiliar, there are many excellent C++ books that can provide much greater detail on inheritance and virtual functions.

The procedure for linking the dialog box procedure (DlgProc) with the corresponding C++ class for the dialog box is nearly identical to the steps covering on the WndProc earlier. The only difference is that Windows CE supports the DWL_USER offset, so it is not necessary to create a new window class with extra space for the dialog boxes. The DWL_USER offset can be used with SetWindowLong and GetWindowLong for storing and retrieving the C++ object pointer.

TravelManager Application

The source code for the TravelManager application started in this chapter can be found on the accompanying CD-ROM. Refer to Appendix

A, "Getting Started with the CD-ROM," for information on accessing the source code on the CD-ROM.

Because this chapter lays the foundation for an application that will be extended in additional chapters, the source code for the initial Travel-Manager application is also listed at the end of this chapter.

This initial version of the application has many important components and classes. The main classes and components of the application include the following:

- **TravelManagerApp**. The application class has a Create method for creating the main window and a Run method for holding the message loop.

- **Window**. The base class from which all subsequent window classes will be derived.

- **MainWindow**. The class for the main window, which has methods for creating the main window, creating the command bar, and processing certain messages.

- **DlgProc**. The dialog box procedure dispatches messages to the correct object.

- **WndProc**. The window procedure, which dispatches messages to the correct object.

- **WinMain**. The entry point into the application, which creates the application class and waits for it to exit.

```
#include <windows.h>
#include "resource.h"
#include "commctrl.h"

// Class name and window title
WCHAR szClassName[] = TEXT("TRVLMGR");
WCHAR szTitle[] = TEXT("TravelManager");

// The application class
class TravelManagerApp
{
```

```
public:
    TravelManagerApp();
    ~TravelManagerApp(){}

    BOOL Create(HINSTANCE);
    int Run();
    HINSTANCE m_hInst;
};

class Window
{
public:
    Window() {}
    ~Window() {}

    virtual BOOL Create() {return FALSE;}

    virtual void WMCreate(HWND) {}
    virtual void WMPaint() {}

    virtual LRESULT WMCommand(HWND, UINT, WPARAM, LPARAM) { return 0;
➡}

    HWND m_hWnd;
};

// The main window class
class MainWindow : public Window
{
public:
    MainWindow(TravelManagerApp *);
    ~MainWindow() {}

    BOOL Create();
    void CreateCommandBar();

    void WMCreate(HWND);
    LRESULT WMCommand( HWND, UINT, WPARAM, LPARAM );

    TravelManagerApp * m_pApp;
    HWND m_hwndCB;
    HWND m_hwndCombo;
};
```

```
// forward declaration
BOOL APIENTRY DlgProc( HWND, UINT, WPARAM, LPARAM);

// Implementation of MainWindow methods
MainWindow::MainWindow(TravelManagerApp * pApp)
{
    m_pApp = pApp;
}

void MainWindow::WMCreate(HWND hWnd)
{
    m_hWnd = hWnd;

        LONG lStyle = GetWindowLong(hWnd, GWL_STYLE);
        lStyle & ~WS_CAPTION;
        SetWindowLong(hWnd, GWL_STYLE, lStyle);

    CreateCommandBar();

}

void MainWindow::CreateCommandBar()
{
    static TBBUTTON tbButton[] = {
        {0,            0,              TBSTATE_ENABLED, TBSTYLE_SEP,
➥0, 0, 0, -1},
        {0,            0,              TBSTATE_ENABLED, TBSTYLE_SEP,
➥0, 0, 0, -1},
        {STD_CUT,      ID_EDIT_CUT,    TBSTATE_ENABLED,
➥TBSTYLE_BUTTON, 0, 0, 0,  0},
        {STD_COPY,     ID_EDIT_COPY,   TBSTATE_ENABLED,
➥TBSTYLE_BUTTON, 0, 0, 0, -1},
        {STD_PASTE,    ID_EDIT_PASTE,  TBSTATE_ENABLED,
➥TBSTYLE_BUTTON, 0, 0, 0, -1},
        {0,            0,              TBSTATE_ENABLED, TBSTYLE_SEP,
➥0, 0, 0,  0},
        {15,    ID_VIEW_ITINERARY,   TBSTATE_ENABLED,
➥TBSTYLE_CHECKGROUP, 0, 0, 0, -1},
        {16,    ID_VIEW_EXPENSES,    TBSTATE_ENABLED,
➥TBSTYLE_CHECKGROUP, 0, 0, 0, -1},
        {17,    ID_VIEW_NOTES,    TBSTATE_ENABLED, TBSTYLE_CHECKGROUP,
➥0, 0, 0, -1},
        {0,            0,              TBSTATE_ENABLED, TBSTYLE_SEP,
➥0, 0, 0,  0},
    };
```

```
static TCHAR * tooltips[] = {
        L"",
        L"",
        L"Cut",
        L"Copy",
        L"Paste",
        L"Itinerary",
        L"Expenses",
        L"Notes",
        L"Help",
        L"Exit"
};

m_hwndCB = CommandBar_Create(m_pApp->m_hInst, m_hWnd,
➥ID_COMMANDBAR);

CommandBar_InsertMenubar(m_hwndCB, m_pApp->m_hInst,
➥IDM_MAIN_MENU, 0);

CommandBar_AddBitmap(m_hwndCB, HINST_COMMCTRL,
➥IDB_STD_SMALL_COLOR, 15, 0, 0);

CommandBar_AddBitmap(m_hwndCB, m_pApp->m_hInst, IDB_ITINERAR, 1,
➥0, 0);
CommandBar_AddBitmap(m_hwndCB, m_pApp->m_hInst, IDB_EXPENSES, 1,
➥0, 0);
CommandBar_AddBitmap(m_hwndCB, m_pApp->m_hInst, IDB_NOTES,   1,
➥0, 0);

CommandBar_AddButtons(m_hwndCB, sizeof(tbButton)/
➥sizeof(TBBUTTON), tbButton);

m_hwndCombo = CommandBar_InsertComboBox(m_hwndCB, m_pApp-
➥>m_hInst, COMBOWIDTH,
                                    CBS_DROPDOWNLIST ¦ WS_VSCROLL,
➥ID_COMBO, COMBOPOSITION);

CommandBar_AddAdornments(m_hwndCB, CMDBAR_HELP, NULL);

CommandBar_AddToolTips(m_hwndCB, 10, tooltips);

HMENU hMenu = CommandBar_GetMenu(m_hwndCB,0);
CheckMenuItem(hMenu, ID_VIEW_ITINERARY, MF_CHECKED);
```

```
    SendMessage(m_hwndCB, TB_SETSTATE, (WPARAM)ID_VIEW_ITINERARY,
➥MAKELONG(TBSTATE_ENABLED¦TBSTATE_CHECKED,0));

    if (m_hwndCombo)
    {
        SendMessage(m_hwndCombo, CB_ADDSTRING, 0,
➥(LPARAM)L"Airline");
        SendMessage(m_hwndCombo, CB_ADDSTRING, 0, (LPARAM)L"Car
➥Rental");
        SendMessage(m_hwndCombo, CB_ADDSTRING, 0, (LPARAM)L"Hotel");
        SendMessage(m_hwndCombo, CB_ADDSTRING, 0,
➥(LPARAM)L"Expenses");
        SendMessage(m_hwndCombo, CB_ADDSTRING, 0, (LPARAM)L"Notes");

        SendMessage(m_hwndCombo, CB_SETCURSEL, 0, 0);
    }

}

LRESULT MainWindow::WMCommand( HWND hWnd,  UINT msg, WPARAM wParam,
➥LPARAM lParam )
{
    WORD notifyCode = HIWORD(wParam);

    if ( notifyCode == 0)
    {
        switch (LOWORD(wParam))
        {
        case ID_HELP_ABOUT:
            DialogBoxParam(m_pApp->m_hInst, TEXT("AboutBox"), hWnd,
➥(DLGPROC)DlgProc, NULL);
            break;
        case ID_VIEW_ITINERARY:
        case ID_VIEW_EXPENSES:
        case ID_VIEW_NOTES:
                    // Check the appropriate menu item
            HMENU hMenu = CommandBar_GetMenu(m_hwndCB,0);
            CheckMenuItem(hMenu, ID_VIEW_ITINERARY, MF_UNCHECKED);
            CheckMenuItem(hMenu, ID_VIEW_EXPENSES, MF_UNCHECKED);
            CheckMenuItem(hMenu, ID_VIEW_NOTES, MF_UNCHECKED);
            CheckMenuItem(hMenu, LOWORD(wParam), MF_CHECKED);

                    // Toggle the appropriate command bar button
            SendMessage(m_hwndCB, TB_SETSTATE,
```

```
➥(WPARAM)ID_VIEW_ITINERARY, MAKELONG(TBSTATE_ENABLED,0));
            SendMessage(m_hwndCB, TB_SETSTATE,
➥(WPARAM)ID_VIEW_EXPENSES, MAKELONG(TBSTATE_ENABLED,0));
            SendMessage(m_hwndCB, TB_SETSTATE, (WPARAM)ID_VIEW_NOTES,
➥MAKELONG(TBSTATE_ENABLED,0));
            SendMessage(m_hwndCB, TB_SETSTATE,
➥(WPARAM)LOWORD(wParam),
                    MAKELONG(TBSTATE_ENABLED¦TBSTATE_CHECKED,0));

                    // Select something in theh combo box
        if (LOWORD(wParam) == ID_VIEW_ITINERARY)
        {
                        SendMessage(m_hwndCombo, CB_SETCURSEL,
➥0, 0);
        }
        if (LOWORD(wParam) == ID_VIEW_EXPENSES)
        {
                        SendMessage(m_hwndCombo, CB_SETCURSEL,
➥3, 0);
        }
        if (LOWORD(wParam) == ID_VIEW_NOTES)
        {
                        SendMessage(m_hwndCombo, CB_SETCURSEL,
➥4, 0);
        }

        break;
    }
    return 0;
    }

    if ( notifyCode == CBN_SELCHANGE )
    {
            // Clear view buttons and menu items
        SendMessage(m_hwndCB, TB_SETSTATE, (WPARAM)ID_VIEW_ITINERARY,
➥MAKELONG(TBSTATE_ENABLED,0));
        SendMessage(m_hwndCB, TB_SETSTATE, (WPARAM)ID_VIEW_EXPENSES,
➥MAKELONG(TBSTATE_ENABLED,0));
        SendMessage(m_hwndCB, TB_SETSTATE, (WPARAM)ID_VIEW_NOTES,
➥MAKELONG(TBSTATE_ENABLED,0));

        HMENU hMenu = CommandBar_GetMenu(m_hwndCB,0);
        CheckMenuItem(hMenu, ID_VIEW_ITINERARY, MF_UNCHECKED);
        CheckMenuItem(hMenu, ID_VIEW_EXPENSES, MF_UNCHECKED);
```

```
            CheckMenuItem(hMenu, ID_VIEW_NOTES, MF_UNCHECKED);

        int iSel = SendMessage(m_hwndCombo, CB_GETCURSEL, 0, 0);
            if (iSel < 3)
            {
                    SendMessage(m_hwndCB, TB_SETSTATE,
➥(WPARAM)ID_VIEW_ITINERARY,
MAKELONG(TBSTATE_ENABLED¦TBSTATE_CHECKED,0));
                CheckMenuItem(hMenu, ID_VIEW_ITINERARY, MF_CHECKED);
            }
            else if (iSel == 3)
            {
                    SendMessage(m_hwndCB, TB_SETSTATE,
➥(WPARAM)ID_VIEW_EXPENSES,
MAKELONG(TBSTATE_ENABLED¦TBSTATE_CHECKED,0));
            CheckMenuItem(hMenu, ID_VIEW_EXPENSES, MF_CHECKED);
            }
            else //iSel = 4
            {
                    SendMessage(m_hwndCB, TB_SETSTATE,
➥(WPARAM)ID_VIEW_NOTES, MAKELONG(TBSTATE_ENABLED¦TBSTATE_CHECKED,0));
            CheckMenuItem(hMenu, ID_VIEW_NOTES, MF_CHECKED);
            }

    return 0;
    }

    return 0;
}


BOOL MainWindow::Create()
{
    HWND hWnd = CreateWindow(szClassName,   // class name
                            szTitle,         // window title
                            WS_VISIBLE,      // styles
                            0,               // x position
                            0,               // y position
                            CW_USEDEFAULT,   // width
                            CW_USEDEFAULT,   // height
                            NULL,            // parent
                            NULL,            // menu
                            m_pApp->m_hInst, // instance handle
                            this);           // user data
```

```
            // Did CreateWindow succeed?
            if ( hWnd == 0 )
            {
                return (FALSE);
            }

            ShowWindow(hWnd, SW_SHOW);
            UpdateWindow(hWnd);

            return(TRUE);
        }

BOOL APIENTRY DlgProc( HWND hDlg, UINT message, WPARAM wParam, LPARAM
➥lParam)
{
    switch (message)
    {
    case WM_INITDIALOG:
        SetWindowLong(hDlg, DWL_USER, lParam);
        return (TRUE);

    case WM_COMMAND:
        Window * pWindow = (Window *)GetWindowLong(hDlg, DWL_USER);
                if (pWindow == NULL)
                {
                if ((wParam == IDOK) ¦¦ (wParam == IDCANCEL))
                    {
                            EndDialog(hDlg, TRUE);
                                return (TRUE);
                }
                }
                else
                {
                            return( pWindow->WMCommand(hDlg, message,
➥wParam, lParam) );
                }
        break;
    }
    return (FALSE);
}
```

```
LRESULT CALLBACK WndProc( HWND hWnd,  UINT msg, WPARAM wParam, LPARAM
➥lParam )
{
    if (msg == WM_CREATE)
    {
        LPCREATESTRUCT lpStruct = (LPCREATESTRUCT) lParam;
        Window * pWindow = (Window *) lpStruct->lpCreateParams;
        SetWindowLong(hWnd, 0, (LONG)pWindow);
        pWindow->WMCreate(hWnd);
        return 0;
    }

    Window * pWindow = (Window *)GetWindowLong(hWnd, 0);
    switch (msg)
    {
      case WM_COMMAND:
        return( pWindow->WMCommand(hWnd, msg, wParam, lParam) );
        break;

      case WM_DESTROY:
        delete pWindow;
        PostQuitMessage(0);
        break;

      default:
        return (DefWindowProc(hWnd, msg, wParam, lParam));
    }

    return (0);
}


// Implementation of TravelManagerApp methods
TravelManagerApp::TravelManagerApp()
{
    // API call to initialize common controls
    InitCommonControls();
}


BOOL TravelManagerApp::Create(HINSTANCE hInstance)
{
    WNDCLASS  wc;
```

```
    m_hInst = hInstance;

    wc.style         =  0 ;
    wc.lpfnWndProc   = (WNDPROC) WndProc;
    wc.cbClsExtra    = 0;
    wc.cbWndExtra    = 4;
    wc.hInstance     = m_hInst;
    wc.hIcon         = NULL;
    wc.hCursor       = NULL;
    wc.hbrBackground = (HBRUSH) GetStockObject(WHITE_BRUSH);
    wc.lpszMenuName  = NULL;
    wc.lpszClassName = szClassName;

    if ( !RegisterClass(&wc) )
    {
        return FALSE;
    }

    // RegisterClass worked, so create the window
    MainWindow * pMainWindow = new MainWindow(this);

    if ( !pMainWindow )
    {
        return FALSE;
    }

    if ( !pMainWindow->Create() )
    {
        return FALSE;
    }
    return TRUE;
}

int TravelManagerApp::Run()
{
    MSG msg;

    // Main window was created, start the message loop
    while ( GetMessage(&msg, NULL, 0, 0) != FALSE )
    {
        TranslateMessage (&msg) ;
        DispatchMessage(&msg);
    }
```

```
        return(msg.wParam);
}

int WINAPI WinMain ( HINSTANCE hInstance,
                     HINSTANCE hPrevInstance,
                     LPWSTR lpCmdLine,
                     int nCmdShow )
{
    // Is there another instance already running
    if ( hPrevInstance != 0 )
    {
        return -1;
    }

    TravelManagerApp * pApp = new TravelManagerApp();

    if ( !pApp )
    {
        return -1;
    }

    if ( pApp->Create(hInstance) == FALSE )
    {
        return -1;
    }

    BOOL exitVal = pApp->Run();

    delete pApp;

    return exitVal;
}
```

CHAPTER 7

Controls

I n the last chapter, a command bar was created that was comprised
of a menu with button and combo box controls. You also created
a dialog box that contained icon, text, and button controls. These
controls are preconstructed elements in Windows CE that enable different Windows CE applications to look and act alike.

Controls have been part of the operating system since the earliest days
of Windows. Windows CE carries on the tradition of controls by supporting nearly all the controls that are part of Windows 95. Support
for Windows 95 controls enables a Windows CE application to have the
same look and feel as a Windows 95 application. Table 7.1 summarizes
the controls from Windows 95 and their support under Windows CE.

Table 7.1

Windows 95 Controls Supported Under Windows CE

Control	Supported	Comments
Check boxes	Yes	
Column headings	Yes	
Command bars	Yes	The command bar only supports drop-down menus, drop-down combo boxes, and toolbar buttons.
Command buttons	Yes	
Drop-down combo boxes	Yes	
Drop-down list boxes	Yes	
Group boxes	Yes	
List boxes	Yes	
List views	Yes	
Progress indicators	Yes	
Property sheet	Yes	The Apply button is not supported.
Rich text edit	No	
Scroll bars	Yes	
Slider (aka trackbar)	Yes	
Status bar	Yes	
Static text fields	Yes	
Tabs	Yes	
Text boxes	Yes	
Tree views	Yes	
Toolbars	No	Toolbars are supported using the command bar.
Tooltips	Yes	Tooltips are supported only for command bar buttons.
Up-down buttons	Yes	This control can be used to create spin box controls.

Control Basics

Controls are created either as part of a dialog box template structure or through the CreateWindow function because controls themselves are windows. The type of control is specified by the class name, such as button, edit, or SysListView32. Other attributes that must be specified when creating a control window include a child window identifier, size, position information, and the control's parent window. Style information is also used when creating the control; these styles specify the look and functionality of the control. Styles for each control will be defined in the following sections.

A program interacts with a control by sending messages to the control. These messages enable the application to set and query information about the control. In addition, the control notifies the application of various events by sending the control's parent window a message. This interaction with controls follows the same mechanisms as it would under Win32. The messages allowed for each control will be defined throughout this chapter.

Common Styles

In addition to control-specific styles, there are a number of window styles that can also be used when creating controls. The WS_BORDER style specifies that the control has a thin border. The WS_VISIBLE style creates a window that is initially visible. The WS_GROUP and WS_TABSTOP are used to set which controls can be tabbed. The WS_CHILD style creates a child window. The WS_DISABLED style creates a window that is initially disabled. The WS_HSCROLL and WS_VSCROLL add horizontal or vertical scroll bars to the window.

Note

Windows CE does not support the following window styles: WS_CHILDWINDOW, WS_ICONIC, WS_MAXIMIZE, WS_MAXIMIZEBOX, WS_MINIMIZE, WS_MINIMIZEBOX, WS_OVERLAPPED, WS_OVERLAPPEDWINDOW, WS_POPUPWINDOW, WS_SIZEBOX, WS_THICKFRAME, WS_TILED, and WS_TILEDWINDOW.

Common Messages and Functions

There are a few messages that can be used with multiple controls. These messages include WM_CUT, WM_COPY, WM_PASTE, and WM_CLEAR for dealing with the clipboard; the WM_SETFONT and WM_GETFONT for setting and retrieving the font used in the control; and the WM_SETTEXT and WM_GETTEXT for setting and getting the window's text (or the `SetWindowText` and `GetWindowText` functions). Another variation of the WM_SETTEXT and WM_GETTEXT messages are the functions `GetDlgItemText` and `SetDlgItemText`, which enable manipulation of a control in a dialog box by specifying the control ID.

Button Control

One of the most versatile predefined controls is the button control. This control is used to display push buttons, check boxes, radio buttons, and even group boxes. Essentially, a button control defines a small rectangular region that usually changes state when clicked.

Button Styles

The appearance of the button's control is specified through style flags. The style flags available in Windows CE are listed in Table 7.2.

Table 7.2	
Button Styles in Windows CE	
Style	Description
BS_3STATE	Creates a button that is the same as a check box, except that the box can be grayed as well as checked or unchecked. Use the grayed state to show that the state of the check box is not determined.
BS_AUTO3STATE	Creates a button that is the same as a three-state check box, except that the box changes its state when the user selects it. The state cycles through checked, grayed, and unchecked.

Style	Description
BS_AUTOCHECKBOX	Creates a button that is the same as a check box, except that the check state automatically toggles between checked and unchecked each time the user selects the check box.
BS_AUTORADIOBUTTON	Creates a button that is the same as a radio button, except that when the user selects it, Windows automatically sets the button's check state to checked and automatically sets the check state for all other buttons in the same group to unchecked.
BS_BITMAP	Specifies that the button displays a bitmap.
BS_BOTTOM	Places text at the bottom of the button rectangle.
BS_CENTER	Centers text horizontally in the button rectangle.
BS_CHECKBOX	Creates a small, empty check box with text. By default, the text is displayed to the right of the check box. To display the text to the left of the check box, combine this flag with the BS_RIGHTBUTTON style.
BS_DEFPUSHBUTTON	Creates a push button that behaves like a BS_PUSHBUTTON-style button, but also has a heavy black border. If the button is in a dialog box, the user can select the button by pressing the Enter key, even when the button does not have the input focus. This style is useful for enabling the user to quickly select the most likely (default) option.
BS_GROUPBOX	Creates a rectangle in which other controls can be grouped. Any text associated with this style is displayed in the rectangle's upper-left corner.

continues

Table 7.2

Button Styles in Windows CE, continued

Style	Description
BS_ICON	Specifies that the button displays an icon.
BS_LEFT	Left-aligns the text in the button rectangle. However, if the button is a check box or radio button that does not have the BS_RIGHTBUTTON style, the text is left-aligned on the right side of the check box or radio button.
BS_NOTIFY	Enables a button to send BN_DBLCLK, BN_KILLFOCUS, and BN_SETFOCUS notification messages to its parent window. Note that buttons send the BN_CLICKED notification message regardless of whether it has this style.
BS_OWNERDRAW	Creates an owner-drawn button. The owner window receives a WM_MEASUREITEM message when the button is created and a WM_DRAWITEM message when a visual aspect of the button has changed. Do not combine the BS_OWNERDRAW style with any other button styles.
BS_PUSHBUTTON	Creates a push button that posts a WM_COMMAND message to the owner window when the user selects the button.
BS_PUSHLIKE	Makes a button (such as a check box, three-state check box, or radio button) look and act like a push button. The button looks raised when it isn't pushed or checked, and sunken when it is pushed or checked.

Style	Description
BS_RADIOBUTTON	Creates a small circle with text. By default, the text is displayed to the right of the circle. To display the text to the left of the circle, combine this flag with the BS_RIGHTBUTTON style. Use radio buttons for groups of related, but mutually exclusive choices.
BS_RIGHT	Right-aligns text in the button rectangle. However, if the button is a check box or radio button that does not have the BS_RIGHTBUTTON style, the text is right-aligned on the right side of the check box or radio button.
BS_RIGHTBUTTON	Positions a radio button's circle or a check box's square on the right side of the button rectangle.
BS_TOP	Places text at the top of the button rectangle.
BS_VCENTER	Places text in the middle (vertically) of the button rectangle.

Note

Windows CE does not support the BS_LEFTTEXT, BS_MULTILINE, BS_TEXT, or BS_USERBUTTON styles.

Button Messages

An application programmatically manipulates a button control by sending messages to it. The message can affect the style and state of the button. The valid messages to send to a button control are listed in Table 7.3.

Table 7.3

Button Messages	
Message	Description
BM_GETCHECK	Used to retrieve the state of a radio button or check box. The return value indicates the state.
Value	Meaning
0	unchecked
1	checked
2	indeterminate (applies only to BS_(AUTO)3STATE styles.)
BM_SETCHECK	Used to set the check state of a radio button or check box.
BM_GETSTATE	Used to determine the state of the button.
BM_SETSTATE	Used to set the state of the button. A WPARAM of TRUE highlights the button; FALSE removes any highlighting.
BM_SETSTYLE	Used to change the style of the button.
BM_CLICK	Simulates the user clicking a button. This message causes the button to receive a WM_LBUTTONDOWN and a WM_LBUTTONUP message, and the button's parent window receives a BN_CLICKED notification message.

Button Notifications

Despite the wide range of appearances that the button control can take, it provides one main notification message, BN_CLICKED. This notification is sent by Windows CE when the user taps the button with the stylus or selects the highlighted button by pressing the Enter key. The parent window of the button control receives the BN_CLICKED notification in the form of a WM_COMMAND message.

The TravelManager application handles the BN_CLICKED notification when it processes the WM_COMMAND message for the ItineraryView window. That process appears as the following code:

```
ItineraryView::WMCommand( HWND hWnd, UINT msg, WPARAM wParam, LPARAM
➥lParam )
{
    WORD notifyCode = HIWORD(wParam);
        WORD id = LOWORD(wParam);

        if (notifyCode == BN_CLICKED  && id == IDC_BUTTON1)
        {
                FlightInfoDlg * pDlg = new
➥FlightInfoDlg(m_pMainWindow);
                pDlg->Create();
                return 1;
        }
        return 0;
}
```

Static Controls

Static controls define a simple text field, box, or rectangle used to label, box, or separate other controls. Static controls take no input and provide no output.

Static Styles

The styles valid when creating a static control are listed in Table 7.4.

Table 7.4

Static Control Styles

Style	Description
SS_BITMAP	Specifies that a bitmap is to be displayed in the static control. The error code text is the name of a bitmap—not a file name—defined elsewhere in the resource file. The style ignores the *nWidth* and *nHeight* parameters, and the control automatically sizes itself to accommodate the bitmap.
SS_CENTER	Specifies a simple rectangle and centers the error code text in the rectangle. The text is formatted before it is displayed, and words that extend past the end of a line are automatically wrapped to the beginning of the next centered line.
SS_CENTERIMAGE	Specifies that the midpoint of a static control with the SS_BITMAP or SS_ICON style is to remain fixed when the control is resized. The four sides are adjusted to accommodate a new bitmap or icon. If a static control has the SS_BITMAP style and the bitmap is smaller than the control's client area, the client area is filled with the color of the pixel in the upper-left corner of the bitmap. If a static control has the SS_ICON style, the icon does not appear to paint the client area.
SS_ICON	Specifies an icon displayed in the dialog box. The given text is the name of an icon (not a file name) defined elsewhere in the resource file. The style ignores the *nWidth* and *nHeight* parameters, and the icon automatically sizes itself.

Style	Description
SS_LEFT	Specifies a simple rectangle and left-aligns the given text in the rectangle. The text is formatted before it is displayed, and words that extend past the end of a line are automatically wrapped to the beginning of the next left-aligned line.
SS_LEFTNOWORDWRAP	Specifies a simple rectangle and left-aligns the given text in the rectangle. Tabs are expanded but words are not wrapped, and text that extends past the end of a line is clipped.
SS_NOPREFIX	Prevents interpretation of any ampersand (&) characters in the control's text as accelerator prefix characters. These are displayed with the ampersand removed and the next character in the string underlined. This static control style may be included with any of the defined static controls. An application can combine SS_NOPREFIX with other styles by using the bitwise or (|) operator. This can be useful when file names or other strings that may contain an ampersand (&) must be displayed as a static control in a dialog box.
SS_NOTIFY	Sends the parent window STN_CLICKED and STN_DBLCLK notification messages when the user clicks or double-clicks the control.
SS_RIGHT	Specifies a simple rectangle and right-aligns the given text in the rectangle. The text is formatted before it is displayed, and words that extend past the end of a line are automatically wrapped to the beginning of the next right-aligned line.

Note

> Windows CE does not support the SS_BLACKFRAME, SS_BLACKRECT, SS_GRAYFRAME, SS_GRAYRECT, SS_METARECT, SS_RIGHTIMAGE, SS_SIMPLE, SS_WHITEFRAME, or SS_WHITERECT styles.

Static Control Messages

Due to the fact that static controls provide little functionality, no messages or functions are specific to static controls. It is common, however, to use the general WM_SETTEXT message (or corresponding SetWindowText function) with static controls. For dialog boxes, the SetDlgItemText function makes it convenient to change the text of the control. The TravelManager application uses SetDlgItemText to change the text of static controls in response to the user selecting entries out of the tree control in the Alternate Flight Lookup dialog box.

```
        SetDlgItemText(hWnd, IDC_FROM, L"Seattle");
SetDlgItemText(hWnd, IDC_TO, L"Indianapolis");
        SetDlgItemText(hWnd, IDC_DEPARTS, L"8:20 am");
        SetDlgItemText(hWnd, IDC_ARRIVES, L"4:45 pm");
        SetDlgItemText(hWnd, IDC_AIRLINE, L"Delta");
        SetDlgItemText(hWnd, IDC_CONNECTION, L"Atlanta");
        SetDlgItemText(hWnd, IDC_LAYOVER, L"1:10");
```

At this stage in the development of the TravelManager application, the data displayed in the static controls is hard-coded. The text to display would eventually come out of a database or other mechanism and be selectively displayed based on the node selected in the tree control.

Static Notifications

As noted previously, static controls with the SS_NOTIFY style enable the parent to receive STN_CLICKED and STD_DBLCLK notification messages when the user clicks or double-clicks the control.

Scroll bar Control

A scroll bar control designates a rectangle that contains a scroll box and has direction arrows at both ends. The scroll bar sends a notification message to its parent window whenever the user clicks the control. The parent window is responsible for updating the position of the scroll box if necessary. Scroll bar controls have the same appearance and function as scroll bars used in ordinary windows. Unlike scroll bars, however, scroll bar controls can be positioned anywhere in a window for use whenever scrolling input is needed for a window.

Scroll Bar Control Styles

The valid styles when creating a scroll bar control are listed in Table.7.5.

Table 7.5

Scroll Bar Control Styles

Style	Description
SBS_HORZ	Designates a horizontal scroll bar. If the SBS_TOPALIGN style is not specified, the scroll bar has the height, width, and position specified by the parameters of `CreateWindow`.
SBS_LEFTALIGN	Aligns the left edge of the scroll bar with the left edge of the rectangle defined by the parameters of `CreateWindow`. The scroll bar has the default width for system scroll bars. Use this style with the SBS_VERT style.
SBS_SIZEBOX	Designates a size box with the height, width, and position specified by the parameters of `CreateWindow`.
SBS_TOPALIGN	Aligns the top edge of the scroll bar with the top edge of the rectangle defined by the parameters of `CreateWindow`. The scroll bar has the default height for system scroll bars. Use this style with the SBS_HORZ style.

continues

Table 7.5

Scroll Bar Control Styles, continued

Style	Description
SBS_VERT	Designates a vertical scroll bar. If you do not specify the SBS_LEFTALIGN style, the scroll bar has the height, width, and position specified by the parameters of CreateWindow.

Note

Windows CE does not support the SBS_BOTTOMALIGN, SBS_RIGHTALIGN, SBS_SIZEBOXBOTTOMRIGHTALIGN, or SBS_SIZEGRIP styles.

Scroll Bar Control Messages and Functions

The scroll bar control supports two messages (and their corresponding functions) for getting and setting information specific to the scroll bar control. The two messages and their corresponding functions and descriptions are shown in Table 7.6.

Table 7.6

Scroll Bar Control Messages

Message	Function	Description
SBM_GETSCROLLINFO	GetScrollInfo	Retrieves the parameters of a scroll bar including the minimum and maximum scrolling positions, the page size, and the position of the scroll box (thumb).

Message	Function	Description
SBM_SETSCROLLINFO	SetScrollInfo	Sets the parameters of a scroll bar, including the minimum and maximum scrolling positions, the page size, and the position of the scroll box (thumb).

Scroll Bar Control Notifications

An application is notified of scroll events through the WM_HSCROLL and WM_VSCROLL messages. These events are received in the form of a WM_COMMAND message and are shown in Table 7.7.

Table 7.7

Scroll Bar Control Notifications

Notification	Description
WM_HSCROLL	Indicates that a scroll event has occurred with a horizontal scroll bar.
WM_VSCROLL	Indicates that a scroll event has occurred with a vertical scroll bar.

Edit Control

Edit controls are rectangular child windows into which the user can type text from the keyboard. Edit controls are simple mechanisms for enabling data entry. The TravelManager application uses edit controls in the Add/Edit Expense dialog box shown in Figure 7.1.

Edit Control Styles

The styles shown in Table 7.8 are valid when creating an edit control.

Figure 7.1

The Add/Edit
Expense dialog
box.

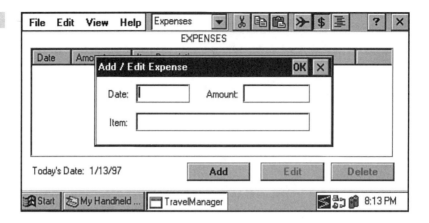

Table 7.8

Edit Control Styles

Style	Description
ES_AUTOHSCROLL	Automatically scrolls text to the right by 10 characters when the user types a character at the end of the line. When the user presses the Enter key, the control scrolls all text back to position zero.
ES_AUTOVSCROLL	Automatically scrolls text up one page when the user presses the Enter key on the last line.
ES_CENTER	Centers text in a multiline edit control.
ES_COMBOBOX	Indicates that the edit control is part of a combo box.
ES_LEFT	Left-aligns text.
ES_LOWERCASE	Converts all characters to lowercase as they are typed into the edit control.
ES_MULTILINE	Designates a multiline edit control.

Style	Description
ES_NOHIDESEL	Causes the edit control to show selection even when the control does not have focus.
ES_NUMBER	Permits only digits to be entered into the edit control.
ES_OEMCONVERT	Converts text entered in the edit control from the Windows character set to the OEM character set and then back to the Windows set. This style is most useful for edit controls that contain file names.
ES_PASSWORD	Displays an asterisk (*) for each character typed into the edit control.
ES_READONLY	Prevents the user from typing or editing text in the edit control.
ES_RIGHT	Right-aligns text in a multiline edit control.
ES_UPPERCASE	Converts all characters to uppercase as they are typed into the edit control.
ES_WANTRETURN	Specifies that a carriage return be inserted when the user presses the Enter key while entering text into a multiline edit control in a dialog box.

Edit Control Messages and Functions

Edit controls support a variety of messages to control the behavior of the control. The text of the edit control can be set and retrieved using the WM_SETTEXT and WM_GETTEXT messages or their corresponding functions (SetWindowText, GetDlgItemText, and so on).

The TravelManager application uses edit controls in the adding and editing of expense items in the Expenses view. See ExpAddEditDlg::WMCommand and ExpAppEditDlg::WMInitDialog for an example of setting and getting text from an edit control.

Other messages specific to edit controls are listed in Table 7.9.

Table 7.9

Edit Control Messages	
Message	Description
EM_CANUNDO	Determines whether an edit-control operation can be undone; that is, whether the control can respond to the EM_UNDO message.
EM_CHARFROMPOS	Retrieves the zero-based character index and zero-based line index of the character nearest the specified point in an edit control.
EM_EMPTYUNDOBUFFER	Resets the undo flag of an edit control. The undo flag is set whenever an operation within the edit control can be undone.
EM_FINDWORDBREAK	Finds the next word break before or after the specified character position, or retrieves information about the character at that position.
EM_FMTLINES	Sets the inclusion flag of soft linebreak characters on or off within a multiline edit control. A soft linebreak consists of two carriage returns and a linefeed is inserted at the end of a line that is broken because of wordwrapping.
EM_GETFIRSTVISIBLELINE	Determines the uppermost visible line in an edit control.
EM_GETHANDLE	Retrieves a handle of the memory currently allocated for a multiline edit control's text.
EM_GETLIMITTEXT	Retrieves the current text limit, in characters, for an edit control.
EM_GETLINE	Copies a line of text from an edit control and places it in a specified buffer.
EM_GETLINECOUNT	Retrieves the number of lines in a multiline edit control.

Message	Description
EM_GETMARGINS	Retrieves the widths of the left and right margins for an edit control.
EM_GETMODIFY	Determines whether the content of an edit control has been modified.
EM_GETPASSWORDCHAR	Retrieves the password character displayed in an edit control when the user enters text.
EM_GETRECT	Retrieves the formatting rectangle of an edit control. The *formatting rectangle* is the limiting rectangle of the text. The limiting rectangle is independent of the size of the edit-control window.
EM_GETSEL	Retrieves the starting and ending character positions of the current selection in an edit control.
EM_GETTHUMB	Retrieves the position of the scroll box (thumb) in a multiline edit control.
EM_GETWORDBREAKPROC	Retrieves the address of the current wordwrap function.
EM_LIMITTEXT	Limits the amount of text the user may enter into an edit control.
EM_LINEFROMCHAR	Retrieves the index of a line that contains the specified character index in a multiline edit control. A *character index* is the number of characters from the beginning of the edit control.
EM_LINEINDEX	Retrieves the character index of a line in a multiline edit control. The *character index of a line* is the number of characters from the beginning of the edit control to the specified line.
EM_LINELENGTH	Retrieves the length of a line, in characters, in an edit control.
EM_LINESCROLL	Scrolls the text vertically or horizontally in a multiline edit control.

continues

Table 7.9

Edit Control Messages, continued

Message	Description
EM_POSFROMCHAR	Retrieves the coordinates of the specified character in an edit control.
EM_REPLACESEL	Replaces the current selection in an edit control with the specified text.
EM_SCROLL	Scrolls the text vertically in a multiline edit control. This message is equivalent to sending a WM_VSCROLL message to the edit control.
EM_SCROLLCARET	Scrolls the caret into view in an edit control.
EM_SETHANDLE	Sets the handle of the memory that will be used by a multiline edit control.
EM_SETLIMITTEXT (EM_LIMITTEXT)	Sets the text limit for an edit control. The *text limit* is the maximum amount of text, in bytes, that the edit control can contain.
EM_SETMARGINS	Sets the widths of the left and right margins for an edit control. The message redraws the control to reflect the new margins.
EM_SETMODIFY	Sets or clears the modification flag for an edit control. The *modification flag* indicates whether the text within the edit control has been modified. It is automatically set whenever the user changes the text.
EM_SETPASSWORDCHAR	Sets or removes the password character for a single-line edit control when the user types text.
EM_SETREADONLY	Sets or removes the read-only style (ES_READONLY) of an edit control.

Message	Description
EM_SETRECT	Sets the formatting rectangle of a multi-line edit control. The *formatting rectangle* is the limiting rectangle of the text. The limiting rectangle is independent of the size of the edit control window. When the edit control is first created, the formatting rectangle is the same as the client area of the edit control window. By using the EM_SETRECT message, an application can make the formatting rectangle larger or smaller than the edit control window.
EM_SETRECTNP	Sets the formatting rectangle of a multi-line edit control. The formatting rectangle is the limiting rectangle of the text. The EM_SETRECTNP message is identical to the EM_SETRECT message, except that the edit control window is not redrawn.
EM_SETSEL	Selects a range of characters in an edit control.
EM_SETTABSTOPS	Sets the tab stops in a multiline edit control.
EM_SETWORDBREAKPROC	Replaces the default wordwrap function with an application-defined wordwrap function.
EM_UNDO	Undoes the last edit control operation.

Edit Control Notifications

Edit controls generate various notifications regarding the state of the edit control. These notifications are described in Table 7.10.

Table 7.10

Edit Control Messages	
Notification	Description
EN_CHANGE	Indicates the user has modified text in an edit control.
EN_ERRSPACE	Indicates the edit control cannot allocate enough memory to meet a specific request.
EN_HSCROLL	Indicates the user has clicked the edit control's horizontal scroll bar.
EN_KILLFOCUS	Indicates the user has selected another control.
EN_MAXTEXT	Indicates, when inserting text, the user has exceeded the specified number of characters for the edit control. Insertion has been truncated. This message is also sent either when an edit control does not have the ES_AUTOHSCROLL style and the number of characters to be inserted exceeds the width of the edit control or when an edit control does not have the ES_AUTOVSCROLL style and the total number of lines to be inserted exceeds the height of the edit control.
EN_SETFOCUS	Indicates the user has selected this edit control.
EN_UPDATE	Indicates the user has altered the text in the edit control, and Windows is about to display the new text.
EN_VSCROLL	Indicates the user has clicked the edit control's vertical scroll bar.

List Box Control

List box controls are used to display lists of strings. The strings are displayed in a scrollable columnar list within a rectangle.

List Box Control Styles

List boxes permit various creation styles. These styles are discussed in detail in Table 7.11.

Table 7.11

List Box Control Styles

Style	Description
LBS_DISABLENOSCROLL	Shows a disabled vertical scroll bar for the list box when the box does not contain enough items to scroll. If you do not specify this style, the scroll bar is hidden when the list box does not contain enough items.
LBS_EXTENDEDSEL	Permits multiple items to be selected by using the Shift key and the mouse or a special key combination.
LBS_HASSTRINGS	Specifies that a list box contains items consisting of strings. The list box maintains the memory and addresses for the strings so the application can use the LB_GETTEXT message to retrieve the text for a particular item. By default, all list boxes except owner-drawn list boxes have this style. You can create an owner-drawn list box with or without this style.
LBS_MULTICOLUMN	Specifies a multicolumn list box that is scrolled horizontally. The LB_SETCOLUMNWIDTH message sets the width of the columns.
LBS_MULTIPLESEL	Turns string selection on or off each time the user clicks or double-clicks a string in the list box. The user can select any number of strings.
LBS_NOINTEGRALHEIGHT	Specifies that the size of the list box is exactly the size specified by the application when it created the list box. Normally, Windows sizes a list box so that the list box does not display partial items.

continues

Table 7.11

List Box Control Styles, continued	
Style	Description
LBS_NOREDRAW	Specifies that the list box's appearance is not updated when changes are made. You can change this style at any time by sending a WM_SETREDRAW message.
LBS_NOSEL	Specifies that the list box contains items that can be viewed but not selected.
LBS_NOTIFY	Notifies the parent window with an input message whenever the user clicks or double-clicks a string in the list box.
LBS_SORT	Sorts strings in the list box alphabetically.
LBS_USETABSTOPS	Enables a list box to recognize and expand tab characters when drawing its strings. The default tab positions are 32 dialog box units. A *dialog box unit* is a horizontal or vertical distance. One horizontal dialog box unit is equal to one-fourth of the current dialog box base-width unit. Windows calculates these units based on the height and width of the current system font.
LBS_WANTKEYBOARDINPUT	Specifies that the owner of the list box receives WM_VKEYTOITEM messages whenever the user presses a key and the list box has the input focus. This enables an application to perform special processing on the keyboard input.

Note

Windows CE does not support the LBS_NODATA, LBS_OWNERDRAWFIXED, LBS_OWNERDRAWVARIABLE, or LBS_STANDARD styles.

List Box Control Messages and Functions

List box controls support a number of messages used to control the functionality of the control. These messages are described in Table 7.12.

Table 7.12

List Box Control Messages	
Message	Description
LB_ADDFILE	Adds the specified file name to a list box that contains a directory listing.
LB_ADDSTRING	Adds a string to a list box. If the list box does not have the LBS_SORT style, the string is added to the end of the list. Otherwise, the string is inserted into the list and the list is sorted.
LB_DELETESTRING	Deletes a string in a list box.
LB_DIR	Adds a list of file names to a list box.
LB_FINDSTRING	Finds the first string in a list box that contains the specified prefix.
LB_FINDSTRINGEXACT	Finds the first list box string that matches the string specified in the lpszFind parameter.
LB_GETANCHORINDEX	Retrieves the index of the anchor item, which is the item from which a multiple selection starts. A multiple selection spans all items from the anchor item to the caret item.

continues

Table 7.12

List Box Control Messages, continued	
Message	Description
LB_GETCARETINDEX	Determines the index of the item that has the focus rectangle in a multiple-selection list box. The item may or may not be selected.
LB_GETCOUNT	Retrieves the number of items in a list box.
LB_GETCURSEL	Retrieves the index of the currently selected item, if any, in a single-selection list box.
LB_GETHORIZONTALEXTENT	Retrieves from a list box the scrollable width, in pixels, by which the list box can be scrolled horizontally if the list box has a horizontal scroll bar.
LB_GETITEMDATA	Retrieves the application-defined 32-bit value associated with the specified list box item.
LB_GETITEMHEIGHT	Retrieves the height of items in a list box.
LB_GETITEMRECT	Retrieves the dimensions of the rectangle that binds a list box item as it is currently displayed in the list box.
LB_GETLOCALE	Retrieves the current locale of the list box. You can use the locale to determine the correct sorting order of displayed text for list boxes with the LBS_SORT style. Locale is also used to determine the correct sorting order of text added by the LB_ADDSTRING message.
LB_GETSEL	Retrieves the selection state of an item.
LB_GETSELCOUNT	Retrieves the total number of selected items in a multiple-selection list box.

Message	Description
LB_GETSELITEMS	Fills a buffer with an array of integers that specify the item numbers of selected items in a multiple-selection list box.
LB_GETTEXT	Retrieves a string from a list box.
LB_GETTEXTLEN	Retrieves the length of a string in a list box.
LB_GETTOPINDEX	Retrieves the index of the first visible item in a list box. Initially, the item with index 0 is at the top of the list box, but if the list box contents have been scrolled, another item may be at the top.
LB_INITSTORAGE	Allocates memory for storing list box items. An application sends this message before adding a large number of items to a list box.
LB_INSERTSTRING	Inserts a string into a list box. Unlike the LB_ADDSTRING message, the LB_INSERTSTRING message does not cause a list with the LBS_SORT style to be sorted.
LB_ITEMFROMPOINT	Retrieves the zero-based index of the item nearest to the specified point in a list box.
LB_RESETCONTENT	Removes all items from a list box.
LB_SELECTSTRING	Searches a list box for an item that begins with the characters in a specified string. If a matching item is found, the item is selected.
LB_SELITEMRANGE	Selects one or more consecutive items in a multiple-selection list box.
LB_SELITEMRANGEEX	Selects one or more consecutive items in a multiple-selection list box.

continues

Table 7.12

List Box Control Messages, continued	
Message	Description
LB_SETANCHORINDEX	Sets the anchor item, which is the item from which a multiple selection starts. A multiple selection spans all items from the anchor item to the caret item.
LB_SETCARETINDEX	Sets the focus rectangle to the item at the specified index in a multiple-selection list box. If the item is not visible, it is scrolled into view.
LB_SETCOLUMNWIDTH	Sets the width, in pixels, of all columns in the list box.
LB_SETCOUNT	Sets the count of items in a list box created with the LBS_NODATA style and not created with the LBS_HASSTRINGS style.
LB_SETCURSEL	Selects a string and scrolls it into view, if necessary. When a new string is selected, the list box removes the highlight from the previously selected string.
LB_SETHORIZONTALEXTENT	Sets the scrollable width, in pixels, by which a list box can be scrolled horizontally. If the width of the list box is smaller than this value, the horizontal scroll bar horizontally scrolls items in the list box. If the width of the list box is equal to or greater than this value, the horizontal scroll bar is hidden.
LB_SETITEMDATA	Sets a 32-bit value associated with the specified item in a list box.

Message	Description
LB_SETITEMHEIGHT	Sets the height, in pixels, of items in a list box. If the list box has the LBS_OWNERDRAWVARIABLE style, this message sets the height of the item specified by the index parameter. Otherwise, this message sets the height of all items in the list box.
LB_SETLOCALE	Sets the current locale of the list box. You can use the locale to determine the correct sorting order of displayed text (for list boxes with the LBS_SORT style) and of text added by the LB_ADDSTRING message.
LB_SETSEL	Selects a string in a multiple-selection list box.
LB_SETTABSTOPS	Sets the tab-stop positions in a list box.
LB_SETTOPINDEX	Ensures that a particular item in a list box is visible.

List Box Control Notifications

List box controls generate notifications indicating some event has occurred. These notifications are listed in Table 7.13.

Table 7.13

List Box Control Notifications	
Notification	**Description**
LBN_DBLCLK	Indicates a string has been double-clicked.
LBN_ERRSPACE	Indicates the list box cannot allocate enough memory to meet a specific request.

continues

Table 7.13

List Box Control Notifications, continued	
Notification	Description
LBN_KILLFOCUS	Indicates the list box has lost keyboard focus.
LBN_SELCANCEL	Indicates the user has canceled the selection in the list box.
LBN_SELCHANGE	Indicates the selection in the list box is about to change.
LBN_SETFOCUS	Indicates the list box has received keyboard focus.

Combo Box Control

A combo box control is a pre-built combination of an edit control and a list box. A combo box enables the user to select from a range of values while taking up much less space than a list box control. In the previous chapter, the TravelManager application used a combo box in the command bar.

Combo Box Control Styles

The creation styles that the combo box supports are listed in Table 7.14.

Table 7.14

Combo Box Control Styles	
Style	Description
CBS_AUTOHSCROLL	Automatically scrolls the text in an edit control to the right when the user types a character at the end of the line. If this style is not set, only text that fits within the rectangular boundary is permitted.

Style	Description
CBS_DISABLENOSCROLL	Shows a disabled vertical scroll bar in the list box when the box does not contain enough items to scroll. Without this style, the scroll bar is hidden when the list box does not contain enough items.
CBS_DROPDOWN	Displays a combo box where the list box is not displayed unless the user selects an icon next to the edit control.
CBS_DROPDOWNLIST	Similar to CBS_DROPDOWN, except that the edit control is replaced by a static text item that displays the current selection in the list box.
CBS_HASSTRINGS	Specifies that an owner-drawn combo box contains items consisting of strings. The combo box maintains the memory and address for the strings, so the application can use the CB_GETLBTEXT message to retrieve the text for a particular item.
CBS_LOWERCASE	Converts to lowercase any uppercase characters entered into the edit control of a combo box.
CBS_NOINTEGRALHEIGHT	Specifies that the size of the combo box is exactly the size specified by the application when it created the combo box. Normally, Windows sizes a combo box so that it does not display partial items.
CBS_OEMCONVERT	Converts text entered in the combo box edit control from the Windows character set to the OEM character set and then back to the Windows set. This style is most useful for combo boxes that contain file names and applies only to combo boxes created with the CBS_DROPDOWN style.
CBS_SORT	Automatically sorts strings entered into the list box.
CBS_UPPERCASE	Converts to uppercase any lowercase characters entered into the edit control of a combo box.

Note	Windows CE does not support CBS_SIMPLE, CBS_OWNERDRAWFIXED, and CBS_OWNERDRAWVARIABLE.

Combo Box Control Messages

Combo box controls accept certain messages, which are identified in Table 7.15.

Table 7.15

Combo Box Control Messages

Message	Description
CB_ADDSTRING	Adds a string to the list box of a combo box. If the combo box does not have the CBS_SORT style, the string is added to the end of the list. Otherwise, the string is inserted into the list, and the list is sorted.
CB_DELETESTRING	Deletes a string in the list box of a combo box.
CB_DIR	Adds a list of file names to the list box of a combo box.
CB_FINDSTRING	Searches the list box of a combo box for an item beginning with the characters in a specified string.
CB_FINDSTRINGEXACT	Finds the first list box string in a combo box that matches the string specified in the lpszFind parameter.
CB_GETCOUNT	Retrieves the number of items in the list box of a combo box.
CB_GETCURSEL	Retrieves the index of the currently selected item, if any, in the list box of a combo box.

Message	Description
CB_GETDROPPEDCONTROLRECT	Retrieves the screen coordinates of the drop-down list box of a combo box.
CB_GETDROPPEDSTATE	Determines whether the list box of a combo box is dropped down.
CB_GETDROPPEDWIDTH	Retrieves the minimum acceptable width, in pixels, of the list box of a combo box with the CBS_DROPDOWN or CBS_DROPDOWNLIST style.
CB_GETEDITSEL	Retrieves the starting and ending character positions of the current selection in the edit control of a combo box.
CB_GETEXTENDEDUI	Determines whether a combo box has the default user interface or the extended user interface.
CB_GETHORIZONTALEXTENT	Retrieves from a combo box the scrollable width, in pixels, by which the list box can be scrolled horizontally. This is applicable only if the list box has a horizontal scroll bar.
CB_GETITEMDATA	Retrieves the application-supplied 32-bit value associated with the specified item in the combo box.
CB_GETITEMHEIGHT	Determines the height of list items or the selection field in a combo box.
CB_GETLBTEXT	Retrieves a string from the list of a combo box.
CB_GETLBTEXTLEN	Retrieves the length, in characters, of a string in the list of a combo box.

continues

Table 7.15

Message	Description
Combo Box Control Messages, continued	
CB_GETLOCALE	Retrieves the current locale of the combo box. The locale is used to determine the correct sorting order of displayed text for combo boxes with the CBS_SORT style and text added by using the CB_ADDSTRING message.
CB_GETTOPINDEX	Retrieves the zero-based index of the first visible item in the list box portion of a combo box. Initially, the item with index 0 is at the top of the list box, but if the list box contents have been scrolled, another item may be at the top.
CB_INITSTORAGE	Allocates memory for storing a large number of list box items.
CB_INSERTSTRING	Inserts a string into the list box of a combo box at the specified position.
CB_LIMITTEXT	Limits the length of the text the user may type into the edit control of a combo box.
CB_RESETCONTENT	Removes all items from the list box and edit control of a combo box.
CB_SELECTSTRING	Searches the list of a combo box for an item that begins with the characters in a specified string. If a matching item is found, it is selected and copied to the edit control.

Message	Description
CB_SETCURSEL	Selects a string in the list of a combo box. If necessary, the list scrolls the string into view. The text in the edit control of the combo box changes to reflect the new selection, and any previous selection in the list is removed.
CB_SETDROPPEDWIDTH	Sets the maximum acceptable width, in pixels, of the list box of a combo box with the CBS_DROPDOWN or CBS_DROPDOWNLIST style.
CB_SETEDITSEL	Selects characters in the edit control of a combo box.
CB_SETEXTENDEDUI	Selects either the default user interface or the extended user interface for a combo box that has the CBS_DROPDOWN or CBS_DROPDOWNLIST style.
CB_SETHORIZONTALEXTENT	Sets the width, in pixels, by which a list box can be scrolled horizontally (the scrollable width).
CB_SETITEMDATA	Sets the 32-bit value associated with the specified item in a combo box.
CB_SETITEMHEIGHT	Sets the height of list items or the selection field in a combo box.
CB_SETLOCALE	Sets the current locale of the combo box. If the combo box has the CBS_SORT style and strings are added using CB_ADDSTRING, the locale of a combo box affects how list items are sorted.

continues

Table 7.15

Combo Box Control Messages, continued

Message	Description
CB_SETTOPINDEX	Ensures that a particular item is visible in the list box of a combo box. The system scrolls the list box contents so that either the specified item appears at the top of the list box or the maximum scroll range has been reached.
CB_SHOWDROPDOWN	Shows or hides the list box of a combo box that has the CBS_DROPDOWN or CBS_DROPDOWNLIST style.

Combo Box Control Notifications

Combo box controls generate notifications in response to actions by the user or the system. These notifications are sent in the form of WM_COMMAND messages. The TravelManager application processes the CBN_SELCHANGE notification from the combo box on the command bar, which is referenced in the following:

```
LRESULT MainWindow::WMCommand( HWND hWnd,  UINT msg, WPARAM wParam,
➥LPARAM lParam )
{
    WORD notifyCode = HIWORD(wParam);

        ... code removed ...

    if ( notifyCode == CBN_SELCHANGE )
    {
        ... process CBM_SELCHANGE ...
```

An application can process the following combo box control notification messages shown in Table 7.16.

Table 7.16

Combo Box Control Notifications

Notification	Description
CBN_CLOSEUP	Indicates the list box part of the combo box has been closed.
CBN_DROPDOWN	Indicates the list box part of the combo box is about to be made visible.
CBN_EDITCHANGE	Indicates that the text in the edit portion of the combo box may have been altered.
CBN_EDITUPDATE	Indicates the edit control portion of the combo box is about to display altered text.
CBN_ERRSPACE	Indicates the combo box cannot allocate enough memory to meet a specific request.
CBN_KILLFOCUS	Indicates that the combo box has lost keyboard focus.
CBN_SELCHANGE	Indicates that the selection in the list box part of the combo box has changed.
CBN_SELENDCANCEL	Indicates the user selected an item but then selected another control or closed the dialog box.
CBN_SELENDOK	Indicates the user selected a list item and then closed the list.
CBN_SETFOCUS	Indicates the combo box has received keyboard focus.

List View Control

The list view control is a new common control that was added with Windows 95. The list view control is used to display any arrangement of icons with labels, or columnar lists of text, with or without icons. An example of list view control can be seen in Windows 95 Explorer. A list view control has four possible views: icon, small icon, list, and report. The report view makes it convenient to produce multicolumn list boxes. The TravelManager application uses a list view control in the Itinerary-Air dialog box and in the Expenses dialog box (see Figure 7.2 and Figure 7.3).

Figure 7.2

Itinerary-Air dialog box.

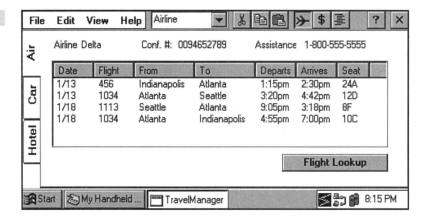

Figure 7.3

Expenses dialog box.

List View Control Styles

The window styles shown in Table 7.17 are specific to list view controls.

Table 7.17

List View Control Styles

Style	Description
LVS_ALIGNLEFT	Specifies that items are left-aligned in icon and small icon view.
LVS_ALIGNTOP	Specifies that items are aligned with the top of the list view control in icon and small icon view.
LVS_AUTOARRANGE	Specifies that icons are automatically kept arranged in icon and small icon view.
LVS_BUTTON	Specifies that item icons look like buttons in icon view.
LVS_EDITLABELS	Permits item text to be edited in place. The parent window must process the LVN_ENDLABELEDIT notification message.
LVS_ICON	Specifies icon view.
LVS_LIST	Specifies list view.
LVS_NOCOLUMNHEADER	Specifies that a column header is not displayed in report view. By default, columns have headers in report view.
LVS_NOLABELWRAP	Displays item text on a single line in icon view. By default, item text may wrap in icon view.
LVS_NOSCROLL	Disables scrolling. All items must be within the client area.
LVS_NOSORTHEADER	Specifies that column headers do not work like buttons. This style is useful if clicking a column header in report view does not carry out an action, such as sorting.

continues

Table 7.17

| List View Control Styles, continued | |
Style	Description
LVS_OWNERDRAWFIXED	Enables the owner window to paint items in report view. The list view control sends a WM_DRAWITEM message to paint each item; it does not send separate messages for each subitem. The itemData member of the DRAWITEMSTRUCT structure contains the item data for the specified list view item.
LVS_REPORT	Specifies report view.
LVS_SHAREIMAGELISTS	Specifies that the control does not take ownership of the image lists assigned to it; that is, it does not destroy the image lists when it is destroyed. This style enables the same image lists to be used with multiple list view controls.
LVS_SHOWSELALWAYS	Always shows the selection highlight, even if the control is not activated.
LVS_SINGLESEL	Enables only one item at a time to be selected. By default, multiple items may be selected.
LVS_SMALLICON	Specifies small icon view.
LVS_SORTASCENDING	Sorts items based on item text in ascending order.
LVS_SORTDESCENDING	Sorts items based on item text in descending order.

List View Control Messages and Functions

An application sends messages to a list view control to alter its appearance, add or change items and columns, and so on. Each message has a corresponding function (macro) that can be used instead of sending the message explicitly.

The TravelManager application uses many `ListView` functions, including: `ListView_InsertColumn`, `ListView_GetItemCount`, `ListView_GetNextItem`, `ListView_GetItemText`, and `ListView_SetItemText`. The following code (from ItineraryView::Create) shows how TravelManager creates the columns for the Itinerary-Air list view and then inserts some dummy data.

```
HWND hwndLV = GetDlgItem(dlg, IDC_AIRLIST);

LV_COLUMN lvc;

// Initialize the LV_COLUMN structure.
lvc.mask    = LVCF_FMT | LVCF_WIDTH | LVCF_TEXT;
lvc.fmt     = LVCFMT_LEFT;

lvc.cx      = 50;
lvc.pszText = L"Date";
ListView_InsertColumn(hwndLV, 0, &lvc);
lvc.cx      = 50;
lvc.pszText = L"Flight";
ListView_InsertColumn(hwndLV, 1, &lvc);
lvc.cx      = 75;
lvc.pszText = L"From";
ListView_InsertColumn(hwndLV, 2, &lvc);
lvc.cx      = 75;
lvc.pszText = L"To";
ListView_InsertColumn(hwndLV, 3, &lvc);
lvc.cx      = 50;
lvc.pszText = L"Departs";
ListView_InsertColumn(hwndLV, 4, &lvc);
lvc.cx      = 50;
lvc.pszText = L"Arrives";
ListView_InsertColumn(hwndLV, 5, &lvc);
lvc.cx      = 40;
lvc.pszText = L"Seat";
ListView_InsertColumn(hwndLV, 6, &lvc);

    // Insert some dummy date; real data will eventually come
➥from our database
    static TCHAR * szAirData[4][7] =
    {
    {L"1/
```

```
13",L"456",L"Indianapolis",L"Atlanta",L"1:15pm",L"2:30pm",L"24A"},
        {L"1/13",L"1034",L"Atlanta",L"Seattle",L"3:20pm",L"4:42pm",
➥L"12D"},
        {L"1/18",L"1113",L"Seattle",L"Atlanta",L"9:05pm",L"3:18pm",
➥L"8F"},
        {L"1/18",L"1034",L"Atlanta",L"Indianapolis",L"4:55pm",
➥L"7:00pm",L"10C"}
        };

    LV_ITEM lvi;
    lvi.mask = LVIF_TEXT;
    lvi.iSubItem = 0;

    int i,k;
    for (i=0; i<4; i++)
    {
            lvi.iItem = i;
            lvi.pszText = szAirData[i][0];
            lvi.cchTextMax = 6;
            ListView_InsertItem(hwndLV, &lvi);

            for (k=1; k<7; k++)
            {
                    ListView_SetItemText(hwndLV, i, k,
➥szAirData[i][k]);
            }
    }
```

Table 7.18 shows the available list view messages and their corresponding macros.

Table 7.18

List View Control Messages

Message	Function	Description
LVM_ARRANGE	ListView_Arrange	Arranges the items in large icon view based on the flag's set.

Message	Function	Description
LVM_CREATEDRAGIMAGE	ListView_CreateDragImage	Creates a drag image for the specified item.
LVM_DELETEALLITEMS	ListView_DeleteAllItems	Removes all items from a list view window.
LVM_DELETECOLUMN	ListView_DeleteColumn	Removes a column from a list view window.
LVM_DELETEITEM	ListView_DeleteItem	Removes a single item from a list view window.
LVM_EDITLABEL	ListView_EditLabel	Begins in-place editing of an item's text label. This message selects and sets the focus to the item.
LVM_ENSUREVISIBLE	ListView_EnsureVisible	Ensures that an item is entirely or partially visible by scrolling the list view window if necessary.

continues

Table 7.18

List View Control Messages, *continued*		
Message	Function	Description
LVM_FINDITEM	ListView_FindItem	Searches for an item in a list view control.
LVM_GETBKCOLOR	ListView_GetBkColor	Retrieves the background color of the list view window.
LVM_GETCALLBACKMASK	ListView_GetCallbackMask	Retrieves the callback mask for a list view window.
LVM_GETCOLUMN	ListView_GetColumn	Retrieves the attributes of a specified column.
LVM_GETCOLUMNWIDTH	ListView_GetColumnWidth	Retrieves the width of a column in list view or details view.
LVM_GETCOUNTPERPAGE	ListView_GetCountPerPage	Calculates the number of items that can fit vertically in the visible area in list view or details view.

Message	Function	Description
LVM_GETEDITCONTROL	ListView_GetEditControl	Retrieves the handle of the edit window used to edit an item's text label in place.
LVM_GETIMAGELIST	ListView_GetImageList	Retrieves the handle of an image list used for drawing items.
LVM_GETITEM	ListView_GetItem	Retrieves the attributes of an item.
LVM_GETITEMCOUNT	ListView_GetItemCount	Retrieves the number of items in a list view control.
LVM_GETITEMPOSITION	ListView_GetItemPosition	Retrieves the position of an item in large icon view or small icon view.
LVM_GETITEMRECT	ListView_GetItemRect	Retrieves the bounding rectangle for an item in the current view.
LVM_GETITEMSTATE	ListView_GetItemState	Retrieves the state of an item.

continues

Table 7.18

List View Control Messages, continued

Message	Function	Description
LVM_GETITEMTEXT	ListView_GetItemText	Retrieves the text of an item or a subitem.
LVM_GETNEXTITEM	ListView_GetNextItem	Searches for the next item, starting from a specified item.
LVM_GETORIGIN	ListView_GetOrigin	Retrieves the list view origin point, which is needed for setting the item position.
LVM_GETSTRINGWIDTH	ListView_GetStringWidth	Retrieves the minimum column width necessary to display the given string. The returned width takes the current font and column margins of the list view control (but not the width of a small icon) into account.

Message	Function	Description
LVM_GETTEXTBKCOLOR	ListView_GetTextBkColor	Retrieves the background text color in a list view window.
LVM_GETTEXTCOLOR	ListView_GetTextColor	Retrieves the color of the text in a list view window.
LVM_GETTOPINDEX	ListView_GetTopIndex	Retrieves the index of the first visible item in a list view window.
LVM_GETVIEWRECT	ListView_GetViewRect	Retrieves the bounding rectangle of all items in large icon view.
LVM_HITTEST	ListView_HitTest	Determines which item is at a specified position in a list view window.
LVM_INSERTCOLUMN	ListView_InsertColumn	Inserts a new column in a list view window.
LVM_INSERTITEM	ListView_InsertItem	Inserts a new item in a list view window.

continues

Table 7.18

List View Control Messages, continued		
Message	Function	Description
LVM_REDRAWITEMS	ListView_RedrawItems	Forces a redraw of a range of items in a list view control.
LVM_SCROLL	ListView_Scroll	Scrolls the contents of a list view window.
LVM_SETBKCOLOR	ListView_SetBkColor	Sets the background color of a list view window.
LVM_SETCALLBACKMASK	ListView_SetCallbackMask	Sets the callback mask for a list view window.
LVM_SETCOLUMN	ListView_SetColumn	Sets the attributes of a column in a list view control.
LVM_SETCOLUMNWIDTH	ListView_SetColumnWidth	Sets the width of a column in details view or list view.
LVM_SETIMAGELIST	ListView_SetImageList	Sets the image list used for drawing items in a list view control.

Message	Function	Description
LVM_SETITEM	ListView_SetItem	Sets an item's attributes.
LVM_SETITEMCOUNT	ListView_SetItemCount	Sets the item count of a list view control.
LVM_SETITEMPOSITION	ListView_SetItemPosition	Sets the position of an item in large icon view or small icon view relative to the list view rectangle.
LVM_SETITEMSTATE	ListView_SetItemState	Sets the state of an item.
LVM_SETITEMTEXT	ListView_SetItemText	Sets the text of an item or a subitem.
LVM_SETTEXTBKCOLOR	ListView_SetTextBkColor	Sets the background text color in a list view window.
LVM_SETTEXTCOLOR	ListView_SetTextColor	Sets the text color in a list view window.
LVM_SORTITEMS	ListView_SortItems	Sorts items in a list view control, using an application-defined comparison function.
LVM_UPDATE	ListView_Update	Updates an item.

List View Control Notifications

A list view control sends notification messages to its owner window when events occur in the control. In the Expenses view, the TravelManager application responds to the LVN_ITEMCHANGED notification and enables or disables the Edit and Delete push buttons. It also responds to the NM_DBLCLK notification to bring up the Add/Edit dialog box for the expense that is double-clicked (double-tapped).

```
LRESULT ExpensesView::WMNotify( HWND hWnd,  UINT msg, WPARAM wParam,
LPARAM lParam )
{
        if (wParam == IDC_EXPLIST)
        {
                // Note: lParam can really point to a couple different
➥struct
                // types, but the first element of all of them is the
➥NMHDR
                // struct. That's how we can cast lParam to one thing
➥here
                // and then to something else after we determine what
➥the
                // notification code is.
                NMHDR FAR * pNMHdr = (NMHDR FAR *)lParam;

                HWND hwndLV = GetDlgItem(hWnd, IDC_EXPLIST);

                if (pNMHdr->code == LVN_ITEMCHANGED)
            {
                        NM_LISTVIEW * pnmh = (NM_LISTVIEW *) lParam;

                        int iCurSel = ListView_GetNextItem (hwndLV, -
➥1, LVNI_SELECTED);
                        if (iCurSel == -1)
                        {
                                EnableWindow( GetDlgItem(hWnd,
➥IDC_EDIT), FALSE);
                                EnableWindow( GetDlgItem(hWnd,
➥IDC_DELETE), FALSE);
                         }
                        else
                        {
                                EnableWindow( GetDlgItem(hWnd,
➥IDC_EDIT), TRUE);
```

```
                                EnableWindow( GetDlgItem(hWnd,
➥IDC_DELETE), TRUE);
                        }
                }
                else if (pNMHdr->code == NM_DBLCLK)
                {
                        int iCurSel = ListView_GetNextItem (hwndLV,
➥-1, LVNI_SELECTED);
                        if (iCurSel != -1)
                        {
                                ExpAddEditDlg * pDlg;
                                pDlg = new ExpAddEditDlg(m_pMainWindow,
➥TRUE, hwndLV);

                                pDlg->Create();
                        }
                }
        }
        return TRUE;
}
```

The possible notifications from the list view control are described in Table 7.19.

Table 7.19

List View Control Notifications

Notification	Description
LVN_BEGINDRAG	Indicates that a drag-and-drop operation involving the left mouse button is being initiated.
LVN_BEGINLABELEDIT	Indicates the start of label editing for an item.
LVN_BEGINRDRAG	Indicates that a drag-and-drop operation involving the right mouse button is being initiated.
LVN_COLUMNCLICK	Indicates that a column was clicked.
LVN_DELETEALLITEMS	Indicates that all items in the control were deleted.
LVN_DELETEITEM	Indicates that an item was deleted.

continues

Table 7.19	

List View Control Notifications, continued

Notification	Description
LVN_ENDDRAG	Indicates the end of default processing for a drag-and-drop operation involving the left mouse button.
LVN_ENDLABELEDIT	Indicates the end of label editing for an item.
LVN_ENDRDRAG	Indicates the end of default processing for a drag-and-drop operation involving the right mouse button.
LVN_GETDISPINFO	Requests a list view control's parent window to provide information needed to display or sort an item.
LVN_INSERTITEM	Indicates that a new item was inserted.
LVN_ITEMCHANGED	Indicates that an item has changed.
LVN_ITEMCHANGING	Indicates that an item is changing.
LVN_KEYDOWN	Indicates that a key has been pressed.
LVN_SETDISPINFO	Notifies a list view control's parent window that it must update the information it maintains for an item.

Tree View Control

The tree view control provides a way to display a hierarchical list of items. Each item has a label and optionally can have a bitmap associated with it. An example of a tree view control can be found in the Travel-Manager application. The tree control is used in the Alternate Flight Lookup dialog box, which is shown in Figure 7.4.

Tree View Control Styles

The tree view styles specify the appearance of the tree view control. A list of tree view styles can be found in Table 7.20.

Figure 7.4

TravelManager's
Tree control.

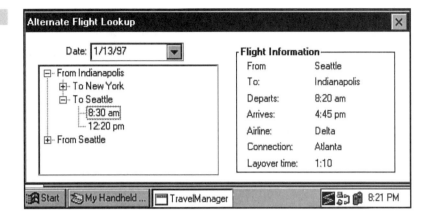

Table 7.20

Tree View Control Styles

Style	Description
TVS_DISABLEDRAGDROP	Prevents the tree view control from sending TVN_BEGINDRAG notification messages.
TVS_EDITLABELS	Enables the user to edit the labels of tree view items.
TVS_HASBUTTONS	Displays plus (+) and minus (-) buttons next to parent items. The user clicks the buttons to expand or collapse a parent item's list of child items. To include buttons with items at the root of the tree view, TVS_LINESATROOT must also be specified.
TVS_HASLINES	Uses lines to show the hierarchy of items.
TVS_LINESATROOT	Uses lines to link items at the root of the tree view control. This value is ignored if TVS_HASLINES is not also specified.
TVS_SHOWSELALWAYS	Uses the system highlight colors to draw the selected item.

Tree View Control Messages and Functions

An application sends messages to a tree view control to alter its appearance, add or change items, and so on. Each message has a corresponding function (macro) that can be used instead of sending the message explicitly.

In the FlightInfoDlg::WMInitDialog, the TravelManager application creates the items in the tree using the TreeView_InsertItem function. The data inserted into the tree is hard-coded here, but would eventually come from the database.

```
TV_INSERTSTRUCT TreeCtrlItem;

    // lParam can hold any value we want; we'll use 0 to mean the
➥node
    // has children and non-zero to mean it is a leaf node.
    TreeCtrlItem.hParent = TVI_ROOT;
    TreeCtrlItem.hInsertAfter = TVI_LAST;
    TreeCtrlItem.item.mask = TVIF_TEXT | TVIF_PARAM;
    TreeCtrlItem.item.pszText = L"From Indianapolis";
    TreeCtrlItem.item.lParam = 0;
    HTREEITEM hTreeItem1 = TreeView_InsertItem(hwndTree,
➥&TreeCtrlItem);

    TreeCtrlItem.hParent = hTreeItem1;
    TreeCtrlItem.item.pszText = L"To New York";
    TreeCtrlItem.item.lParam = 0;
    HTREEITEM hTreeItem2= TreeView_InsertItem(hwndTree,
➥&TreeCtrlItem);

    TreeCtrlItem.hParent = hTreeItem2;
    TreeCtrlItem.item.pszText = L"10:00 am";
    TreeCtrlItem.item.lParam = 1;
    TreeView_InsertItem(hwndTree, &TreeCtrlItem);

... etc. ...
```

Table 7.21 shows the available tree view messages and their corresponding macros.

Table 7.21

Tree View Control Messages

Message	Function	Description
TVM_CREATEDRAGIMAGE	TreeView_CreateDragImage	Creates a drag image for the specified item.
TVM_DELETEITEM	TreeView_DeleteAllItems	Deletes all items in a tree view window.
TVM_DELETEITEM	TreeView_DeleteItem	Deletes a specified item from a tree view window.
TVM_EDITLABEL	TreeView_EditLabel	Begins in-place editing of an item's text label. The text is replaced by a single-line edit window containing the original text in a selected and focused state.
TVM_ENSUREVISIBLE	TreeView_EnsureVisible	Ensures that an item is visible and expands the parent item or scrolls the tree view window if necessary.

continues

Table 7.21

Tree View Control Messages, continued		
Message	Function	Description
TVM_EXPAND	TreeView_Expand	Expands or collapses the list of child items associated with a parent item.
TVM_GETNEXTITEM	TreeView_GetChild	Retrieves the child of a specified tree view item.
TVM_GETCOUNT	TreeView_GetCount	Returns the number of items in a tree view window.
TVM_GETDROPHILITE	TreeView_GetDrop-Hilight	Retrieves the target of a drag-and-drop operation.
TVM_GETEDITCONTROL	TreeView_GetEditControl	Retrieves the handle of the edit control being used for in-place editing of an item's text label.
TVM_GETNEXTITEM	TreeView_GetFirstVisible	Retrieves the first visible item of a tree view control.
TVM_GETIMAGELIST	TreeView_GetImageList	Retrieves the handle of the image list associated with a tree view window.

Tree View Control Messages

TVM_GETINDENT	TreeView_GetIndent	Retrieves the amount, in pixels, that child items are indented relative to their parent item.
TVM_GETITEM	TreeView_GetItem	Retrieves information about an item.
TVM_GETITEMRECT	TreeView_GetItemRect	Retrieves the bounding rectangle and visibility state of an item.
TVM_GETNEXTITEM	TreeView_GetNextItem	Retrieves the next item that matches a specified relationship.
TVM_GETNEXTITEM	TreeView_GetNextSibling	Retrieves the next sibling of an item.
TVM_GETNEXTITEM	TreeView_GetNextVisible	Retrieves the next visible item follow-ing the speci-fied tree view item.
TVM_GETNEXTITEM	TreeView_GetParent	Retrieves the parent of an item.
TVM_GETNEXTITEM	TreeView_GetPrevSibling	Retrieves the previous sibling of an item.

continues

Table 7.21

Tree View Control Messages, continued		
Message	Function	Description
TVM_GETNEXTITEM	TreeView_GetPrevVisible	Retrieves the first visible item preceding the specified tree view item.
TVM_GETNEXTITEM	TreeView_GetRoot	Retrieves the root of an item.
TVM_GETNEXTITEM	TreeView_GetSelection	Retrieves the currently selected item.
TVM_GETVISIBLECOUNT	TreeView_GetVisibleCount	Retrieves the count of items that will fit into the tree view window.
TVM_HITTEST	TreeView_HitTest	Retrieves the tree view item that occupies the specified point. This message is generally used for drag-and-drop operations.
TVM_INSERTITEM	TreeView_InsertItem	Inserts a new item in a tree view window.

Message	Function	Description
TVM_SELECTITEM	TreeView_Select	Selects, scrolls into view, or redraws an item.
TVM_SELECTITEM	TreeView_SelectDropTarget	Selects an item as the drop target.
TVM_SELECTITEM	TreeView_SelectItem	Selects an item.
TVM_SETIMAGELIST	TreeView_SetImageList	Sets the image list for a tree view window and redraws it.
TVM_SETINDENT	TreeView_SetIndent	Sets the amount of indention for a child item.
TVM_SETITEM	TreeView_SetItem	Sets the attributes of an item.
TVM_SORTCHILDREN	TreeView_SortChildren	Sorts the child items of a given parent item.
TVM_SORTCHILDRENCB	TreeView_SortChildrenCB	Sorts items using an application-defined comparison function.

Tree View Control Notifications

A tree view control sends the following WM_NOTIFY notification
messages to its parent window. In the Alternate Flight Lookup
dialog box, the TravelManager application processes the
TVN_SELCHANGED notification and sets the static text accordingly.
(The text will eventually come from the database rather than be hard-
coded.)

```
LRESULT FlightInfoDlg::WMNotify( HWND hWnd,  UINT msg, WPARAM wParam,
Table 7.21
➡LPARAM lParam )
{
    NM_TREEVIEW * pnmh = (NM_TREEVIEW *) lParam;

    switch (pnmh->hdr.code)
    {
        case TVN_SELCHANGED:
            {
                    if (pnmh->itemNew.lParam != 0)
                    {
                            SetDlgItemText(hWnd, IDC_FROM,
➡L"Seattle");
                            SetDlgItemText(hWnd, IDC_TO,
➡L"Indianapolis");
                            SetDlgItemText(hWnd, IDC_DEPARTS,
➡L"8:20 am");
                            SetDlgItemText(hWnd, IDC_ARRIVES,
➡L"4:45 pm");
                            SetDlgItemText(hWnd, IDC_AIRLINE,
➡L"Delta");
                            SetDlgItemText(hWnd, IDC_CONNECTION,
➡L"Atlanta");
                            SetDlgItemText(hWnd, IDC_LAYOVER,
➡L"1:10");
                    }
                    else
                    {
                            SetDlgItemText(hWnd, IDC_FROM, L"<not
➡selected>");
                            SetDlgItemText(hWnd, IDC_TO, L"<not
➡selected>");
                            SetDlgItemText(hWnd, IDC_DEPARTS,
```

```
➥L"<not selected>");
                                    SetDlgItemText(hWnd, IDC_ARRIVES,
➥L"<not selected>");
                                    SetDlgItemText(hWnd, IDC_AIRLINE,
➥L"<not selected>");
                                    SetDlgItemText(hWnd, IDC_CONNECTION,
➥L"<not selected>");
                                    SetDlgItemText(hWnd, IDC_LAYOVER,
➥L"<not selected>");
                        }
                }
            break;
        }
        return 0;
```

The possible notifications from the tree view control are listed in Table 7.22.

Table 7.22

Tree View Control Notifications

Notification	Description
TVN_BEGINDRAG	Indicates that a drag-and-drop operation involving the left mouse button is being initiated.
TVN_BEGINLABELEDIT	Indicates the start of label editing for an item.
TVN_BEGINRDRAG	Indicates the initiation of a drag-and-drop operation involving the right mouse button.
TVN_DELETEITEM	Indicates that an item has been deleted.
TVN_ENDLABELEDIT	Indicates the end of label editing for an item.
TVN_GETDISPINFO	Requests that a tree view control's parent window provides information needed to display or sort an item.
TVN_ITEMEXPANDED	Indicates that a parent item's list of child items has expanded or collapsed.

continues

Table 7.22

Tree View Control Notifications, continued	
Notification	Description
TVN_ITEMEXPANDING	Indicates that a parent item's list of child items is about to expand or collapse.
TVN_KEYDOWN	Indicates that the user pressed a key and the tree view control has the input focus.
TVN_SELCHANGED	Indicates that the selection has changed from one item to another.
TVN_SELCHANGING	Indicates that the selection is about to change from one item to another.
TVN_SETDISPINFO	Notifies a tree view control's parent window that it must update the information it maintains about an item.

Tab Control

A tab control is similar to a set of notebook dividers: It separates topics or sections of information and helps you locate a particular topic or section easily. A tab control is also helpful for dividing information when there's not enough screen real-estate. The TravelManager uses a tab control to divide the itinerary information up into three parts: Air, Car, Hotel (see Figure 7.5).

Figure 7.5

Tab control.

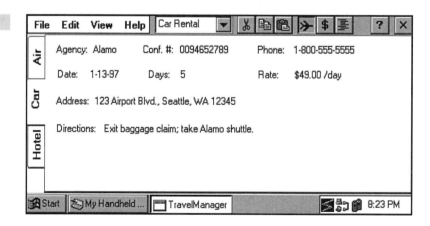

In the ItineraryView::Create function, the tab control is created using
CreateWindow function. The size of the tab control is determined by
getting the client size of the main window and then accounting for the
size of the command bar.

```
BOOL ItineraryView::Create()
{
  RECT rect;

  int iFlags = WS_CHILD¦WS_VISIBLE¦WS_TABSTOP¦WS_CLIPSIBLINGS¦
                 TCS_MULTILINE¦TCS_VERTICAL;

  GetClientRect(m_pMainWindow->m_hWnd, &rect);
  rect.top += CommandBar_Height(m_pMainWindow->m_hwndCB);

  HWND hwndTab = CreateWindow(WC_TABCONTROL,  L"",iFlags,
               rect.left, rect.top, rect.right - rect.left,
               rect.bottom - rect.top, m_pMainWindow->m_hWnd,
               (HMENU)12345, m_pMainWindow->m_pApp->m_hInst,
➥NULL);

  m_hWnd = hwndTab;
```

Tab Control Styles

The window styles listed in Table 7.23 are specific to tab controls.

Table 7.23

Tab Control Styles	
Style	Description
TCS_BUTTONS	Specifies that tabs appear as buttons and no border is drawn around the display area.
TCS_FIXEDWIDTH	Specifies that all tabs are the same width. This style cannot be combined with the TCS_RIGHTJUSTIFY style.

continues

Table 7.23

Tab Control Styles, continued

Style	Description
TCS_FOCUSNEVER	Specifies that the tab control never receives the input focus.
TCS_FOCUSONBUTTONDOWN	Specifies that tabs receive the input focus when clicked.
TCS_FORCEICONLEFT	Aligns icons with the left edge of each fixed-width tab. This style can only be used with the TCS_FIXEDWIDTH style.
TCS_FORCELABELLEFT	Aligns labels with the left edge of each fixed-width tab; that is, it displays the label immediately to the right of the icon instead of centering it. This style can only be used with the TCS_FIXEDWIDTH style, and it implies the TCS_FORCEICONLEFT style.
TCS_MULTILINE	Displays multiple rows of tabs, if necessary, so all tabs are visible at once.
TCS_OWNERDRAWFIXED	Specifies that the parent window is responsible for drawing tabs.
TCS_RAGGEDRIGHT	Does not stretch each row of tabs to fill the entire width of the control. This style is the default style.
TCS_RIGHTJUSTIFY	Increases the width of each tab, if necessary, so that each row of tabs fills the entire width of the tab control. This window style is ignored unless the TCS_MULTILINE style is also specified.
TCS_SINGLELINE	Displays only one row of tabs. The user can scroll to see more tabs, if necessary. This style is the default.

Style	Description
TCS_TABS	Specifies that tabs appear as tabs and that a border is drawn around the display area. This style is the default.
TCS_TOOLTIPS	Specifies that the tab control has a tooltip control associated with it.

Tab Control Messages and Functions

An application sends messages to a tree view control for various reasons: to alter its appearance, add or change items, and so on. Each message has a corresponding function (macro) that can be used instead of sending the message explicitly.

After creating the tab control window, the TravelManager application uses a variety of tab control functions to create the individual pages (tabs). The tabs are positioned vertically along the right side rather than the top due to the vertical real estate space on Windows CE. Although the tab control is not able to rotate the text for the tab, that limitation can be overcome by creating the vertical text as a bitmap and then using the bitmap for the tab. In order to put images on a tab, they must be stored in an image list.

```
HBITMAP     hbitmap;
HIMAGELIST  hTabImage = ImageList_Create(15, 38, ILC_COLOR, 3, 0);

// Load the icons and add them to the image list
hbitmap = LoadBitmap(m_pMainWindow->m_pApp->m_hInst, L"IDB_AIR");
ImageList_Add(hTabImage, hbitmap, NULL);
DeleteObject(hbitmap);
hbitmap = LoadBitmap(m_pMainWindow->m_pApp->m_hInst, L"IDB_CAR");
ImageList_Add(hTabImage, hbitmap, NULL);
DeleteObject(hbitmap);
hbitmap = LoadBitmap(m_pMainWindow->m_pApp->m_hInst, L"IDB_HOTEL");
ImageList_Add(hTabImage, hbitmap, NULL);
DeleteObject(hbitmap);

TabCtrl_SetPadding(hwndTab,5,5);
TabCtrl_SetImageList(hwndTab, hTabImage);
```

After loading the images into the image list, the image for a particular tab control is specified in the iImage member of the TC_ITEM structure. Each of the dialog boxes that will be used as the pages for the tab control are also created. All the dialog boxes are created now enabling a pointer to the dialog box to be stored in the tab control (the lParam member).

```
TC_ITEM item;
HWND dlg, dlg2, dlg3;

item.cchTextMax= 32;

item.mask      = (UINT)TCIF_IMAGE | TCIF_PARAM;
item.iImage = 0;
dlg = CreateDialogParam( m_pMainWindow->m_pApp->m_hInst,
➡L"ITINERARY_AIR", hwndTab,
DlgProc, (LPARAM)this );
g_ModelessDlg = dlg;
item.lParam = (LPARAM)dlg;
TabCtrl_InsertItem (hwndTab, 0, (TC_ITEM FAR*)&item);

item.iImage = 1;
dlg2 = CreateDialogParam( m_pMainWindow->m_pApp->m_hInst,
➡L"ITINERARY_CAR", hwndTab,
DlgProc, (LPARAM)this );
item.lParam = (LPARAM)dlg2;
TabCtrl_InsertItem (hwndTab, 1, (TC_ITEM FAR*)&item);

item.iImage = 2;
dlg3 = CreateDialogParam( m_pMainWindow->m_pApp->m_hInst,
➡L"ITINERARY_HOTEL", hwndTab,
DlgProc, (LPARAM)this );
item.lParam = (LPARAM)dlg3;
TabCtrl_InsertItem (hwndTab, 2, (TC_ITEM FAR*)&item);
```

Finally, you determine the size of the client area for the tab control and adjust the size of each of the pages (dialog boxes) to fit, as follows:

```
TabCtrl_AdjustRect(hwndTab, FALSE, &rect);
MoveWindow(dlg, rect.left, 2, rect.right-rect.left, rect.bottom-
➡rect.top, TRUE);
MoveWindow(dlg2, rect.left, 2, rect.right-rect.left, rect.bottom-
➡rect.top, FALSE);
```

```
  ShowWindow(dlg2, SW_HIDE);
  MoveWindow(dlg3, rect.left, 2, rect.right-rect.left, rect.bottom-
➡rect.top, FALSE);
  ShowWindow(dlg3, SW_HIDE);
```

Table 7.24 shows the available tab control messages and their corresponding macros.

Table 7.24

Tab Control Messages

Message	Function	Description
TCM_ADJUSTRECT	TabCtrl_AdjustRect	Calculates a tab control's display area given a window rectangle or calculates the window rectangle that would correspond to a specified display area.
TCM_DELETEALLITEMS	TabCtrl_DeleteAllItems	Removes all items from a tab control.
TCM_DELETEITEM	TabCtrl_DeleteItem	Removes an item from a tab control.
TCM_GETCURFOCUS	TabCtrl_GetCurFocus	Returns the index of the item that has the focus in a tab control.
TCM_GETCURSEL	TabCtrl_GetCurSel	Determines the currently selected tab in a tab control.
TCM_GETIMAGELIST	TabCtrl_GetImageList	Retrieves the image list associated with a tab control.

continues

Table 7.24

Tab Control Messages, continued		
Message	Function	Description
TCM_GETITEM	TabCtrl_GetItem	Retrieves information about a tab in a tab control.
TCM_GETITEMCOUNT	TabCtrl_GetItemCount	Retrieves the number of tabs in the tab control.
TCM_GETITEMRECT	TabCtrl_GetItemRect	Retrieves the bounding rectangle for a tab in a tab control.
TCM_GETROWCOUNT	TabCtrl_GetRowCount	Retrieves the current number of rows of tabs in a tab control.
TCM_GETTOOLTIPS	TabCtrl_GetToolTips	Retrieves the handle to the tooltip control associated with a tab control.
TCM_HITTEST	TabCtrl_HitTest	Determines which tab, if any, is at a specified screen position.
TCM_INSERTITEM	TabCtrl_InsertItem	Inserts a new tab in a tab control.
TCM_REMOVEIMAGE	TabCtrl_RemoveImage	Removes an image from a tab control's image list.
TCM_SETCURFOCUS	TabCtrl_SetCurFocus	Sets the focus to a specified tab in a tab control.
TCM_SETCURSEL	TabCtrl_SetCurSel	Selects a tab in a tab control.

Message	Function	Description
TCM_SETIMAGELIST	TabCtrl_SetImageList	Assigns an image list to a tab control.
TCM_SETITEM	TabCtrl_SetItem	Sets some or all of a tab's attributes.
TCM_SETITEMEXTRA	TabCtrl_SetItemExtra	Sets the number of bytes per tab reserved for application-defined data in a tab control.
TCM_SETITEMSIZE	TabCtrl_SetItemSize	Sets the width and height of tabs in a fixed-width or owner-drawn tab control.
TCM_SETPADDING	TabCtrl_SetPadding	Sets the amount of space (padding) around each tab's icon and label in a tab control.
TCM_SETTOOLTIPS	TabCtrl_SetToolTips	Assigns a tooltip control to a tab control.

Tab Control Notifications

A tree view control sends the following notification messages to its parent window in the form of WM_NOTIFY messages. The Travel Manager application handles the TCN_SELCHANGING and TCN_SELCHANGE notifications to hide and display the appropriate dialog boxes.

```
LRESULT MainWindow::WMNotify( HWND hWnd,  UINT msg, WPARAM wParam,
LPARAM lParam )
{
    TC_ITEM tcItem;
    int iTab;
```

```
    LPNMHDR pnmh = (LPNMHDR) lParam;
    HWND hwndTabCtrl;

    switch (pnmh->code)
    {
        case TCN_SELCHANGING:
        hwndTabCtrl = GetDlgItem(hWnd, 12345);
                iTab = TabCtrl_GetCurSel(hwndTabCtrl);
        tcItem.mask = TCIF_PARAM;
        TabCtrl_GetItem(hwndTabCtrl, iTab, &tcItem);
        ShowWindow((HWND)(tcItem.lParam), SW_HIDE);
        return FALSE;
                break;
                case TCN_SELCHANGE:
        hwndTabCtrl = GetDlgItem(hWnd, 12345);
                iTab = TabCtrl_GetCurSel(hwndTabCtrl);
        tcItem.mask = TCIF_PARAM;
        TabCtrl_GetItem(hwndTabCtrl, iTab, &tcItem);
        ShowWindow((HWND)(tcItem.lParam), SW_SHOW);
        SendMessage(m_hwndCombo, CB_SETCURSEL, iTab, 0);
        return FALSE;
                break;
    default:
        return (DefWindowProc(hWnd, msg, wParam, lParam));
    }
    return FALSE;
}
```

The possible tree control notifications are listed in Table 7.25.

Table 7.25

Tree View Control Notifications

Notification	Description
TCN_KEYDOWN	Indicates that a key has been pressed.
TCN_SELCHANGE	Indicates that the currently selected tab has changed.
TCN_SELCHANGING	Indicates that the currently selected tab is about to change.

TravelManager Application—Chapter 7

Quite a lot has been added to the TravelManager application since the last chapter. Most of the user interface elements are now in place in the application. New C++ classes created in this chapter include the following:

- **ItineraryView**. The class that encapsulates the components of the itinerary view, such as the tab control and its pages.

- **ExpensesView**. The class that encapsulates the view dealing with listing, adding, editing and deleting of expenses.

- **NotesView**. The class for our view that enables the entry of notes (and eventually the saving of the notes).

- **ExpAddEditDlg**. The class that permits the entry of new expenses and the editing of current expenses.

Although the visible interface is nearly complete, most of the data that is displayed is just hard-coded static data. In the coming chapters, the capability to get that data from the database will be added.

For the sake of space, the entire TravelManager application is not relisted here. The accompanying CD-ROM contains the source code and project file changes to the TravelManager application developed in each chapter. See Appendix A, "Getting Started with the CD-ROM," for information on accessing the source code on the CD-ROM.

Input and Output

The previous chapters have shown the importance of windows, dialog boxes, and controls when interacting with the user. Many other mechanisms in Windows CE aid in providing information to the user and getting information from the user. These mechanisms include such things as the keyboard, the display, notifications, timers, and audio output.

This chapter examines various means of interaction with the user in Windows CE. Many input and output mechanisms in Windows CE are nearly identical to those in Win32. This chapter will briefly cover all those mechanisms, while focusing on those mechanisms that are unique only to Windows CE, as well as pointing out differences between Windows CE and Win32.

Keyboard Input

In Windows CE, keyboard input conventions are similar to those for other versions of Windows. This similarity exists for both the physical layout of the keyboard and for the way Windows CE notifies applications of keyboard events.

Keyboard Hardware

Although Windows CE may eventually support devices without keyboards, the hardware requirements for the initial Handheld PCs define a basic keyboard layout that is as close to the PC keyboard as possible. Due to the obvious space constraints however, there are some common keys that are not supported, including Insert, Scroll Lock, Pause, Num Lock, Print Screen, and all the function keys. Windows CE applications should avoid functionality that requires these keys.

Tip

> In Windows CE, Shift+Backspace is equivalent to the Delete key.

Keyboard Functionality in Windows CE

With the exception of a few unsupported keyboard-related API functions, the way a Windows CE program interacts with the keyboard is identical to programs under other versions of Windows. Usually that means applications do not monitor direct keyboard input at all.

Similarly, Windows CE, like other Windows versions, handles most keyboard functionality itself. When a user uses the keyboard, an application is interested more in the effect of the keystrokes. For instance, if the user selects an option on a menu, Windows CE notifies the application that a menu option was selected; it doesn't determine how the selection was made (the application shouldn't care whether the menu option was selected using the keyboard or the stylus/mouse).

There are some instances, however, where an application does want to monitor the actual keystrokes from the keyboard. As in Win32, all applications essentially share the keyboard, and the operating system delivers keyboard messages to the correct window. The window that receives the keyboard message is the window with the *input focus,* which is either the active window or a child of the active window.

Most child windows have controls such as push buttons, edit controls, or list boxes. When a child window has input focus, then the active window is the control's parent (for example, the dialog box). A window can determine when it has focus by trapping the WM_SETFOCUS and WM_KILLFOCUS messages.

Applications receive messages about keyboard events through both keystroke and character messages. The keystroke messages correspond directly to the pressing of keys on the keyboard; Windows CE interprets those keystrokes and, if applicable, delivers additional character messages. For instance, pressing and releasing the "A" key generates two keystroke messages (one for the key going down; one for the key going up). Windows CE then assists by interpreting the character for that key press. For instance, normally, pressing the A key would result in a character of lowercase a. However, depending on the status of the Shift, Ctrl, and Caps Lock keys, that A key could result in an uppercase A or perhaps a special character.

When a key is pressed, Windows CE delivers either a WM_KEYDOWN or a WM_SYSKEYDOWN message to the window with input focus. When the key is released, Windows CE delivers either a WM_KEYUP or WM_SYSKEYUP message. The SYS messages refer to system keystroke messages. *System keystrokes messages* are usually generated for keys pressed in combination with the Alt key.

The character messages that Windows CE delivers are WM_CHAR, WM_SYSCHAR, WM_DEADCHAR, and WM_SYSDEADCHAR. *Dead character messages* are used with non-U.S. keyboards in which certain keys are defined to add a diacritic to a letter.

Keyboard Functions

Table 8.1 lists all the Win32 keyboard-related functions and provides a description of their functionality as supported by Windows CE.

Table 8.1

Keyboard Functions

Function	Description
ActivateKeyboardLayout	Not supported for Windows CE.
EnableWindow	Enables or disables mouse and keyboard input to the specified window or control.
GetActiveWindow	Retrieves the window handle of the active window.
GetAsyncKeyState	Determines whether a key is up or down at the time the function is called.
GetFocus	Retrieves the handle of the keyboard focus window.
GetKeyboardLayoutName	Not supported for Windows CE.
GetKeyboardState	Not supported for Windows CE.
GetKeyNameText	Not supported for Windows CE.
GetKeyState	Retrieves the status of the specified virtual key.
IsWindowEnabled	Determines whether the specified window is enabled for touch screen input and keyboard input.
keybd_event	Synthesizes a keystroke.
LoadKeyboardLayout	Not supported for Windows CE.
MapVirtualKey	Translates (maps) a virtual-key code into a scan code or character value.
OemKeyScan	Not supported for Windows CE.
RegisterHotKey	Not supported for Windows CE.
SetActiveWindow	Makes the specified window the active window.

Function	Description
`SetFocus`	Sets the keyboard focus to the specified window.
`SetKeyboardState`	Not supported for Windows CE.
`ToAscii`	Not supported for Windows CE.
`ToUnicode`	Not supported for Windows CE.
`UnloadKeyboardLayout`	Not supported for Windows CE.
`UnregisterHotKey`	Not supported for Windows CE.
`VkKeyScan`	Not supported for Windows CE.

Keyboard Messages

Table 8.2 lists the Win32 keyboard messages and a description of their Windows CE functionality.

Table 8.2

Keyboard Messages

Message	Description
WM_ACTIVATE	Sent when a window is being activated or deactivated.
WM_CHAR	Sent to the window with the keyboard focus when a WM_KEYDOWN message is translated by the `TranslateMessage` function. WM_CHAR contains the character code of the key that was pressed.
WM_DEADCHAR	Sent to the window with the keyboard focus when a WM_KEYUP message is translated by the `TranslateMessage` function. WM_DEADCHAR specifies a character code generated by a dead key.

continues

Table 8.2

Keyboard Messages, continued	
Message	Description
WM_HOTKEY	Not supported for Windows CE.
WM_KEYDOWN	Sent to the window with the keyboard focus when a nonsystem key is pressed.
WM_KEYUP	Sent to the window with the keyboard focus when a nonsystem key is released.
WM_KILLFOCUS	Sent to a window immediately before it loses the keyboard focus.
WM_SETFOCUS	Sent to a window after it has gained the keyboard focus.
WM_SYSCHAR	Sent to the window with the keyboard focus when a WM_SYSKEYDOWN message is translated by the `TranslateMessage` function. It specifies the character code of a system character key (a character key that is pressed while the Alt key is down).
WM_SYSDEADCHAR	Sent to the window with the keyboard focus when a WM_SYSKEYDOWN message is translated by the `TranslateMessage` function. WM_SYSDEADCHAR specifies the character code of a system dead key (a dead key that is pressed while holding down the Alt key).
WM_SYSKEYDOWN	Sent to the window with the keyboard focus when the user holds down the Alt key and then presses another key.
WM_SYSKEYUP	Sent to the window with the keyboard focus when the user releases a key that was pressed while the Alt key was held down.

TravelManager Keyboard Use

Most of the keyboard input that the TravelManager application relies on is done through controls on dialog boxes. Because Windows CE dialog controls handle their own keyboard input, the TravelManager application does not have to deal with the specifics of using the keyboard for input into edit controls or choosing menu options.

One instance, however, exists in which the TravelManager application does have to handle low-level keyboard use. To show stylus use and drawing operations (discussed later in this chapter), a new view—the Draw view—has been added to the application. In the Draw view, the user can use the stylus to draw on the screen, and then clear the screen by pressing a key on the keyboard.

To implement drawing functionality, make the following changes to Windows CE:

1. Add virtual WMChar method to the Window class.

2. Modify WndProc to catch WMChar messages and call the WMChar method of the Window class.

3. Implement the WMChar method of the DrawView class as shown in the following code:

```
LRESULT DrawView::WMChar(HWND, UINT, WPARAM, LPARAM)
{
    InvalidateRect (m_hWnd, NULL, TRUE);

    UpdateWindow(m_hWnd);

    sndPlaySound(L"\\Windows\\close.wav", SND_SYNC);

    return 0;
}
```

Note

In the previous code, the calls to `InvalidateRect` and `UpdateWindow` will cause the window to be repainted, thereby clearing the contents of the window.

Stylus Input

One apparent difference between Windows CE and other versions of Windows is the absence of a familiar staple of Windows: the mouse. Although original versions of Windows never required a mouse, the mouse has certainly become a standard input device. Window CE, on the other hand, achieves similar functionality through the addition of a touch screen and stylus.

In Windows CE, the stylus is used to perform the actions previously associated with a mouse: clicking, double-clicking, and dragging. In pen/stylus notation, those actions would be referred to as tapping, double-tapping, and dragging. Win32 enables those actions to be initiated by one of three buttons on the mouse (although the mouse usually only has two buttons). Windows CE obviously can't support three buttons, but it does try to emulate the most common "right-button click" when the user taps on the screen while holding down the Alt key.

Stylus Functionality in Windows CE

Although the methods for generating the mouse/stylus events are quite different between Windows CE and other versions of Windows, the way applications interpret those events is quite similar. Windows CE uses the same WM_LBUTTONDOWN, WM_LBUTTONUP, and WM_LBUTTONDBLCLK as Win32. These messages signal when the user has pressed on the touch screen, let up from the touch screen, or double-tapped on the screen, respectively.

As previously stated, Windows CE enables the same functionality as right-clicking by using the Alt key when tapping. However, Windows CE does not interpret those events and deliver any RBUTTON messages. Instead, an application should use the GetAsyncKeyState when processing the WM_LBUTTONDOWN message to determine if the user is simulating a right-button click.

Another difference in Windows CE is cursor support. Because there is no mouse cursor on the Windows CE display, cursor support is greatly reduced. The only cursor function supported is SetCursor, and even it is very constrained. The only cursor support available to an application is the functionality to display the "wait cursor."

Like Win32, stylus/mouse messages go to the window in which the user clicks. It is possible for an application to "capture" the stylus/mouse so that the application receives messages even when the stylus/mouse is used outside the window. An application can use the `SetCapture` and `ReleaseCapture` functions to manipulate capture of the stylus/mouse messages.

Win32 applications can receive many non-client area mouse messages. On the other hand, due to the precious nature of the Windows CE screen real estate, Windows CE windows do not have any non-client areas. Windows CE applications will never get any WM_NC*xxx* messages.

Stylus/Mouse Functions

Table 8.3 lists all the Win32 mouse-related functions and provides a description of their functionality as supported by Windows CE.

Table 8.3

Stylus/Mouse Functions

Function	Description
DragDetect	Not supported for Windows CE.
GetCapture	Retrieves the handle of the window (if any) that has captured the stylus.
GetDoubleClickTime	Retrieves the current double-click time for the stylus.
mouse_event	Not supported for Windows CE.
ReleaseCapture	Releases the stylus capture from a window in the current thread and restores normal stylus input processing.

continues

Table 8.3

Stylus/Mouse Functions, continued	
Function	Description
SetCapture	Sets the stylus capture to the specified window belonging to the current thread. After a window has captured the stylus, all stylus input is directed to that window. Only one window at a time can capture the stylus.
SetDoubleClickTime	Not supported for Windows CE.
SwapMouseButton	Not supported for Windows CE.

Cursor Functions

Table 8.4 lists all the Win32 cursor-related functions and provides a description of their functionality as supported by Windows CE.

Table 8.4

Cursor Functions	
Function	Description
ClipCursor	Not supported for Windows CE.
CopyCursor	Not supported for Windows CE.
CreateCursor	Not supported for Windows CE.
DestroyCursor	Not supported for Windows CE.
GetClipCursor	Not supported for Windows CE.
GetCursor	Not supported for Windows CE.
GetCursorPos	Not supported for Windows CE.
LoadCursor	Not supported for Windows CE.
LoadCursorFromFile	Not supported for Windows CE.
SetCursor	Establishes the cursor shape. For Windows CE, it can only turn on or off the wait cursor.
SetCursorPos	Not supported for Windows CE.

Function	Description
SetSystemCursor	Not supported for Windows CE.
ShowCursor	Not supported for Windows CE.

Stylus/Mouse Messages

Table 8.5 lists Win32 mouse messages and a description of their Windows CE functionality.

Table 8.5

Stylus/Mouse Messages

Message	Description
WM_CAPTURECHANGED	Sent to the window that is losing the mouse capture.
WM_LBUTTONDBLCLK	Sent when the user double-taps the touch-screen while the cursor is in the client area of a window. If the stylus is not captured, the message is posted to the window beneath the cursor. Otherwise, the message is sent to the window that has captured the stylus.
WM_LBUTTONDOWN	Sent when the user presses the touch-screen while the cursor is in the client area of a window. If the stylus is not captured, the message is posted to the window beneath the cursor. Otherwise, the message is sent to the window that has captured the stylus.
WM_LBUTTONUP	Sent when the user releases the stylus from the touch-screen while the cursor is in the client area of a window. If the stylus is not captured, the message is posted to the window beneath the cursor. Otherwise, the message is sent to the window that has captured the stylus.

continues

Table 8.5

Stylus/Mouse Messages, continued	
Message	Description
WM_MBUTTONDBLCLK	Not supported for Windows CE.
WM_MBUTTONDOWN	Not supported for Windows CE.
WM_MBUTTONUP	Not supported for Windows CE.
WM_MOUSEACTIVATE	Not supported for Windows CE.
WM_MOUSEMOVE	Posted to a window when the stylus moves. If the stylus is not captured, the message is posted to the window that contains the cursor. Otherwise, the message is posted to the window that has captured the mouse.
WM_NCHITTEST	Not supported for Windows CE.
WM_NCLBUTTONDBLCLK	Not supported for Windows CE.
WM_NCLBUTTONDOWN	Not supported for Windows CE.
WM_NCLBUTTONUP	Not supported for Windows CE.
WM_NCMBUTTONDBLCLK	Not supported for Windows CE.
WM_NCMBUTTONDOWN	Not supported for Windows CE.
WM_NCMBUTTONUP	Not supported for Windows CE.
WM_NCMOUSEMOVE	Not supported for Windows CE.
WM_NCRBUTTONDBLCLK	Not supported for Windows CE.
WM_NCRBUTTONDOWN	Not supported for Windows CE.
WM_NCRBUTTONUP	Not supported for Windows CE.
WM_RBUTTONDBLCLK	Not supported for Windows CE.
WM_RBUTTONDOWN	Not supported for Windows CE.
WM_RBUTTONUP	Not supported for Windows CE.

TravelManager Stylus or Mouse Use

Although stylus input is fundamental to any Windows CE application, most of the functionality is handled automatically by the operating system. Tapping on the menu bar, tapping on the drop-down box of a combo box, or double-tapping on an item in a list are all handled by Windows CE, which then performs some action.

The Draw view of the TravelManager application is one area where the application processes basic stylus input. In order to implement drawing onto the screen, the application catches the WM_LBUTTONDOWN, WM_LBUTTONUP, and WM_MOUSEMOVE messages in the WndProc function and dispatches them to virtual methods of the Window class. These WMLButtonDown, WMLButtonUp, and WM-MouseMove methods of the DrawView class then perform the drawing operations. The code for the aforementioned methods is shown in the display output section of this chapter.

Timer Input

Although not directly related to user interaction, one mechanism an application can use for input is timers. Like Win32, the Windows CE timer is an input device that periodically notifies an application when a specified interval of time has elapsed. Timers can obviously be used to display time, but timers can also be used to update information on the screen, implement an autosave feature, or dismiss an initial "splash" screen.

Timer Functionality in Windows CE

The fairly simple timer functionality in Win32 is unchanged in Windows CE. An application starts a timer by calling the SetTimer function. One of the parameters to the SetTimer function is an integer specifying the interval at which Windows CE sends WM_TIMER messages to the application. When an application is done using the timer, the KillTimer function stops the timer messages.

As in Win32, an application can choose to have the timer messages sent to one of two places. The first, and easiest method, is to have the timer-messages sent directly to the window procedure for a given window. The other method is to have Windows CE call a given function within the application when the timer goes off.

Timer Functions

Table 8.6 lists timer-related functionality supported by Windows CE.

Table 8.6

Timer Functions

Function	Description
SetTimer	Creates a timer with the specified interval value (specified in milliseconds).
KillTimer	Destroys the specified timer. The system searches the message queue for any pending WM_TIMER messages associated with the timer and removes them.

TravelManager Timer Use

The TravelManager implements a simple use of a timer. Until now, after the About box was displayed (by the user choosing the About menu option), the dialog box could only be closed by the user pressing the OK button. To show simple timer functionality, the About box in the TravelManager application now closes when the user presses OK, or after 15 seconds have elapsed.

The first change to the TravelManager application to implement this feature is to catch the WM_TIMER message in the DlgProc function and to dispatch it to a new virtual WMTimer message in the Window class.

The AboutDlg class starts a timer in the WMInitDialog method by calling the SetTimer function, specifying NULL for a callback procedure so that the timer message will be sent back to this dialog box.

```
SetTimer(hDlg, 1, 15000, NULL);
```

When the timer goes off, the WM_TIMER message will be caught in DlgProc and dispatched to the WMTimer method of the AboutDlg class. This method stops the timer using the KillTimer function and closes the dialog box (the notification function is described later in this chapter).

```
LRESULT AboutDlg::WMTimer( HWND hDlg, UINT, WPARAM wParam, LPARAM )
{
    PegHandleAppNotifications(L"trvlmgr.exe");
    KillTimer(hDlg, 1);
    EndDialog(hDlg, TRUE);
    return 0;

}
```

Display Output

Previous chapters covered many methods for putting information on the screen. In the first "Hello Windows CE" application, a window was created on the screen and displayed the text Hello Windows CE in the center of the window. The TravelManager application uses windows, dialog boxes, and other controls to present information on the screen.

Whether an application writes text to the screen or asks Windows CE to display entire dialog boxes, the actual displaying of graphics on the video display is the job of the Graphics Device Interface (GDI) subsystem. The GDI subsystem provides a low-level, but common, interface to the display hardware. In Windows CE, the GDI functionality is actually part of the Graphics, Windowing, and Events Subsystem (GWES).

The Win32 GDI subsystem supports a variety of graphics functions, which can be divided into the following categories:

Lines and curves

Filled areas

Bitmaps

Text

Mapping modes and transforms

Metafiles

Regions

Paths

Clipping

Palettes

Printing

The Windows CE GDI subsystem supports a subset of the Win32 GDI functions. Given the large number of GDI related functions, this section concentrates mainly on the differences between Windows CE and Win32.

Many GDI functions from Win32 do not make sense for the small footprint of Windows CE-based devices, or they place too much of a burden on the limited system resources. As a result, Windows CE has excluded many Win32 GDI functions. The following list describes some of the functions or categories of the GDI subsystem that currently are not supported in Windows CE:

- **Printing and the device contexts**. These are used to store attributes that govern how the GDI operates on printers.

- **TrueType fonts**. Windows CE supports only raster fonts. There are seven rasterized system fonts available in several sizes that are stored in ROM.

- **Color and custom palettes**. Colors are mapped to two-bit-per-pixel grayscale. The Visual C++ IDE provides a resource editor for creating bitmaps and icons with the grayscale palette.

- **Coordinate space transformation functions**. Examples include `SetMapMode`, `GetMapMode`, `SetViewportExt`, and `SetWindowExt`.

- **Metafiles**. All pictorial information is stored as bitmaps.

- **bit block transfers**. The system provides only limited support for bit block transfers (BitBlt).

- **current point**. The concept of a current point is not supported, so most line drawing functions are not available. (PolyLine is used instead.)

- **Cursors**. Except for the wait cursor (the spinning hourglass), cursors are not supported. Applications cannot show active targets by changing the size or shape of the cursor.

- **Arc** or **Pie**. Neither Arc nor Pie is supported in Windows CE. To create an arc, use Ellipse with an appropriately defined clipping region.

- **GetBitmapBits** and **GetDIBBits**. These functions are not supported.

- **GetStockObject**. Cannot be used with DEFAULT_PALETTE or any font other than SYSTEM_FONT.

In most application functionality using GDI functions, knowing the screen or display size is very important. The standard screen size for the initial generation of Handheld PCs is 480×240 pixels. However, future Handheld PCs have already been announced that will utilize larger screen resolutions.

Tip

Applications should use the `GetSystemMetrics` function call (with SM_CXSCREEN and SM_CYSCREEN) to get the full screen size. Also be sure to subtract the height of any command bar in order to get the usable screen size.

Due to the limited functionality, the Windows CE SDK documentation suggests writing bitmaps to Windows CE using DIBSections. In order to do this, the following sequence of steps may be useful:

1. Determine the size of the source bitmap (HBITMAP) using GetObject.

2. Create a DIBSection of that size and appropriate bit depth.

3. Select both the source and the DIBSection into memory DCs and Blt source to DIBSection.

4. Open the file and write the BITMAPFILEHEADER.

5. Write the BITMAPINFO.

6. Write the bits.

7. Close the file, delete the DIBSection, and so on.

A DIBsection can't be used like a palette device to simply change the color table to get a different image. Color 0 is black, color 1 is dark gray, color 2 is light gray, and color 3 is white. Creating a color table that tries to map otherwise will fail. In order to change a portion of an image from dark gray to light gray, all the relevant bits must be changed from 1 to 2.

Painting and Drawing Functions

Table 8.7 lists most of the GDI-related functions and provides a description of their functionality as supported by Windows CE.

Table 8.7

GDI Functions	
Function	Description
BeginPaint	Prepares the specified window for painting and fills a PAINTSTRUCT structure with information about the painting.

Function	Description
BitBlt	Performs a bit-block transfer of the color data corresponding to a rectangle of pixels from the specified source device context into a destination device context. (The only supported raster operations are SRCCOPY, SRCAND, SRCPAINT, and SRCINVERT. Mirroring is not supported.)
DrawAnimatedRects	Not supported for Windows CE.
DrawCaption	Not supported for Windows CE.
DrawEdge	Draws one or more edges of a rectangle.
DrawFocusRect	Draws a rectangle in the style used to indicate that the rectangle has the focus.
DrawFrameControl	Not supported for Windows CE.
DrawState	Not supported for Windows CE.
DrawStateProc	Not supported for Windows CE.
DrawTextEx	Not supported for Windows CE.
EndPaint	Marks the end of painting in the specified window. This function is required for each call to the BeginPaint function, but only after painting is complete.
ExcludeUpdateRgn	Not supported for Windows CE.
GdiFlush	Not supported for Windows CE.
GdiGetBatchLimit	Not supported for Windows CE.
GdiSetBatchLimit	Not supported for Windows CE.
GetBkColor	Returns the current background color for the specified device context.
GetBkMode	Returns the current background mix mode for a specified device context. The background mix mode of a device context affects text, hatched brushes, and pen styles that are not solid lines.
GetBoundsRect	Not supported for Windows CE.

continues

Table 8.7

GDI Functions, continued

Function	Description
GetDC	Retrieves a handle of a display device context (DC) for the client area of the specified window. The display device context can be used in subsequent GDI functions to draw in the client area of the window.
GetDeviceCaps	Retrieves device-specific information about a specified device.
GetPixel	Retrieves the red, green, blue (RGB) color value of the pixel at the specified coordinates.
GetROP2	Not supported for Windows CE.
GetStockObject	Retrieves a handle to one of the predefined stock pens, brushes, or fonts. Windows CE does not support the following stock objects: ANSI_FIXED_FONT, ANSI_VAR_FONT, OEM_FIXED_FONT, SYSTEM_FIXED_FONT, DEFAULT_PALETTE.
GetSystemMetrics	Retrieves the dimensions (widths and heights) of Windows display elements and system configuration settings. All dimensions retrieved by GetSystemMetrics are in pixels.
GetUpdateRect	Retrieves the coordinates of the smallest rectangle that completely encloses the update region of the specified window in client coordinates. If there is no update region, GetUpdateRect retrieves an empty rectangle and sets all coordinates to zero.
GetUpdateRgn	Retrieves the update region of a window by copying it into the specified region. The coordinates of the update region are relative to the upper-left corner of the window (that is, they are client coordinates).
GetWindowDC	Retrieves the device context (DC) for the entire window, including title bar, menus, and scroll bars.

Function	Description
GrayString	Not supported for Windows CE.
InvalidateRect	Adds a rectangle to the specified window's update region. The update region represents the portion of the window's client area that must be redrawn.
InvalidateRgn	Not supported for Windows CE.
LineTo	Not supported for Windows CE.
LockWindowUpdate	Not supported for Windows CE.
MaskBlt	Combines the color data for the source and destination bitmaps using the specified mask and raster operation. Note: Windows CE supports only raster operations of SRCCOPY and SRCINVERT.
MoveTo	Not supported for Windows CE.
OutputProc	Not supported for Windows CE.
PatBlt	Paints the given rectangle using the brush that is currently selected into the specified device context. The brush color and the surface color(s) are combined by using the given raster operation.
Polygon	Draws a polygon consisting of two or more vertices connected by straight lines. The polygon is outlined by using the current pen and filled by using the current brush and the polygon fill mode. However, note: only convex polygons are supported in Windows CE.
Polyline	Draws a series of line segments by connecting the points in the specified array.
PaintDesktop	Not supported for Windows CE.
RedrawWindow	Not supported for Windows CE.
ReleaseDC	Releases a device context (DC), which frees it for use by other applications. The effect of the ReleaseDC function depends on the type of device context.

continues

Table 8.7

GDI Functions, continued	
Function	Description
ResetDisplay	Not supported for Windows CE.
SetBkColor	Sets the current background color to the specified color value, or to the nearest physical color if the device cannot represent the specified color value.
SetBkMode	Sets the background mix mode of the specified device context. The background mix mode is used with text, hatched brushes, and pen styles that are not solid lines.
SetBoundsRect	Not supported for Windows CE.
SetPixel	Sets the pixel at the specified coordinates to the specified color.
SetRectRgn	Not supported for Windows CE.
SetROP2	Not supported for Windows CE.
StretchBlt	Copies a bitmap from a source rectangle into a destination rectangle, stretching or compressing the bitmap to fit the dimensions of the destination rectangle, if necessary. Windows stretches or compresses the bitmap according to the stretching mode currently set in the destination device context.
UpdateWindow	Updates the client area of the specified window by sending a WM_PAINT message to the window if the window's update region is not empty. The function sends a WM_PAINT message directly to the window procedure of the specified window, bypassing the application queue. If the update region is empty, no message is sent.
ValidateRect	Validates the client area within a rectangle by removing the rectangle from the update region of the specified window.
ValidateRgn	Not supported for Windows CE.
WindowFromDC	Not supported for Windows CE.

Table 8.8 lists the Win32 GDI messages and a description of their Windows CE functionality.

Table 8.8		
GDI Messages		
Message	Description	
WM_DISPLAYCHANGE	Not supported for Windows CE.	
WM_ERASEBKGND	Sent to prepare an invalidated portion of a window for painting.	
WM_ICONERASEBKGND	Not supported for Windows CE.	
WM_NCPAINT	Not supported for Windows CE.	
WM_PAINT	Sent to inform an application that part or all of the window's client area is invalid and must be repainted.	
WM_PAINTICON	Not supported for Windows CE.	
WM_PRINT	Not supported for Windows CE.	
WM_PRINTCLIENT	Not supported for Windows CE.	
WM_SETREDRAW	Sent to enable or disable changes in the window from being redrawn.	

TravelManager Display Output Use

The TravelManager application's use of direct display output is limited to the new Draw view. In this view, the user is able to use the stylus to draw lines on the display. This functionality is implemented by catching certain messages when the user touches the stylus to the screen, moves the stylus, and releases the stylus from the screen. The functionality of this view is encapsulated in the DrawView class.

The Create method of the DrawView class creates a new window to draw in, as well as a four-pixel wide solid pen that will be used to draw lines.

```
BOOL DrawView::Create()
{
    RECT rect;

    int iFlags = WS_CHILD|WS_VISIBLE;

    GetClientRect(m_pMainWindow->m_hWnd, &rect);
    rect.top += CommandBar_Height(m_pMainWindow->m_hwndCB);

    m_hWnd = CreateWindow(szClassName,  L"",iFlags,
                 rect.left, rect.top, rect.right - rect.left,
                 rect.bottom - rect.top, m_pMainWindow->m_hWnd,
(HMENU)1234,
                 m_pMainWindow->m_pApp->m_hInst, this);

    LOGPEN lf;
    lf.lopnStyle = PS_SOLID;
    lf.lopnWidth.x = 4;
    lf.lopnColor = 0;

    m_hPen = CreatePenIndirect(&lf);

    return TRUE;
}
```

The following code demonstrates how the WMPaint method essentially clears the window and writes a string of text to the upper-left corner of the window.

```
void DrawView::WMPaint()
{
    PAINTSTRUCT ps;
    RECT rect;

    HDC hdc = BeginPaint (m_hWnd, &ps);

    GetClientRect(m_hWnd, &rect);
    FillRect(hdc, &rect, (HBRUSH)GetStockObject(WHITE_BRUSH));

    ExtTextOut(hdc, 5, 4, ETO_OPAQUE, &rect, szClear,
wcslen(szClear), NULL);

    EndPaint (m_hWnd, &ps);
    ReleaseDC(m_hWnd, hdc);
}
```

The WMLButtonDown, WMLButtonUp, and WMMouseMove methods track whether the stylus is up or down, give the points of the stylus, and then draw the line between the specific points.

```
LRESULT DrawView::WMLButtonDown(HWND, UINT, WPARAM, LPARAM lParam)
{
    bLBDown = TRUE;

    line[0].x = LOWORD(lParam);
    line[0].y = HIWORD(lParam);

    return 0;
}

LRESULT DrawView::WMLButtonUp(HWND, UINT, WPARAM, LPARAM)
{
    bLBDown = FALSE;
    return 0;
}

LRESULT DrawView::WMMouseMove(HWND, UINT, WPARAM, LPARAM lParam)
{
    if ( bLBDown == TRUE )
    {
        HDC hdc = GetDC(m_hWnd);

        line[1].x = LOWORD(lParam);
        line[1].y = HIWORD(lParam);

        if((line[0].x != line[1].x) ¦¦ (line[0].y != line[1].y))
        {
            HPEN oldPen = (HPEN)SelectObject(hdc, m_hPen);

            Polyline(hdc, line, 2);

            SelectObject(hdc, oldPen);

            //reset value of initial point to end point
            line[0] = line[1];
        }

        ReleaseDC(m_hWnd, hdc);
    }
    return 0;
}
```

Clipboard Input and Output

The Windows CE clipboard supports the same functionality as Win32; the clipboard enables data to be transferred from one application to another. The clipboard supports various formats that describe the type of data on the clipboard. Windows CE supports the following formats:

CF_GDIOBJFIRST through CF_GDIOBJLAST

CF_DSPBITMAP

CF_DSPENHMETAFILE

CF_DSPMETAFILEPICT

CF_DSPTEXT

CF_HDROP

CF_LOCALE

CF_OWNERDISPLAY

CF_PRIVATEFIRST through CF_PRIVATELAST

Another restriction with the Windows CE clipboard is that it does not perform any implicit conversions between formats. Also, data to be set into the clipboard should be allocated using the `LocalAlloc` function.

Clipboard Functions

Table 8.9 lists the Win32 clipboard functions and provides a description of their functionality as supported by Windows CE.

Table 8.9

Clipboard Functions

Function	Description
ChangeClipboardChain	Not supported for Windows CE.
CloseClipboard	Closes the clipboard.

Function	Description
CountClipboardFormats	Retrieves the number of different data formats currently on the clipboard.
EmptyClipboard	Empties the clipboard and frees handles to data in the clipboard.
EnumClipboardFormats	Enumerates the data formats that are currently available on the clipboard.
GetClipboardData	Retrieves data from the clipboard in a specified format.
GetClipboardDataAlloc	This function is provided for Windows CE only. It works like the GetClipboardData function except it returns a handle to the memory allocated for the clipboard data in the caller's process.
GetClipboardFormatName	Retrieves the name of the specified registered format from the clipboard.
GetClipboardOwner	Retrieves the window handle of the current owner of the clipboard.
GetClipboardViewer	Not supported for Windows CE.
GetOpenClipboardWindow	Retrieves the handle of the window that currently has the clipboard open.
GetPriorityClipboard Format	Returns the first format in the specified available clipboard list.
IsClipboardFormat Available	Determines whether the clipboard contains data in the specified format.
OpenClipboard	Opens the clipboard for examination and prevents other applications from modifying the clipboard content.
RegisterClipboard	Registers a new clipboard for mat. This Formatformat can then be used as a valid clipboard format.
SetClipboardData	Places data on the clipboard in a specified clipboard format.
SetClipboardViewer	Not supported for Windows CE.

TravelManager Clipboard Use

There are many possibilities for clipboard use in the TravelManager application. It is often useful to be able to copy most application-generated data to the clipboard and to be able to paste data into fields where data entry is required.

Although the TravelManager certainly does not reach its potential for clipboard use, it does provide some clipboard support as an example of how the clipboard can be used.

In response to a ID_EDIT_COPY menu option (or the command bar button), the TravelManager application copies the contents of the Notes view edit control to the clipboard. The Copy method of the NotesView class performs the clipboard functionality.

```
void NotesView::Copy()
{
    DWORD length = SendDlgItemMessage(m_hWnd, IDC_EDIT1,
WM_GETTEXTLENGTH, 0, 0);
        TCHAR *pString = (TCHAR *) LocalAlloc( LPTR , (length *
sizeof(TCHAR) + sizeof(TCHAR)));

    if (GetDlgItemText(m_hWnd, IDC_EDIT1, pString, length+1) == 0)
    {
        LocalFree(pString);
        return; //nothing to copy
    }

    if (OpenClipboard(m_hWnd))
    {
        EmptyClipboard();
        SetClipboardData(CF_UNICODETEXT, pString);
        CloseClipboard();
    }
}
```

Sound Output

A small but powerful feature of Windows CE is the capability for an application to easily play a sound. Applications can use a sound to get the user's attention, provide feedback on the progress of an operation, or play back a recorded dictation.

Sound Output in Windows CE

The entire functionality for sound output in Windows CE is accomplished through one API function, `sndPlaySound`. The parameters to `sndPlaySound` are LPCSTR lpszSound and UINT fuSound, which are described as follows:

- **LPCSTR lpszSound**. String that specifies the sound to play.

  The lpszSound parameter specifies the sound to play. This parameter can be an entry in the registry, a pointer to an image of a .wav file that identifies a system sound, or the name of a waveform-audio file. If the function does not find the entry, the parameter is treated as a file name. If this parameter is NULL, any currently playing sound is stopped.

- **UINT fuSound**. Flags for playing the sound.

  The fuSound parameter specifies a flag for playing the sound. The available flags are listed in Table 8.10.

Table 8.10

Sound Output Flags

Value	Meaning
SND_ASYNC	The sound is played asynchronously and the function returns immediately after beginning the sound. To terminate an asynchronously played sound, call `sndPlaySound` with lpszSound set to NULL.
SND_LOOP	The sound plays repeatedly until `sndPlaySound` is called again with the lpszSound parameter set to NULL. You must also specify the SND_ASYNC flag to loop sounds.
SND_MEMORY	The parameter specified by lpszSound points to an image of a waveform sound in memory.

continues

Table 8.10

Sound Output Flags, continued	
Value	Meaning
SND_NODEFAULT	If a sound cannot be found, the function returns silently without playing the default sound.
SND_NOSTOP	If a sound is currently playing, the function immediately returns FALSE, without playing the requested sound.
SND_SYNC	The sound is played synchronously and the function does not return until the sound ends.
SND_ALIAS	Interprets lpszSound only as an event name to be found in the registry.
SND_FILENAME	Interprets lpszSound only as a file name to be loaded from the filesystem (.wav extension optional).

TravelManager Sound Use

To illustrate sound use, the TravelManger application plays a sound when the Draw view is cleared by the user when he presses a key on the keyboard. Pressing the key will end up calling the WMChar method of the DrawView. In addition to clearing the screen, the WMChar method also plays the close.wav sound file.

```
LRESULT DrawView::WMChar(HWND, UINT, WPARAM, LPARAM)
{
    InvalidateRect (m_hWnd, NULL, TRUE);

    UpdateWindow(m_hWnd);

    sndPlaySound(L"\\Windows\\close.wav", SND_SYNC);

    return 0;
}
```

Notifications

As you've seen so far, most of the input and output methods available in Windows CE are slimmed-down versions of features available in Win32. However, notification support is a feature that is only available with Windows CE. This special set of functions enables Windows CE to notify the user or an application of various events, whether the device is on or off. Windows CE, for example, might play a sound or flash the LED light in a schedule application just prior to a scheduled meeting.

Notification Types

Windows CE can generate two main types of notifications: user notifications and application notifications.

User notifications are designed to alert the user about an event at a specific time. The user may be alerted by the appearance of an icon in the notification area of the taskbar, a sound, the display of a message, the flashing of the LED light, or the vibrating of the device. The user is usually required to acknowledge the notification in some way—for instance, clicking the OK button in the dialog box that notifies the user of an appointment.

The application has control of which notification options to use; however, the user should be able to choose notification preferences. Applications can display the system-provided notification options dialog box, which enables the user to choose the preferred notification option. This mechanism also enables the application to recognize which notification options the host device supports. Not all Handheld PCs, for example, may support a notification LED light, and none currently support the notification option of vibrating the device.

Application notifications are designed to alert applications about some system event or that a specific time has been reached. When the given system event or time has been reached, Windows CE automatically starts the application that requested notification of the event or time. When the application starts as the result of a notification, a command-line parameter identifies the event that occurred.

The main difference between a user notification and an application notification is that a user notification is handled entirely by the Windows CE operating system (such as displaying a dialog box, playing a sound, and so on). For an application notification, Windows CE starts the requested application but does no other processing of the notification. In addition, a user notification alerts the user of some event, whereas an application notification alerts an application (which in turn may alert the user).

Programming Windows CE Notifications

Windows CE uses notifications to communicate with the user and Windows CE-based applications. A notification is a signal from the operating system that an event has occurred. This could be a timer event or a system event such as establishing a network connection. An application registers a notification for an event and the system generates a notification when the event occurs.

Windows CE provides an application programming interface (API) that can be used to register events and select options that determine the type of notification. The following sections describe the notification API.

Setting User Notifications

An application registers a user notification for a timer event using the PegSetUserNotification function. The PegSetUserNotification function takes these parameters:

- **HANDLE**. Handle of the notification to overwrite, or zero.

- **TCHAR***. Name of the application that owns this notification.

- **SYSTEMTIME***. Time when the notification is to occur.

- **PEG_USER_NOTIFICATION***. Notification parameters.

The return value from PegSetUserNotification is a handle to the notification that is used in other notification API functions.

The application must specify the time when the notification will occur and the name of the associated application. At the specified time, the system places the primary icon of the application into the taskbar. If the specified time has already passed, the system immediately places the icon in the taskbar.

Tip

> An icon placed into the taskbar is called a *taskbar annunciator.*

The taskbar can contain multiple annunciator icons at the same time for different applications. Only one instance of an icon for any given application will be displayed at any time.

If the user taps the annunciator icon, the system starts a new instance of the corresponding application with a command line containing the APP_RUN_TO_HANDLE_NOTIFICATION string constant, which tells the application why it has been started. If an instance of the application is already running, the new instance would use an application-defined message to send the notification to the previous instance. The new instance would then shut down.

User notifications exist in registered or active states. From the time an application calls PegSetUserNotification until the time the user is notified, the notification is registered. From the time the user is notified until the user handles the event, the notification is active. In other words, a registered notification has been seen by the system but not yet by the user; after the notification is seen by the user, it is active.

Determining User Notification Preferences

All user notifications include a taskbar annunciator. The user can also be notified of an event in one of the following ways (although not all devices support all options):

- Displaying a dialog box.

- Flashing the light-emitting diode (LED) light.

- Playing a .wav file.

- Vibrating the device.

An application should determine user notification preferences prior to setting a user notification. An application uses the `PegGetUser NotificationPreferences` function to get the user's preferences for a particular notification. The parameters to `PegGetUserNotification Preferences` are as follows:

- **HWND**. Parent window for dialog box.

- **PEG_USER_NOTIFICATION**. Pointer to notification structure.

The function displays a dialog box containing the options available on the particular device—only options supported on that device will be displayed. After the user has completed the dialog box, Windows CE fills the PEG_USER_NOTIFICATION structure with the options that the user selected. The application then uses this PEG_USER _NOTIFICATION structure as a parameter to the `PegSetUser Notification` function.

Handling User Notifications

The taskbar annunciator for an active notification remains in the taskbar until the user handles the notification. The user can tap the annunciator icon to start the application. Starting the application removes the taskbar annunciator. The application then calls the `PegHandleAppNotifications` function to remove the taskbar annunciator.

Note

If a notification includes a dialog box, tapping the OK button automatically handles the notification.

An application can mark all its active notifications as handled by calling the `PegHandleAppNotifications` function. The function handles notifications only for the given application.

An application can also remove a notification before it becomes active. A user may set an alarm, for example, but then delete the alarm before it has gone off. An application uses the `PegClearUserNotification` function to delete a registered notification. The only parameter to the

`PegClearUserNotification` function is the handle to the notification
that was returned from the `PegSetUserNotification` function. The
`PegClearUserNotification` function has no effect on notifications that
are already active.

Setting System Event Application Notifications

Application notifications are used by the Windows CE operating system
to talk to applications without requiring user intervention. Application
notifications can be generated based on an application-specified system
event or at an application-specified time. An application does not need
to be running when the notification occurs.

Windows CE defines a limited number of system events upon which
notifications can be based. These system events include:

- When data synchronization finishes.

- When a PCMCIA device is changed.

- When an RS232 connection is made.

- When the system time is changed.

- When a full device data restore completes.

Applications register for a system event by calling the PegRunAppAt-
Event function once for each event. The parameters to PegRunAppAt-
Event include the following:

- **TCHAR***. Name of application to run.

- **LONG**. System event at which to run the application.

The system event is specified using one of the following constants:

NOTIFICATION_EVENT_SYNC_END

NOTIFICATION_EVENT_DEVICE_CHANGE

NOTIFICATION_EVENT_RS232_DETECTED

NOTIFICATION_EVENT_TIME_CHANGE

NOTIFICATION_EVENT_RESTORE_END

Whenever the event occurs, the system starts the application with a system-defined command-line parameter. The command line would contain one of the following string constants:

APP_RUN_AFTER_SYNC

APP_RUN_AT_DEVICE_CHANGE

APP_RUN_AT_RS232_DETECT

APP_RUN_AFTER_RESTORE

After a notification is registered for a system event, the notification will occur each time the event happens. An application can deregister for all system events for an application by calling `PegRunAppAtEvent`, specifying NOTIFICATION_EVENT_NONE as the second parameter.

Setting Timer Event Application Notifications

A timer event notification occurs at an application-specified date and time. This type of notification can be useful for situations where user notification mechanisms are not sufficient to provide the user with necessary information to handle an event. Using a timer event application notification, the system can notify the application at the specified time. The application can then display the appropriate notification information.

Applications register for a timer notification using the `PegRunAppAtTime` function. The parameters to the `PegRunAppAtTime` function are as follows:

- **TCHAR***. Name of the application to run.

- **SYSTEMTIME***. Pointer to structure, specifying the time to run the application.

Notification Functions

The functions listed in Table 8.11 are used to create and manage Windows CE notifications.

Table 8.11	

Notification Functions

Function	Description
PegClearUserNotification	Deletes a user notification that was created by a previous call to the function PegSetUserNotification. This function does not operate on notifications that have already gone off (see PegHandle AppNotifications).
PegGetUserNotification Preferences	Queries the user for notification settings by displaying a dialog box showing options that are valid for the current hardware plat form.
PegHandleAppNotifications	Marks as "handled," all notifications previously registered by the given applications that have gone off. The function turns off the sound and LED, stops vibration, and removes the taskbar annunciator.
PegRunAppAtEvent	Starts running an application when the given event occurs.
PegRunAppAtTime	Requests the system to start running the given application at the given time.
PegSetUserNotification	Creates a new user notification or modifies an existing one.

Notification Structures

The PegSetUserNotification and PegGetUserNotificationPreferences functions both use the PEG_USER_NOTIFICATION structure. This structure is passed in the PegGetUserNotificationPreferences function. It contains information used to initialize the user notifications settings dialog box, and receives the user's notification preference entered by way of the dialog box. These user preferences should be saved and considered when setting notifications. The PEG_USER_NOTIFICATION structure is also used when calling PegSetUserNotification to describe what should happen when the notification time is reached.

The structure is defined in the following code:

```
typedef struct UserNotificationType
{
        DWORD ActionFlags;
        TCHAR *pwszDialogTitle;
        TCHAR *pwszDialogText;
        TCHAR *pwszSound;
        DWORD nMaxSound;
        DWORD dwReserved;
} PEG_USER_NOTIFICATION, *PPEG_USER_NOTIFICATION;
```

The members of the PEG_USER_NOTIFICATION are as follows:

- **ActionFlags**. Specifies the action to take when a notification event occurs. This parameter can be a combination of the following flags:

Value	Meaning
PUN_LED	Flashes the LED. The LED continues to flash until the notification is handled.
PUN_VIBRATE	Vibrates the device. No Handheld PCs currently support this option.
PUN_DIALOG	Displays the user notification dialog box. When this structure is passed to the PegSetUserNotification function, the pwszDialogTitle and pwszDialogText members must provide the title and text of the dialog box. The notification dialog box contains an OK button and a snooze button. The snooze button causes the dialog box to be redisplayed in 5 minutes.
PUN_SOUND	Plays the sound specified by the pwszSound member. When passed to PSVN, the pwszSound member must provide the name of the sound file.
PUN_REPEAT	Repeats the pwszSound for 10-15 seconds. Only valid if PUN_SOUND is set.

- **pwszDialogTitle**. Specifies the title of the user notification dialog box. If this parameter is NULL, no dialog box is displayed. The `PegGetUserNotificationPreferences` function ignores this member.

- **pwszDialogText**. Specifies the text of the user notification dialog box. If this parameter is NULL, no dialog box is displayed. The `PegGetUserNotificationPreferences` function ignores this member.

- **pwszSound**. Points to a buffer that contains the unqualified name of a sound file to play. This parameter is ignored if the ActionFlags member does not include the PUN_SOUND flag.

- **nMaxSound**. Specifies the maximum length of the string that the `PegGetUserNotificationPreferences` function can copy into the pwszSound buffer. Because the string may be a path name in a future release, the buffer must be at least the length derived by the following expression: PATH_MAX * sizeof(TCHAR). This member is ignored by the `PegSetUserNotification` function.

- **dwReserved**. Reserved; must be zero.

TravelManager Notification Use

Given the current functionality in the TravelManager application, there isn't much need for user or application notifications. A user notification could possibly be useful for notifying the user of a scheduled airline flight; however, notifying the user five minutes before a flight isn't very useful because he is likely to already be at the airport.

Because notifications are unique to Windows CE, however, an example of their use is beneficial. Like the timer example, the TravelManager application uses a user notification in the About box. When the user chooses to display the About box, the application displays the About box and starts flashing the LED light. When the About box is closed (either by the user pressing the OK button or the timer going off), the notification is handled.

The notification is set in the AboutDlg::WMInitDialog method. It sets the notification method to flash the LED light and sets the notification time to 2 seconds after the current time.

```
void AboutDlg::WMInitDialog(HWND hDlg)
{
    PEG_USER_NOTIFICATION notificationSettings;
    SYSTEMTIME time;

    notificationSettings.ActionFlags = PUN_LED;
    notificationSettings.dwReserved = 0;
    GetLocalTime(&time);
    time.wSecond+=2;

    m_notification = PegSetUserNotification( 0, L"trvlmgr.exe",
&time,
                                    &notificationSettings);
    if (m_notification != 0)
    {
        SetTimer(hDlg, 1, 15000, NULL);
    }
}
```

The notification is handled in either the AboutDlg::WMCommand method or the AboutDlg::WMTimer method, depending on whether the dialog box is being closed by the user or by the timer going off. (The AboutDlg::WMTimer method was discussed in the "Timers," section of this chapter.)

```
LRESULT AboutDlg::WMCommand( HWND hDlg, UINT, WPARAM wParam, LPARAM )
{
    if ((wParam == IDOK) || (wParam == IDCANCEL))
        {
        PegHandleAppNotifications(L"trvlmgr.exe");
        KillTimer(hDlg, 1);
         EndDialog(hDlg, TRUE);
         return (TRUE);
    }
    return FALSE;
}
```

TravelManager Application Input and Output

The changes to the TravelManager application in this chapter include the use of a timer and simple keyboard input. The application also has a new Draw view in which the user can draw lines using the stylus. The TravelManager also took advantage of Windows CE notification functionality to flash the LED light and play a .wav file.

In the interest of space, the entire application will not be re-listed here. A version of the TravelManager application containing only the changes made for this chapter can be found on the companion CD-ROM. See Appendix A, "Getting Started with the CD-ROM," for information on using the CD-ROM.

CHAPTER 9

Registry and File System

There are many instances when an application creates data that should exist after the application has exited. When a user sets the preferences in an application, for example, the application should remember those settings the next time the application is run. As another example, similar expectations arise with an application that is used to explicitly create data, such as Notepad under Windows 95, or Pocket Word in Windows CE. The user expects that once data is entered, it can be saved for later use.

In Windows 95, an application can write all this data to the hard disk so that it can be used again later. In Windows CE, however, no hard disk is really present. Luckily, the Windows CE SDK has blurred the distinction between memory and disk space, making it possible to save data for later use.

A Handheld PC uses RAM to store applications, runtime data, and user data. In addition, some RAM is reserved for use by the Windows CE operating system. The portion that is available to Windows CE applications is called the *object store*. This object store is the space in RAM that is available for applications to store their data.

The object store is comprised of three general parts:

- The registry
- The file system
- The database system

Note

Remember that when the Handheld PC is turned off, power still is being used to maintain the state of the operating system. This includes maintaining the object store and the state of the current running applications.

The Windows CE registry and file system will be covered in this chapter. The Windows CE database system will be covered in Chapter 10, "Windows CE Databases."

The Windows CE Registry

The Window CE system registry is very similar to the registry in Windows 95; it is a central storage location that contains current information about the computer hardware and configuration, installed software applications, settings and preferences, and associations between types of files and the applications that access and manipulate their contents. In early versions of Windows, all this information was scattered between system .ini files (such as win.ini and system.ini) and private application .ini files.

Registry Structure

Basically, the registry is a collection of keys and values. However, unlike .ini files, keys can be nested. Thus, the registry is organized as a tree with a hierarchical structure. All keys are named and can have any number of values and subkeys. A *value* has a name and an optional piece of data, which can be one of many different types, such as binary, numeric, or string.

Each key has a name consisting of one or more printable ANSI characters (characters ranging from values 32 through 127). Key names cannot include a backslash or wildcard characters. The name of each subkey is unique with respect to the key that is immediately above it in the hierarchy. Key names are not localized into other languages, although values may be.

Figure 9.1 shows a graphical representation of the Windows CE registry.

Figure 9.1

The Windows CE registry.

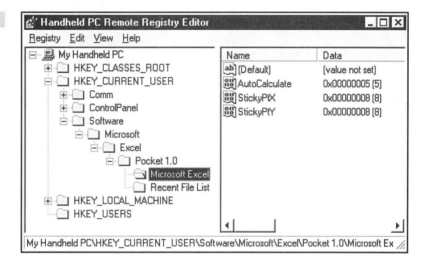

In Figure 9.1, the entries in the left pane are the keys and subkeys; the entries in the right pane are the values for the HKEY_CURRENT_USER\Software\Microsoft\Excel\Pocket 1.0\Microsoft Excel key. This key has no default value, but it does have three other numeric values.

Predefined Keys

An application must open a key before it can add data to the registry. To open a key, an application must supply the handle of another key in the registry that is already open. The system defines standard handles that are always open. An application can use these predefined handles as entry points to the registry.

Windows CE contains only a subset of the predefined keys that are present in Windows 95. Table 9.1 defines the root keys.

Table 9.1

Windows CE Registry Keys

Registry Key	Description
HKEY_CLASSES_ROOT	This key defines document types and the properties associated with those types, such as an icon to display and how to open that type document.
HKEY_CURRENT_USER	This key defines settings for the current user.
HKEY_LOCAL_MACHINE	This key defines settings for the machine.
HKEY_USERS	This key defines the settings and preferences for each user.

Value Types

The registry supports several different data types that an application can use when inserting values into the registry. Table 9.2 lists the supported types.

Table 9.2

Windows CE Registry Data Types

Data Type	Description
REG_BINARY	Binary data in any form.
REG_DWORD	A 32-bit number.
REG_DWORD _LITTLE_ENDIAN	A 32-bit number in little-endian format (same as REG_DWORD). In little-endian format, the most significant byte of a word is the high-order word.
REG_DWORD_BIG _ENDIAN	A 32-bit number in big-endian format. In big-endian format, the most significant byte of a word is the low-order word.

Data Type	Description
REG_EXPAND_SZ	A null-terminated string that contains unexpanded references to environment variables (for example, "%PATH%"). This string will be a Unicode or ANSI string, depending on whether you use the Unicode or ANSI functions.
REG_LINK	A Unicode symbolic link.
REG_MULTI_SZ	An array of null-terminated strings, terminated by two null characters.
REG_NONE	No defined value type.
REG_RESOURCE_LIST	A device-driver resource list.
REG_SZ	A null-terminated Unicode string.

Registry Tools

Windows 95 contains a tool called the Registry Editor that enables direct interaction with the registry. Although not usually needed by end users, this tool permits advanced users fast and easy access to the settings in the registry. In contrast, Windows CE does not contain a direct registry editing tool.

The Windows CE SDK does provide a Remote Registry Editor that can be used to examine and even update the Windows CE registry from a desktop PC. This tool is especially useful for verifying the results of registry programming when developing an application.

Although the end user does not have direct interaction with the registry, applications can interact with the registry in a variety of ways. When an application is installed, the setup mechanism can update the registry, or a desktop application connected to a Windows CE device can update the registry through the remote registry API functions. A Windows CE application's primary function, however, is to interact with the registry using the registry functions in the Windows CE API.

Registry Uses

An application can use the registry in many ways. Most applications use the registry for saving application settings and preferences. Applications can also manipulate settings and preferences for Windows CE itself through entries in the registry.

Registering Filename Extensions

Windows CE supports the notion of file extension identifiers. This enables Windows CE to identify the type associated with a given file extension. The registry information for these file extensions is found under the HKEY_CLASSES_ROOT key. In order for an application to define its file extension, it should accomplish the following duties:

1. Make sure that the file extension does not conflict with one that is already defined in the registry.

2. Enter a new key name—the key name should match the file extension name. (The default value of the key should be an application identifier.) For example, to register files with the extension .abc and an application identifier of abcfile, the key would be as follows:

```
HKEY_CLASSES_ROOT
        .abc = abcfile
```

3. Next, add another key to HKEY_CLASSES_ROOT with the same name as the application identifier just created. (The default value is a text string that describes the file type.)

```
HKEY_CLASSES_ROOT
        abcfile = "ABC Application Document"
```

Generally, an application adds its document type to the registry during installation. The procedure used to install an application onto a Windows CE Handheld PC facilitates adding this information to the registry. The installation procedure itself will be covered in Chapter 12, "Windows CE Application Loader."

Registering an Icon

In addition to creating a string that describes the file type, an application also can set the icon that is displayed for its file extension. To specify the icon, another key is added under the application identifier key, which was created earlier.

```
HKEY_CLASSES_ROOT
        abcfile = "ABC Application Document"
                DefaultIcon = \Windows\abcview.exe, 1
```

The value for the DefaultIcon key consists of a path to a resource (usually an .exe or .dll) and an offset where the icon is located. The icon setting in the registry also can be created when an application is installed. This installation procedure will be covered in Chapter 12.

Saving Application Data

Besides setting information about its document types, an application can use the registry to store a variety of information. An application interacts with the registry using Windows CE API functions. Windows CE supports most of the registry API functions that are available in Win32. The supported functions are described in the following sections.

Applications can place data anywhere in the registry hierarchy. However, applications should create a key (with the application's name) under the HKEY_LOCAL_MACHINE\SOFTWARE and HKEY_CURRENT_USER\SOFTWARE keys.

Opening and Creating Keys

Before an application can add data to the registry, it must create or open a key. To create or open a key, an application refers to the key as a subkey of another currently open key. The four predefined keys are always open; an application does not need to open each subkey individually when opening a key with the other keys above it. However, the application must start from an open key.

An application uses the RegOpenKeyEx to open a key:

```
LONG RegOpenKeyEx(
        HKEY hKey,              // handle of open key or predefined
➥key
        LPCWSTR lpszSubKey,     // address of name of subkey to open
        DWORD ulOptions,        // reserved, must be zero
        REGSAM samDesired,      // not used
        PHKEY phkResult         // address of handle for opened key
);
```

The RegCreateKeyEx function creates the specified key. The system then creates the necessary structure to add the key, including producing any intermediate keys not yet present in the registry. If the key already exists in the registry, the function opens it. The RegCreateKeyEx function is defined as follows:

```
LONG RegCreateKeyEx(
        HKEY hKey,                      // handle of an open key
        LPCWSTR lpszSubKey,             // address of subkey name
        DWORD Reserved,                 // reserved, must be zero
        LPWSTR lpszClass,               // address of class string
        DWORD dwOptions,                // not used, should be zero
        REGSAM samDesired,              // not used, should be zero
        LPSECURITY_ATTRIBUTES lpSecurityAttributes,  // not used
        PHKEY phkResult,                // address of buffer for
➥opened key
        LPDWORD lpdwDisposition         // address of disposition value
➥buffer
);
```

Tip

In Windows CE, the dwOptions and samDesired parameters are ignored and should be set to zero to ensure compatibility with future versions of Windows CE. The lpSecurityAttributes parameter should be set to NULL. Windows CE automatically assigns the key a default security descriptor.

Closing Keys

An application uses the RegCloseKey function to close a key and write the data it contains to the object store. In Windows CE, the data automatically is written to the registry before the RegCloseKey function returns. Other versions of Win32 define a RegFlushKey function, but this is unnecessary in Windows CE.

```
LONG RegCloseKey(
        HKEY hKey        // handle of key to close
);
```

Writing Data to the Registry

An application uses the RegSetValueEx function to associate a value and its data with a key.

```
LONG RegSetValueEx(
        HKEY hKey,                      // handle of key to set value
➥for
        LPCWSTR lpszValueName, // address of value to set
        DWORD Reserved,                 // reserved, must be zero
        DWORD dwType,          // flag for value type
        const BYTE *lpData,             // address of value data
        DWORD cbData           // size of value data
);
```

Deleting Registry Data

An application uses the RegDeleteValue function to delete a value from a key. The RegDeleteKey is used to delete a key, but the key is not actually removed until the last handle to it has been closed.

```
LONG RegDeleteValue(
        HKEY hKey,                      // handle of open key
        LPCWSTR lpszValueName  // address of value name
);
```

```
LONG RegDeleteKey(
        HKEY hKey,                        // handle of open key
        LPCWSTR lpszSubKey                // address of name of subkey
➡to delete
);
```

Finding Registry Data

An application can retrieve both the subkeys and the values of a given key. The `RegEnumKeyEx` and `RegEnumValue` functions are used to enumerate the available subkeys and the values present for a key. The application initially should call the `RegEnumKeyEx` or `RegEnumValue` with the dwIndex parameter set to zero. It then can increment the dwIndex parameter and continue to call the enumeration function until it returns ERROR_NO_MORE_ITEMS. The `RegEnumKeyEx` sequence is defined as follows:

```
LONG RegEnumKeyEx(
        HKEY hKey,                        // handle of key to enumerate
        DWORD dwIndex,           // index of subkey to retrieve
        LPWSTR lpszName,                  // address of buffer for
➡subkey name
        LPDWORD lpcchName,                // address for size of subkey
➡buffer
        LPDWORD lpReserved,      // reserved, must be NULL
        LPWSTR lpszClass,                 // address of buffer for class
➡string
        LPDWORD lpcchClass,               // address for size of class
➡buffer
        PFILETIME lpftLastWriteTime   // not used
);
```

The `RegEnumKeyValue` is defined as follows:

```
LONG RegEnumValue(
        HKEY hKey,                         // handle of key to query
        DWORD dwIndex,            // index of value to query
        LPWSTR lpszValueName, // address of buffer for value string
        LPDWORD lpcchValueName,          // address for size of value
```

```
➥buffer
        LPDWORD lpReserved,    // reserved
        LPDWORD lpType,                // address of buffer for type
➥code
        LPBYTE lpData,         // address of buffer for value data
        LPDWORD lpcbData               // address for size of data
➥buffer
);
```

Retrieving Registry Data

To retrieve information about a particular key, an application uses the
RegQueryInfoKey function. To retrieve a particular value for a key, an
application uses the RegQueryValueEx function. The RegQueryInfoKey
and RegQueryValueEx are defined as follows:

```
LONG RegQueryInfoKey (
        HKEY hKey,                     // handle of key to query
        LPWSTR lpszClass,              // address of buffer for class
➥string
        LPDWORD lpcchClass,            // address of size of class
string buffer
        LPDWORD lpReserved,            // reserved, must be NULL
        LPDWORD lpcSubKeys,            // address of buffer for
➥number of subkeys
        LPDWORD lpcchMaxSubKeyLen,     // address of buffer for
➥longest subkey name length
        LPDWORD lpcchMaxClassLen,      // address of buffer for
➥longest class string length
        LPDWORD lpcValues,             // address of buffer for
➥number of value entries
        LPDWORD lpcchMaxValueNameLen, // address of buffer for
➥longest value name length
        LPDWORD lpcbMaxValueData,      // address of buffer for
➥longest value data length
        LPDWORD lpcbSecurityDescriptor,    // not used, must be
NULL
        PFILETIME lpftLastWriteTime   // not used, must be NULL
);

LONG RegQueryValueEx(
```

```
        HKEY hKey,                          // handle of key to query
        LPCWSTR lpszValueName,              // address of name of value to
➡query
        LPDWORD lpReserved,      // reserved, must be NULL
        LPDWORD lpType,                     // address of buffer for value
➡type
        LPBYTE lpData,           // address of data buffer
        LPDWORD lpcbData                    // address of data buffer size
);
```

Memory and the Registry

On any platform, limiting memory use is important. Windows CE's memory restraints, however, make effective memory use even more critical. To decrease access times and reduce memory requirements, the sizes of registry entries can be limited according to the following guidelines:

- Limit the length of each key name component.

- Limit the number of subkey levels under which a value is stored.

- Do not use the null (default) value name; this wastes the key above the value.

- Do not use many small registry values; use larger values (such as multistrings or binary) rather than many individual strings or integers.

- Do not use the Windows 95 key-naming convention just for the sake of doing so.

- Keep the registry values to a reasonable size; do not add multi-kilobyte values.

Note

Because the registry is not exposed to the end user, registry keys do not need to follow a traditional naming convention.

TravelManager Registry Use

Most applications have many potential registry uses for the system registry. For the TravelManager application, one such use is to save the current view when the user closes the application. This is done so that when the application is restarted, the user sees the same view before he previously closed the application.

The current view is saved to the registry in the SaveCurrentState method of the MainWindow class. This method opens or creates the SOFTWARE\WINDOWS CE PROGRAMMING\ TRAVELMANAGER registry key using the RegCreateKeyEx function. The process then determines the currently visible view and saves that information to the registry using the RegSetValueEx function. The registry is then closed using the RegCloseKey function. TravelManager's SaveCurrentState function is listed as follows:

```
void MainWindow::SaveCurrentState()
{
        HKEY hKey;
        DWORD dwDisp, dwState;
        HRESULT hRes;

        hRes = RegCreateKeyEx(HKEY_LOCAL_MACHINE, L"Software\\Windows
➥CE Programming\\TravelManager", 0, NULL, 0, KEY_ALL_ACCESS, NULL,
➥&hKey, &dwDisp);
        if (hRes != ERROR_SUCCESS)
        {
                MessageBox(NULL, L"CreateKey failed", L"", MB_OK);
                return;
        }
    dwState = 0;
    if (IsWindowVisible(m_pItineraryView->m_hWnd))
        dwState = 1;
    else if (IsWindowVisible(m_pExpensesView->m_hWnd))
        dwState = 2;
    else if (IsWindowVisible(m_pNotesView->m_hWnd))
        dwState = 3;
    else if (IsWindowVisible(m_pDrawView->m_hWnd))
        dwState = 4;
```

```
        hRes = RegSetValueEx(hKey, L"View",0,REG_DWORD, (LPBYTE)&dwState,
➥sizeof(DWORD));
        RegCloseKey(hKey);


}
```

When the TravelManager application is started, it queries any previously saved state information from the registry in the LoadCurrentState method of the MainWindow class. TravelManager first opens the same registry key used in the SaveCurrentState method and then uses the `RegQueryValueEx` function to retrieve the saved view information. After closing the registry, the saved view information is used to display the proper view. The `LoadCurrentState` function is shown as follows:

```
void MainWindow::LoadCurrentState()
{
        HKEY hKey;
        DWORD dwSize, dwValue, dwType;
        HRESULT         hRes;

        hRes = RegOpenKeyEx(HKEY_LOCAL_MACHINE, L"Software\\Windows
➥CE Programming\\TravelManager", 0, KEY_ALL_ACCESS, &hKey);
        if (hRes != ERROR_SUCCESS)
        {
                MessageBox(NULL, L"Error opening registry", L"",
➥MB_OK);
                return;
        }

        dwSize = sizeof(DWORD);
        hRes = RegQueryValueEx(hKey, L"View", 0, &dwType,
➥(LPBYTE)&dwValue, &dwSize);
        if (hRes != ERROR_SUCCESS)
        {
                MessageBox(NULL, L"Error reading registry", L"",
➥MB_OK);
        RegCloseKey(hKey);
        return;
        }

        RegCloseKey(hKey);
```

```
    // Hide all view windows
    ShowWindow(m_pItineraryView->m_hWnd, SW_HIDE);
    ShowWindow(m_pExpensesView->m_hWnd, SW_HIDE);
    ShowWindow(m_pNotesView->m_hWnd, SW_HIDE);
    ShowWindow(m_pDrawView->m_hWnd, SW_HIDE);

    // Uncheck all view menu/buttons
    HMENU hMenu = CommandBar_GetMenu(m_hwndCB,0);
    CheckMenuItem(hMenu, ID_VIEW_ITINERARY, MF_UNCHECKED);
    CheckMenuItem(hMenu, ID_VIEW_EXPENSES, MF_UNCHECKED);
    CheckMenuItem(hMenu, ID_VIEW_NOTES, MF_UNCHECKED);
    CheckMenuItem(hMenu, ID_VIEW_DRAW, MF_UNCHECKED);

    // Toggle the appropriate command bar button
    SendMessage(m_hwndCB, TB_SETSTATE, (WPARAM)ID_VIEW_ITINERARY,
MAKELONG(TBSTATE_ENABLED,0));
    SendMessage(m_hwndCB, TB_SETSTATE, (WPARAM)ID_VIEW_EXPENSES,
MAKELONG(TBSTATE_ENABLED,0));
    SendMessage(m_hwndCB, TB_SETSTATE, (WPARAM)ID_VIEW_NOTES,
➥MAKELONG(TBSTATE_ENABLED,0));
    SendMessage(m_hwndCB, TB_SETSTATE, (WPARAM)ID_VIEW_DRAW,
➥MAKELONG(TBSTATE_ENABLED,0));

    switch (dwValue)
    {
    case 4:
        ShowWindow(m_pDrawView->m_hWnd, SW_SHOW);
        SendMessage(m_hwndCB, TB_SETSTATE, (WPARAM)ID_VIEW_DRAW,
            MAKELONG(TBSTATE_ENABLED¦TBSTATE_CHECKED,0));
        CheckMenuItem(hMenu, ID_VIEW_DRAW, MF_CHECKED);
        break;
    case 3:
        CheckMenuItem(hMenu, ID_VIEW_NOTES, MF_CHECKED);
        SendMessage(m_hwndCB, TB_SETSTATE, (WPARAM)ID_VIEW_NOTES,
            MAKELONG(TBSTATE_ENABLED¦TBSTATE_CHECKED,0));
        ShowWindow(m_pNotesView->m_hWnd, SW_SHOW);
        break;
    case 2:
        CheckMenuItem(hMenu, ID_VIEW_EXPENSES, MF_CHECKED);
        SendMessage(m_hwndCB, TB_SETSTATE, (WPARAM)ID_VIEW_EXPENSES,
            MAKELONG(TBSTATE_ENABLED¦TBSTATE_CHECKED,0));
        ShowWindow(m_pExpensesView->m_hWnd, SW_SHOW);
        break;
    case 1:
```

```
case 0:
default:
    CheckMenuItem(hMenu, ID_VIEW_ITINERARY, MF_CHECKED);
    SendMessage(m_hwndCB, TB_SETSTATE, (WPARAM)ID_VIEW_ITINERARY,
        MAKELONG(TBSTATE_ENABLED¦TBSTATE_CHECKED,0));
    ShowWindow(m_pItineraryView->m_hWnd, SW_SHOW);
    break;
}

}
```

The Windows CE File System

Just as Windows CE enables a portion of RAM to act as the system registry, it also allocates a portion of the RAM to act as the file system. This file system can be manipulated through a subset of the Win32 file system APIs. The following sections examine the structure of the Windows CE file system and the supported APIs for accessing the file system.

File System Structure

The structure of the Windows CE file system is similar to Windows 95 except that no drive letters exist in Windows CE. Instead, the root of the file system is specified with the familiar single backslash. Directories can be created as needed off this root directory. The \Windows directory is important because all ROM files actually appear in this directory. Most files in the \Windows directory are in ROM, but the user or an application also can place files in the \Windows directory. If a file is placed in the \Windows directory that has the same name as a file in ROM, the file in RAM takes precedence. Windows CE does support long file names, which makes it easier to produce unique file names and avoid the possibility of a naming collision.

The Windows CE file system has certain constraints. First, this file system has no concept of a current directory. File specification always must be explicit, not relative to a current directory. Second, no PATH environment variable exists, so Windows CE cannot scan a PATH list to search for a file. The exception to this rule is that Windows CE always looks in the \Windows directory when trying to locate a DLL. For this reason, all EXE and DLL files should be placed in the \Windows directory. Links then can be placed on the desktop or in the My Programs folder.

Because memory is so limited under Windows CE, the entire file system is always compressed at a ratio of about 2:1 to conserve RAM. There is no way to turn off the compression, but you should have no need to do so because this compression is completely transparent. Furthermore, the object store does not use the FAT structure, so no cluster size issues arise and no space is wasted when storing a file. With memory at such a premium, the file system is optimized for size, not speed. The system does, however, do some minimal caching to improve performance.

Working with Directories

Directories exist in Windows CE just as they do in Windows 95. Applications can create directories with the CreateDirectory function and delete directories with the RemoveDirectory function. The CreateDirectory function is defined as follows:

```
BOOL CreateDirectory(
        LPCTSTR lpPathName,                       // pointer to a
➥directory path string
        LPSECURITY_ATTRIBUTES lpSecurityAttributes   // should be
NULL
);
```

In Windows CE, the lpSecurityAttributes parameter is ignored and should be set to NULL. The RemoveDirectory function is defined as follows:

```
BOOL RemoveDirectory(
        LPCTSTR lpPathName      // address of directory to remove
);
```

Creating and Opening Files

An application uses the `CreateFile` function to create, open, or truncate a file, pipe, or communications resource. The application then returns a handle that can be used to access the object. The `CreateFile` function is defined as follows:

```
HANDLE CreateFile(
        LPCTSTR lpFileName,                         // pointer to name of
➥the file
        DWORD dwDesiredAccess,          // access (read/write) mode
        DWORD dwShareMode,              // share mode
        LPSECURITY_ATTRIBUTES lpSecurityAttributes,  // ignored
        DWORD dwCreationDistribution, // how to create
        DWORD dwFlagsAndAttributes,              // file attributes
        HANDLE hTemplateFile            // ignored
);
```

The differences between the Windows CE version of `CreateFile` and the regular Win32 version are detailed in the following list:

- Windows CE requires the use of a colon (:) to identify a communication device.

- In Windows CE, the lpSecurityAttributes parameter is ignored and should be set to NULL.

- The following attribute flags are not supported in Windows CE for the dwFlagsAndAttributes parameter:

     FILE_ATTRIBUTE_OFFLINE

     FILE_ATTRIBUTE_TEMPORARY

- The following file flags are not supported in Windows CE for the dwFlagsAndAttributes parameter:

     FILE_FLAG_OVERLAPPED (However, multiple reads/writes pending on a device at a time are allowed.)

     FILE_FLAG_SEQUENTIAL_SCAN

     FILE_FLAG_NO_BUFFERING

FILE_FLAG_DELETE_ON_CLOSE

FILE_FLAG_BACKUP_SEMANTICS

FILE_FLAG_POSIX_SEMANTICS

- The dwFlagsAndAttributes parameter does not support the SECURITY_SQOS_PRESENT flag in Windows CE or its corresponding values.

- The hTemplateFile parameter is ignored in Windows CE. As a result, CreateFile does not copy the extended attributes to the new file.

Closing and Deleting Files

A file that is opened with the CreateFile function should be closed with the CloseHandle function.

```
BOOL CloseHandle(
        HANDLE hObject // handle to object to close
);
```

An application can remove a file from the object store by using the DeleteFile function.

```
BOOL DeleteFile(
        LPCTSTR lpFileName      // pointer to name of file to delete
);
```

Reading and Writing Data

After a file is opened, an application can read data from it with the ReadFile function. The ReadFile function reads data from the file, starting at the position indicated by the file pointer. After the read operation has been completed, the file pointer is adjusted by the number of bytes actually read.

```
BOOL ReadFile(
        HANDLE hFile,                          // handle of file to
➥read
        LPVOID lpBuffer,                       // buffer to receive
➥data
        DWORD nNumberOfBytesToRead,    // number of bytes to read
        LPDWORD lpNumberOfBytesRead,   // address of number of bytes
➥read
        LPOVERLAPPED lpOverlapped      // must be NULL
);
```

The differences between the Windows CE version of `ReadFile` and the regular Win32 version are detailed in the following list:

- The lpOverlapped parameter must be set to NULL. Windows CE does not allow files to be created with the overlapped attribute.

- Asynchronous read operations on files is not supported in Windows CE.

- The hFile parameter cannot be a socket handle in Windows CE.

Applications use the `WriteFile` function to write data to a file. The `WriteFile` function starts writing data to the file at the position indicated by the file pointer. After the write operation has been completed, the file pointer is adjusted by the number of bytes actually written.

```
BOOL WriteFile(
        HANDLE hFile,                          // handle of file to
➥write to
        LPCVOID lpBuffer,                      // address of data to
➥write to file
        DWORD nNumberOfBytesToWrite,  // number of bytes to write
        LPDWORD lpNumberOfBytesWritten,      // address for # of
➥bytes written
        LPOVERLAPPED lpOverlapped            // must be set to NULL
);
```

Windows CE does not support asynchronous write operations. The lpOverlapped parameter is ignored and should be set to NULL before calling this function.

The WriteFile function typically writes data to an internal buffer that the operating system writes to disk on a regular basis. The FlushFileBuffers function writes all the buffered information for the specified file to memory and is defined as follows:

```
BOOL FlushFileBuffers(
        HANDLE hFile    // open handle to file
);
```

Copying and Moving Files

Applications also can copy or move an existing file. The file to be moved or copied does not need to be opened. Instead, the CopyFile function is used to copy an existing file or a new file, and the MoveFile function is used to rename an existing file or directory.

```
BOOL CopyFile(
        LPCTSTR lpExistingFileName,    // pointer to name of an
➥existing file
        LPCTSTR lpNewFileName, // pointer to name of file to copy to
        BOOL bFailIfExists             // flag for operation if file
exists
);

BOOL MoveFile(
        LPCTSTR lpExistingFileName,    // address of name of the ex-
isting file
        LPCTSTR lpNewFileNam  // address of new name for the file
);
```

Finding Files

An application can use the FindFirstFile function to search a directory for the first file whose name matches the specified search file name (this can include wild cards). FindFirstFile examines subdirectory names as well as file names. The application subsequently can call the FindNextFile function repeatedly to retrieve all files and directories that match the search file name. The FindClose function is used to close the search handle returned from `FindFirstFile` when the search is complete. These three functions are defined as follows:

```
HANDLE FindFirstFile(
        LPCTSTR lpFileName,                  // pointer to name of file to
➥search for
        LPWIN32_FIND_DATA lpFindFileData     // pointer to returned
➥information
);

BOOL FindNextFile(
        HANDLE hFindFile,                    // handle to search
        LPWIN32_FIND_DATA lpFindFileData     // pointer to structure
➥for data on found file
);

BOOL FindClose(
        HANDLE hFindFile       // file search handle
);
```

Retrieving File Information

Windows CE supports a variety of functions to obtain information about a file.

GetFileAttributes returns attributes—such as read only, hidden, and archive—for a specified file or directory. The file does not need to be opened; instead, it is specified by a path.

```
DWORD GetFileAttributes(
        LPCTSTR lpFileName     // address of the name of a file or
➥directory
);
```

GetFileInformationByHandle retrieves information about an open file.

```
BOOL GetFileInformationByHandle(
        HANDLE hFile,  // handle of file
```

```
            LPBY_HANDLE_FILE_INFORMATION lpFileInformation        //
➥address of structure
);
```

GetFileSize retrieves the size, in bytes, of the specified file.

```
DWORD GetFileSize(
        HANDLE hFile,                     // handle of file to get size
➥of
        LPDWORD lpFileSizeHigh      // address of high-order word
➥for file size
);
```

GetFileTime retrieves the date and time that a file was created, last accessed, and last modified.

```
BOOL GetFileTime(
        HANDLE hFile,                               // identifies the file
        LPFILETIME lpCreationTime,        // address of creation
➥time
        LPFILETIME lpLastAccessTime,  // address of last access time
        LPFILETIME lpLastWriteTime          // address of last
➥write time
);
```

Setting File Information

Windows CE applications also can set information about files.

SetFileAttributes sets a file's attributes.

```
BOOL SetFileAttributes(
        LPCTSTR lpFileName,               // address of filename
        DWORD dwFileAttributes // address of attributes to set
);
```

SetFileTime sets the date and time that a file was created, last accessed, or last modified.

```
BOOL SetFileTime(
        HANDLE hFile,  // identifies the file
        const FILETIME *lpCreationTime,      // time the file was
⇒created
        const FILETIME *lpLastAccessTime,    // time the file was
⇒last accessed
        const FILETIME *lpLastWriteTime      // time the file was
⇒last written
);
```

SetEndOfFile moves the end-of-file position for the specified file to the
current position of the file pointer.

```
BOOL SetEndOfFile(
        HANDLE hFile    //handle of file whose EOF is to be set
);
```

SetFilePointer moves the file pointer of an open file.

```
DWORD SetFilePointer(
        HANDLE hFile,                    // handle of file
        LONG lDistanceToMove, // number of bytes to move file pointer
        PLONG lpDistanceToMoveHigh, // address of high-order word of
⇒distance to move
        DWORD dwMoveMethod    // how to move
);
```

TravelManager File System Use

Most of the data displayed in the TravelManager application is stored
in and retrieved from the Windows CE database (covered in the next
chapter). However, one piece of data that is useful to store in the Windows CE File System is the data that the user can type into the Notes
view. By saving the Notes view data in a simple text file, the user poten-
tially could view or edit it using another application, such as Microsoft
Pocket Word.

Data from the Notes view is saved to the Windows CE File System
when the user selects the Save menu option. The request to Save is

carried out by the Save function of the NotesView class. This function determines the length of the data in the edit control on the Notes view and creates a TCHAR array large enough to hold that data. The data retrieved from the edit control is in Unicode and therefore could be written to the Windows CE File System as Unicode. However, to keep the format as a simple text file, the data first is converted from Unicode to a multi-byte character string using the wcstombs function.

After the data is converted, the TravelManager application creates a new directory called Travel Manager using the CreateDirectory function. TravelManager then creates a file called notes.txt in that directory using the CreateFile function. The application then writes the data into the file with the WriteFile function. Finally, the file is closed with the CloseHandle function.

Note that the code responsible for saving data to the File System is not compiled for an emulation build. The file system calls are available under emulation, but are mapped directly to the Win32 file system calls. This means paths to a file would also require a drive letter.

```
void NotesView::Save()
{
#ifndef _WIN32_WCE_EMULATION
    DWORD length = SendDlgItemMessage(m_hWnd, IDC_EDIT1,
➥WM_GETTEXTLENGTH, 0, 0);
        TCHAR *pString = (TCHAR *) LocalAlloc( LPTR , (length *
➥sizeof(TCHAR) + sizeof(TCHAR)));

    if (GetDlgItemText(m_hWnd, IDC_EDIT1, pString, length+1) == 0)
    {
        LocalFree(pString);
        return; //nothing to copy
    }

    // Convert from unicode
    DWORD charlength = (length * sizeof(char));
    char * pMBString = (char *) LocalAlloc(LPTR,
➥charlength+sizeof(char));
    wcstombs(pMBString, pString, charlength);

    CreateDirectory(L"\\Travel Manager", NULL);
```

```
        HANDLE hFile;
        hFile = CreateFile(L"\\Travel Manager\\Notes.txt", GENERIC_WRITE,
            0, NULL, CREATE_ALWAYS, FILE_ATTRIBUTE_NORMAL, NULL);

        DWORD dwWritten;
        if (hFile > 0)
        {
            WriteFile(hFile, pMBString, charlength, &dwWritten, NULL);
            CloseHandle(hFile);
        }
        LocalFree(pString);
#endif

}
```

When the TravelManager application is started, it automatically looks
for this saved data file and reads the contents into the Notes view. After
creating the view, the Create method of the NotesView class then tries
to open an existing notes.txt file in the TravelManager directory. If
successful, the Create method uses the GetFileSize function to determine the size of a buffer needed to hold the contents of the file. The
Create method creates the appropriate buffer, reads the contents into
the buffer with the ReadFile function, and converts the string to Unicode with the mbstowcs function. Finally, the Create method adds the
text to the edit control in the Notes view.

```
BOOL NotesView::Create()
{
    RECT rect;

    GetClientRect(m_pMainWindow->m_hWnd, &rect);
    rect.top += CommandBar_Height(m_pMainWindow->m_hwndCB);

    HWND dlg = CreateDialogParam( m_pMainWindow->m_pApp->m_hInst,
L"NOTES", m_pMainWindow->m_hWnd, DlgProc, (LPARAM)this );
    m_hWnd = dlg;

#ifndef _WIN32_WCE_EMULATION
    HANDLE hFile;
    hFile = CreateFile(L"\\Travel Manager\\Notes.txt", GENERIC_READ,
```

```
        0, NULL, OPEN_EXISTING, FILE_ATTRIBUTE_NORMAL, NULL);

    DWORD length, dwRead;

    if (hFile > 0)
    {
        length = GetFileSize(hFile, NULL);
            char *pMBString = (char *) LocalAlloc( LPTR , (length *
➥sizeof(char) + sizeof(char)));
        ReadFile(hFile, pMBString, length*sizeof(char), &dwRead,
➥NULL);
        CloseHandle(hFile);

        TCHAR *pString = (TCHAR *) LocalAlloc( LPTR , (length *
➥sizeof(TCHAR) + sizeof(CHAR)));
        mbstowcs(pString, pMBString, length);
        SetDlgItemText(m_hWnd, IDC_EDIT1, pString);

    }
#endif

    MoveWindow(dlg, rect.left, rect.top, rect.right-rect.left,
➥rect.bottom-rect.top, FALSE);
    ShowWindow(dlg, SW_HIDE);

    return TRUE;
}
```

TravelManager Application

With the changes from this chapter, the TravelManager application now maintains some persistent data. The current view is saved in the registry so that users will start in the same view in which they last left off. The user also has the ability to save data entered into the Notes view to a file in the Windows CE File System.

In the interest of space, the entire application will not be re-listed here. See Appendix A, "Getting Started with the CD-ROM," for information on accessing the TravelManager application from the companion CD-ROM.

CHAPTER 10

Windows CE Databases

Although Windows CE may eventually be used in many different devices, the first Handheld PCs will more than likely be used as personal information management devices. The standard Windows CE applications will enable the user to manage appointments, phone numbers, and tasks. Commercial Windows CE applications will do a range of tasks, from managing expenses and finances to creating grocery lists.

It is easy enough for applications to manage their own data. Some applications store their data in simple flat files, while other applications use full-fledged relational databases. A unique situation with Windows CE applications, however, is that they are likely extensions of desktop applications and should share relevant data. Each application can be responsible for the management of its own data and the synchronization of data between the desktop and the Handheld device. This is such a common scenario with Windows CE, that much of this functionality is built into the operating system.

Windows CE includes a full set of database functionality that frees every application from having to implement the same functionality. This database functionality allows each application to create and maintain its own database for user data. The calendar and task applications, for instance, that ship with the Handheld PCs use their own database through this functionality.

The standardization of a database for Windows CE also enables applications to easily share data. For instance, because the schedule application in Windows CE maintains its data in a Windows CE database, other applications would be able to access this information.

Windows CE Database Structure

A Windows CE database is not fully relational. However, it is an extremely convenient mechanism for general, structured data storage. Each Windows CE database consists of an arbitrary number of records. Additionally, each record consists of one or more properties.

Note

> For someone familiar with relational databases, a record in a Windows CE database is similar to a row, and the properties would be similar to columns.

For example, an application can store a database of address records, where the properties of each record include a name, street address, city, state, zip code, and telephone number.

Each database includes information about the database such as its name, which is an optional database type identifier that can be used to group multiple databases. The database name is important because all databases share a single namespace.

In addition to the name, the database system also stores sort keys for each database. When a database is created, up to four sort keys can be specified that describe how the records in the database are to be sorted. As data is added to a database, the system uses the specified keys to automatically index the records so that records can be retrieved in a useful order.

Windows CE databases enable only one level of hierarchy, so records cannot contain other records and cannot be contained in more than one database. The maximum size of a record is 128K and the maximum size of a property is 64K. There is also an overhead of 32 bytes per record and 4 bytes per property. In addition, keep in mind that all the strings in Windows CE database are stored as Unicode (which take up more space than single-byte strings).

The fact that an application's database can be modified by another application can present problems. Although an application cannot lock a database to restrict access, the operating system does ensure the integrity of the database records (for instance, if multiple applications are deleting records simultaneously). Applications can also be notified when a database is changed. Windows CE supports several notification messages that signal when another application creates, modifies, or deletes database records. Notifications are covered in more detail in Chapter 8, "Input and Output."

Windows CE performs many management functions on the database: compressing the data when it is inserted, decompressing the data when it is accessed, and ensuring the integrity of the database records. In addition, Windows CE has support to ease synchronization of databases between desktop computers and Windows CE machines.

Applications create and use a Windows CE database through new Windows CE API functions. The following table lists the available database functionality and the corresponding API function.

Database Operation	Windows CE Functions
Create database	PegCreateDatabase
Delete database	PegDeleteDatabase
Enumerate databases	PegFindFirstDatabase, PegFindNextDatabase
Open database	PegOpenDatabase
Seek record	PegSeekDatabase
Read record	PegReadRecordProps
Write record	PegWriteRecordProps
Retrieve object information	PegOidGetInfo
Set database information	PegSetDatabaseInfo

Records and Properties

Records and properties are the building blocks of Windows CE databases. A database is comprised of a number of records, and each record is comprised of one or more properties.

Every record in a Windows CE database is identified by a unique object identifier. This object identifier is assigned by the system when a new record is created. Although an application need not keep track of the record identifiers, they can be used in seeking a database to get to a specific record. The record object identifier is of type PEGOID.

Each property of a given record consists of the property identifier, data type, and data value. The property identifier and data type are combined into a two-part, double word value of type PEGPROPID. The high-order word is an application-defined identifier, and the low-order word is a predefined constant that specifies the property's data type. Windows CE supports integer, string, time, and byte array ("blob") data types. The constants used to specify these types are presented in Table 10.1.

Table 10.1

Windows CE Data Constants

Property Type Constant	Data Type
PEGVT_BLOB	A PEGBLOB structure
PEGVT_FILETIME	A FILETIME structure
PEGVT_I2	A 16-bit signed integer
PEGVT_I4	A 32-bit signed integer
PEGVT_LPWSTR	A null-terminated string
PEGVT_UI2	A 16-bit unsigned integer
PEGVT_UI4	A 32-bit unsigned integer

Records are represented as an array of PEGPROPVAL structures that specify the record's properties. The PEGPROPVAL structure is defined as follows:

```
typedef struct _PEGPROPVAL {
        PEGPROPID propid;
        WORD wLenData;
        WORD wFlags;
        PEGVALUNION val;
} PEGPROPVAL;
```

The PEGPROPVAL structure has the following members:

- **PEGPROPID propid**. Specifies the identifier of the property value where the high-order word is an application-defined value, and the low-order word is a PEGVT_ constant that specifies the data type.

- **WORD wLenData**. Not currently used.

- **WORD wFlags**. Flag set by an application to PEGDB_PROPDELETE to specify the property that is to be deleted, or set by the system to PEGDB_PROPNOTFOUND when updating a record where the specified property is not found.

- **PEGVALUNION val**. Specifies the actual value for simple types, or a pointer for strings or BLOBs.

An array of PEGPROPVAL structures is used when both reading and writing records. When reading records, for example, an application can use the TypeFromPropID function to determine the property type given to the property identifier (PEGPROPID).

Creating and Deleting Databases

Applications can create and delete databases as needed. The number of databases that can exist is limited only by available memory (object store space) on the device.

Windows CE databases are created with the `PegCreateDatabase` function. The parameters to the function include the name and type identifier for the database and the optional sort order specifications. The *sort order specifications* specify the number of sort orders active in the database, with four being the maximum possible. This parameter can be zero if no sort orders are active.

The following table summarizes the parameters to `PegCreateDatabase`.

PegCreateDatabase Parameter	Description
LPWSTR lpszName	The name of the database, which can be up to 32 characters long.
DWORD dwDbaseType	The application-defined type of the database.
WORD wNumSortOrder	Number of sort orders in the rgSortSpecs array. A database can have zero to four sort orders.
SORTORDERSPEC * rgSortSpecs	Pointer to array of sort order descriptions or NULL if zero specified for wNumSortOrder.

If `PegCreateDatabase` is successful, the return value is the object identifier (PEGOID) of the database. The database object identifier is used to open a database in order to manipulate its contents. If the `PegCreateDatabase` function fails, the return value is NULL. The `GetLastError` function can be used to get a specific error code. Possible error codes for `PegCreateDatabase` are listed in the following table.

Error Code	Description
ERROR_DISK_FULL	The object store does not contain enough space to create the new database.

Error Code	Description
ERROR_INVALID_ PARAMETER	A parameter is invalid.
ERROR_DUP_NAME	A database already exists with the specified name.

The `PegDeleteDatabase` function is used to destroy a database. The only parameter to the function is a PEGOID, which is the object identifier of the database to be deleted. If the `PegDeleteDatabase` function succeeds, the return value is TRUE; otherwise, it is FALSE. The `GetLastError` function can be used to get extended error information. Possible error codes are ERROR_INVALID_PARAMETER, meaning a parameter was invalid, or ERROR_SHARING_VIOLATION, meaning another thread has an open handle to the database.

Enumerating Databases

The Windows CE object store can contain an arbitrary number of databases. The `PegFindFirstDatabase` and `PegFindNextDatabase` functions enable an application to enumerate the databases in the object store.

The `PegFindFirstDatabase` begins the enumeration sequence and returns a handle to the enumeration context. This handle is used with the `PegFindNextDatabase` function to obtain the object identifiers for each database. At the end of the enumeration, `PegFindNextDatabase` returns the extended error value ERROR_NO_MORE_ITEMS.

The only parameter to `PegFindFirstDatabase` is a DWORD, which specifies the application-defined database type identifier that can also be used when creating databases. Specifying zero for the database type identifier enumerates all databases in the object store. The return value is a handle to the enumeration context, or ERROR_HANDLE_INVALID if the function fails. Calling `GetLastError` may return ERROR_OUTOFMEMORY, indicating that no memory is available to allocate a database handle.

The only parameter to PegFindNextDatabase is the HANDLE, which identifies the enumeration context. If the function succeeds, the return value is the object identifier of the next database to be enumerated. If the function returns zero, use the GetLastError function to get the extended error value. The extended error value can be ERROR_NO_MORE_ITEMS, meaning the object store contains no more databases, or ERROR_INVALID_PARAMETER, meaning the enumeration context handle is invalid.

When the application is finished enumerating databases, it must close the handle to the enumeration context by using the CloseHandle function.

The following code fragment demonstrates the steps in enumerating Windows CE databases.

```
HANDLE hEnumerator;
PEGOID objectID;

hEnumerator = PegFindFirstDatabase(0);  //enumerate ALL databases

if (hEnumerator == INVALID_HANDLE_VALUE)
{
    ::MessageBox(NULL, L"Invalid handle", L"Error", MB_OK);
    return;
}

while( (objectID = PegFindNextDatabase(hEnumerator)) != 0)
{
    // use the objectID of database
    ...
}

CloseHandle(hEnumDB); // must close handle to enumeration context
```

Opening Databases

In order to access a Windows CE database, an application must first obtain a handle to the database. This handle is then used in other database API functions. The PegOpenDatabase function is used to open a Windows CE database.

To identify the database to open, an application can specify either a database name or a database object identifier. The return value of the PegOpenDatabase function is a handle to the opened database. That handle is then used in subsequent calls to read or modify the database. When an application is finished using the database, it must close the handle by calling the CloseHandle function.

An optional flag to the PegOpenDatabase function is PEGDB_AUTOINCREMENT. This flag directs the system to automatically increment the seek pointer after every call to the PegReadRecordProps function. The seek pointer marks the record that will be read by the next read operation. Applications that intend to read many records at a time can increase performance with the PEGDB_AUTOINCREMENT flag.

Another parameter to PegOpenDatabase is the property identifier of a property to be used as the sort order for the open database handle. The system uses the sort order to determine where to move the seek pointer after each subsequent call to PegReadRecordProps (if the PEGDB_AUTOINCREMENT flag is specified). The sort order also determines the property that the PegSeekDatabase function uses to traverse the database.

Because it is possible for multiple applications to run the same database at the same time, it is possible for one application to change a database currently running on another application. The operating system can notify an application when this occurs through notifications. To receive these notifications, an application specifies a window handle in the PegCreateDatabase function. Windows CE will then send notifications about that database to the specified window.

Table 10.2 summarizes the parameters to the PegOpenDatabase function.

Table 10.2

PegOpenDatabase Parameters

PegOpenDatabase Parameter	Description
PPEGOID poid	Points to the object identifier of the database to be opened. To open a database by name, set the value pointed to by poid to zero, which will enable it to receive the object identifier of the newly opened database when a database name is specified for lpszName.
LPWSTR lpszName	Points to the name of the database to be opened. This parameter is ignored if the value pointed to by poid is non-zero.
PEGPROPID propid	Specifies the property identifier of the primary key for the sort order in which the database is to be traversed. All subsequent calls to PegSeekDatabase assume this sort order. This parameter can be zero if the sort order is not important.
DWORD dwFlags	Specifies an action flag of either PEGDB_AUTOINCREMENT or 0.
HWND hwndNotify	Identifies the window to which notification messages (DB_PEGOID_*) will be posted if another thread modifies the given database while your application has it open. This parameter can be NULL if an application does not need to receive notifications.

If the `PegOpenDatabase` function succeeds, the return value is a handle to the open database. If the function fails, the return value is INVALID_HANDLE_VALUE. To get extended error information, call `GetLastError`. The extended error may be one of the error codes listed in the following table.

Error Code	Description
ERROR_INVALID_PARAMETER	A parameter was invalid.
ERROR_FILE_NOT_FOUND	No database exists with the specified name. This error code applies only if the value pointed to by poid was set to NULL (or zero) when the function was called.
ERROR_NOT_ENOUGH_MEMORY	No memory was available to allocate a database handle.

Sorting Databases

An application normally puts the same kind of information in every record in a given database. Each record in the TravelManager application might contain the airline, flight number, departure time, arrival time, seat number, and so on. In addition, the same property for each record would have the same property identifier (for example, the property identifier for the flight number property of one record would be the same for all other records in that database).

When all the records in a Windows CE database share the same property identifiers, an application can request that the system sort the records based on a given property. The order in which the records are sorted affects the order in which the database seeking function

`PegSeekDatabase` finds records in the database, or the order in which the system advances the seek pointer when using the PEGDB_AUTOINCREMENT flag when opening a database.

Up to four different property identifiers can be specified for sorting when a new database is created. These sort order descriptions are specified with the SORTORDERSPEC structure that contains the identifier of a property on which the database records are to be sorted. This structure also includes a combination of flags that affect the sorting order. The SORTORDERSPEC is defined as follows:

```
typedef struct _SORTORDERSPEC {
        PEGPROPID propid;
        DWORD dwFlags;
} SORTORDERSPEC;
```

The valid values for the dwFlags member are listed in the following table.

Flag	Meaning
PEGDB_SORT_DESCENDING	The sort is done in descending order. By default, the sort is done in ascending order.
PEGDB_SORT_CASEINSENSITIVE	The sort operation is case sensitive. This value is valid only for strings.
PEGDB_SORT_UNKNOWNFIRST	Records that do not contain this property are placed before all the other records. By default, such records are placed after all other records.

An application specifies which sort order to use when it calls the PegOpenDatabase function to open a handle to the database. Only one sort order can be active for each open handle. However, by opening multiple handles to the same database, an application can use more than one sort order.

The possible sort orders for a database are defined when the database is created. An application can change the sort orders for a database after it has been created using the PegSetDatabaseInfo function. However, because the system must revise internal indices it uses to maintain the sort orders, changing sort orders can use a large amount of system resources and may take considerable time to complete.

Seeking and Searching Records

Records in a database are retrieved from wherever the database's seek pointer currently points to. Therefore, an application must seek the desired record before attempting to read or modify data. The PegSeekDatabase function is used to seek a specified record in an open database. The desired record can be specified by its object identifier or by a relational value, such as its "name" property equal to "John Doe." When the PegSeekDatabase function finds the desired record, the seek pointer is positioned at that record. An application can then read or update that record.

The order in which the system finds records depends on the sort order that is active with the open database handle. In other words, when searching for a value of "John Doe," the system searches only the properties that have the same property identifier as the sort order property identifier specified when opening the database. If the Contacts is opened specifying the "Name" property as the sort order, then searching for "John Doe" would search the names. However, if the database was opened specifying the "Zip code" as the sort order, then the same PegSeekDatabase call using "John Doe" would examine all the Zip code properties for that value.

The following table summarizes the parameters to the PegSeekDatabase function.

PegSeekDatabase Parameter	Description
HANDLE hDatabase	Identifies the open database in which to seek.
DWORD dwSeekType	Indicates the type of seek operation to perform.
DWORD dwValue	Specifies a value to use for the seek operation. The meaning of this parameter depends on the value of dwSeekType.
LPDWORD lpdwIndex	Points to a variable that receives the index from the start of the database to the beginning of the record that was found.

There are a variety of seek operations the PegSeekDatabase can perform. The following table describes the possible values for the dwSeek-Type parameter of the PegSeekDatabase function.

Seek Operation	Description
PEGDB_SEEK_PEGOID	Seeks until it finds an object that has the given object identifier specified by the dwValue parameter. This type of seek operation is very efficient.
PEGDB_SEEK_VALUESMALLER	Seeks until it finds the largest value that is smaller than the given value. If none of the records has a smaller value, the seek pointer is left pointing at the end of the database, and the function

Seek Operation	Description
	returns zero. The dwValue parameter is a pointer to a PEG-PROPVAL structure. The cost of this type of operation is O(n).
PEGDB_SEEK_VALUEFIRSTEQUAL	Seeks until it finds the first value that is equal to the given value. If the seek operation fails, the seek pointer is left pointing at the end of the database and the function returns zero. The dwValue parameter is a pointer to a PEGPROPVAL structure. The cost of this type of operation is O(n).
PEGDB_SEEK_VALUENEXTEQUAL	Starting from the current seek position, seeks exactly one position forward in the sorted order and checks if the next record is equal in value to the given value. If so, returns the object identifier of the next record; otherwise, returns zero and leaves the seek pointer at the end of the database. This operation can be

continues

Seek Operation	Description
	used in conjunction with the PEGDB_SEEK_ VALUEFIRSTEQUAL operation to enumerate all records with an equal value. The dwValue parameter specifies the value for which to seek. This is a O(1) operation.
PEGDB_SEEK_VALUEGREATER	Seeks until it finds a value greater than or equal to the given value. If all records are smaller, the seek pointer is left at the end of the database, and the function returns zero. The dwValue parameter is a pointer to a PEG-PROPVAL structure. The cost of this type of operation is O(n).
PEGDB_SEEK_BEGINNING	Seeks until it finds the record at the given position from the beginning of the database. The dwValue parameter specifies the number of the records to seek, and the cost of this type of operation is O(dwValue).

Seek Operation	Description
PEGDB_SEEK_CURRENT	Seeks backward or forward from the current position of the seek pointer for the given number of records. The dwValue parameter specifies the number of records from the current position. The function seeks forward if dwValue is a positive value, or backward if it is a negative value. A forward seek operation is efficient. The cost of a backward seek is $O(n)$.
PEGDB_SEEK_END	Seeks backward for the given number of records from the end of the database. The dwValue parameter specifies the number of records. The cost of this type of operation is $O(n)$.

If the `PegSeekDatabase` is successful, the return value is the PEGOID object identifier of the record. If the search is not successful, the return value is zero. `GetLastError` may return ERROR_INVALID_PARAMETER if a parameter is invalid.

Reading Records

After a database is opened, a fundamental operation is reading information. Data is read from a Windows CE database with the `PegReadRecordProps` function.

Unlike the syntax of a SQL database, an application does not specify the set of records to be read (for example, a "where" clause). Instead, the properties are read from the record at the current location of the seek pointer. When a Windows CE database is opened, the seek pointer is positioned at the first record according to the specified sort order. Additionally, if an application specified the PEGDB_AUTOINCREMENT flag when opening the database, the seek pointer is incremented to the next record in the sort order after each call to the PegReadRecordProps function.

The PegReadRecordsProps function is used to read multiple properties at one time. The application specifies which properties to read through a parameter in the PegReadRecordProps function, which are specified in an array of property identifiers (PEGPROPID). Another parameter specifies the number of property identifiers that are listed in the array. Specifying NULL for the array tells the system to retrieve all the properties for the current record.

Another parameter to the PegReadRecordProps function is a buffer for the results. The application specifies the buffer into which the system is to write the property information and specifies a value indicating the size of the buffer. Although it is possible for an application to call PegReadRecordProps once to determine the size of the buffer necessary and then call the function again to retrieve the data, the system greatly facilitates this common functionality. If the application specifies the PEGDB_ALLOWREALLOC flag, the system will reallocate the buffer if it is too small to hold the property information. If the application specifies NULL for the buffer, the system will allocate and use a buffer of the correct size.

Although an application can read any number of properties from the current record, it is important to note that the system stores records in compressed format and must decompress records before they are read. For efficiency, an application should read all the desired properties in a single call rather than using several separate calls.

If the PegReadRecordProps function is successful, the requested property information is copied into the specified buffer. The resulting buffer consists of an array of PEGPROPVAL structures. By using the

PEGPROPID of each PEGPROPVAL structure, the application can determine the value for each property. For property values that can vary in size, such as strings and BLOBs, the PEGPROPVAL structure contains a pointer to the property's data. The data itself is positioned at the end of the allocated buffer.

If a requested property is not valid for the current record, the PEG-PROPVAL structure for that property will contain the PEGDB_PROPNOTFOUND flag.

The following table summarizes the parameters to the `PegReadRecordProps` function.

PegReadRecordProps Parameter	Description
HANDLE hDbase	Identifies an open database. The database must have been opened by a previous call to the `PegOpenDatabase` function.
DWORD dwFlags	Specifies the read flags. Currently, the only value supported is PEGDB_ALLOWREALLOC. This flag indicates that the `LocalAlloc` function was used to allocate the buffer specified by the lplpBuffer parameter, and indicates that the server can reallocate the buffer if it is not large enough to hold the requested properties.
LPWORD lpcPropID	Indicates the number of property identifiers in the array specified by the rgPropID parameter. If

continues

PegReadRecordProps Parameter	Description
	rgPropID is NULL, this parameter receives the number of properties retrieved.
PEGPROPID * rgPropID	Points to an array of property identifiers for the properties to be retrieved. If this parameter is NULL, the function retrieves all properties in the record.
LPBYTE * lplpBuffer	Address of a pointer to a buffer that receives the requested properties. If the dwFlags parameter includes the PEGDB_ALLOWREALLOC flag, the buffer may be reallocated if necessary. If the PEGDB_ALLOWREALLOC flag is specified and this parameter is NULL, the server uses the LocalAlloc function to allocate a buffer of the appropriate size in the caller's address space and returns a pointer to the buffer.
LPDWORD lpcbBuffer	Points to a variable that contains the size, in bytes, of the buffer specified by the lplpBuffer parameter. When the function returns, lpcbBuffer receives a value that indicates the actual size of the data copied to the buffer. If the buffer was too

PegReadRecordProps Parameter	Description
	small to contain the data, this parameter can be used to calculate the amount of memory to allocate for the buffer if PEGDB_ALLOWREALLOC was not specified.

If the PegReadRecordProps function is successful, the return value is the object identifier (PEGOID) of the record that was read. If the function fails, the return value is zero. An application can use the GetLastError function to get additional error information. GetLastError may return one of the error codes listed in the following table.

Error Code	Description
ERROR_INVALID_PARAMETER	A parameter was invalid.
ERROR_NO_DATA	None of the requested properties were found. The output buffer and the size are valid.
ERROR_INSUFFICIENT_BUFFER	The given buffer was not large enough, and the reallocation failed (if the PEGDB_ALLOWREALLOC flag was specified). The lpcbBuffer parameter will contain the required buffer size.
ERROR_KEY_DELETED	The record that was about to be read was deleted by another thread. If the current record was reached as a result of an autoseek, this error is not

continues

Error Code	Description
	returned, and the next record is returned.
ERROR_NO_MORE_ITEMS	The current seek pointer is at the end of the database.

An application must clean up memory allocated by the
PegReadRecordProps function. However, because all variable-length
data is packed into the end of the result buffer, the only memory that
must be freed is the original pointer to the buffer passed in the call.
Because it is possible for the function to fail but still have allocated
memory on the caller's behalf, an application must free the buffer
pointer if it is non-NULL.

The following code sample demonstrates the process for reading properties from a Windows CE database.

```
PEGOID objId;
HANDLE hDb;
WORD cProps;
LPBYTE pBuf = NULL;
DWORD cbBuf = 0;

hDb = PegOpenDatabase(&objId,   // database object id
                      szDbName, // database name
                      0,        // no sort order
                      PEGDB_AUTOINCREMENT, // flags
                      NULL);    // no window for notifications

while (objId = PegReadRecordProps(hDb,     // database handle
                PEGDB_ALLOWREALLOC, // allow reallocation
                &cProps,  // number of properties read
                NULL,     // read all properties
                &pBuf,    // property data buffer
                &cbBuf))  // size of buffer
```

```
{
    //use the property values just read
}
CloseHandle(hDb); // close the database handle hDb
```

Writing Records

Data is written to a Windows CE database with the
PegWriteRecordProps function. This function can be used to
create new database records or to modify existing records.

As discussed previously, a record is composed of a set of properties. To
write these properties to a database record, an application composes an
array of PEGPROPVAL structures. Each PEGPROPVAL structure
specifies a single property identifier and a corresponding value for that
property.

The PegWriteRecordProps function writes all the requested properties
into the specified record. As with reading properties from records, an
application should write all of a record's properties at one time due to
the overhead encountered when data is saved to the database in a compressed format.

The PegWriteRecordProps function is used to create new database
records and also to modify existing database records. If the record identifier parameter to the function specifies an existing record, the function
updates the properties for that record. If the record identifier parameter
is 0, a new record is added to the database with the specified properties.
The PegWriteRecordProps function does not utilize or move the seek
pointer.

An application can also delete an existing property to a record. Specifying the PEGDB_PROPDELETE flag in the PEGPROPVAL structure
instructs the PegWriteRecordProps function to remove the given property.

The following table summarizes the parameters to the
PegWriteRecordProps function.

PegWriteRecordProps Parameter	Description
HANDLE hDbase	Identifies an open database. The database must have been opened by a previous call to the `PegOpen Database` function.
PEGOID oidRecord	Identifies the record to which the given properties are to be written. If this parameter is zero, a new record is created and filled in with the given properties.
WORD cPropID	Indicates the number of properties in the array specified by the rg PropVal parameter. The cPropID parameter must not be zero.
PEGPROPVAL * rgPropVal	Points to an array of PEG PROPVAL structures that specify the property values to be written to the given record.

If the `PegWriteRecordProps` function succeeds, the return value is the object identifier of the record to which the properties were written. If the function fails, the return value is zero. An application can use the `GetLastError` function to get additional error information. `GetLastError` may return one of the error codes listed in the following table.

Error Code	Description
ERROR_DISK_FULL	There was not enough space in the object store to write the properties.
ERROR_INVALID _PARAMETER	A parameter was invalid.

The following code sample demonstrates the process for writing a record to a Windows CE database.

```
PEGPROPVAL NewProp;   // the new property contains a blob...
PEGBLOB blob;   // the blob contains a byte array...
BYTE * pBuf = NULL;  // ...and here's the actual blob data
UINT cbBuf;   // count of bytes needed in blob
...
// figure out the size needed, then allocate it
pBuf = (BYTE *) LocalAlloc(LMEM_FIXED, cbBuf);
// put the actual data into pBuf here...

// now set up to write the new blob property
NewProp.propid = PEGVT_BLOB;
NewProp.wFlags = 0;
NewProp.val.blob = blob; // blob itself points to the buffer
blob.dwCount = cbBuf;  // count of bytes in the buffer
blob.lpb = pBuf;  // set PEGBLOB field to point to buffer
oid = PegWriteRecordProps(hDb, // database handle
    0, // new record
    1, // one property
    &NewProp); // pointer to the blob property
// perform error handling by checking oid...
```

Deleting Records

An application uses the PegDeleteRecord function to delete a record from a database, supplying the object identifier of the record and the handle to the open database that contains the record. The following table summarizes the available parameters for the PegDeleteRecord function.

PegWriteRecordProps	Description Parameter
hDatabase	Identifies the database from which the record is to be deleted. To delete a record, the database must be open. An application opens a database by calling the PegOpenDatabase function.

continues

PegWriteRecordProps	Description Parameter
oidRecord	Object identifier of the record to be deleted.

Retrieving Object Information

An application can retrieve information about any object in the object store with the PegOidGetInfo function. The objects in the object store include databases, records, directories, and files. An application provides an identifier for an object and a pointer to a PEGOIDINFO structure. The following table lists the possible parameters to the PegOidGetInfo function.

PegOidGetInfo Parameter	Description
PEGOID oid	Identifier of the object for which information is to be retrieved.
PEGOIDINFO *poidInfo	Points to a PEGOIDINFO structure that contains information about the object.

If the call to PegOidGetInfo is successful, the return value is TRUE, and the system has filled in the PEGOIDINFO structure with information about the given object. The PEGOIDINFO structure is defined as follows:

```
typedef struct _PEGOIDINFO {
      WORD wObjType;
      WORD wPad;
      union {
            PEGFILEINFO infFile;
            PEGDIRINFO infDirectory;
            PEGDBASEINFO infDatabase;
            PEGRECORDINFO infRecord;
      };
      } PEGOIDINFO;
```

The PEGOIDINFO structure has the following members:

- **WORD wObjType**. Specifies the type of the object. This parameter can be one of the following values:

Object Type	Description
OBJTYPE_INVALID	The object store contains no valid object that has this object identifier.
OBJTYPE_FILE	The object is a file.
OBJTYPE_DIRECTORY	The object is a directory.
OBJTYPE_DATABASE	The object is a database.
OBJTYPE_RECORD	The object is a record inside a database.

- **WORD wPad**. Aligns the structure on a double word boundary.

- **PEGFILEINFO infFile**. Specifies a PEGFILEINFO structure that contains information about a file. This member is valid only if wObjType is OBJTYPE_FILE.

- **PEGDIRINFO infDirectory**. Specifies a PEGDIRINFO structure that contains information about a directory. This member is valid only if wObjType is OBJTYPE_DIRECTORY.

- **PEGDBASEINFO infDatabase**. Specifies a PEGDBASEINFO structure that contains information about a database. This member is valid only if wObjType is OBJTYPE_DATABASE.

- **PEGRECORDINFO infRecord**. Specifies a PEGRECORDINFO structure that contains information about a record in a database. This member is valid only if wObjType is OBJTYPE_RECORD.

The PEGFILEINFO structure is defined as follows:

```
typedef struct _PEGFILEINFO {
                DWORD dwAttributes;
        PEGOID oidParent;
        WCHAR szFileName[MAX_PATH];
                FILETIME ftLastChanged;
        DWORD dwLength;
} PEGFILEINFO;
```

The PEGOIDINFO structure has the following members:

- **DWORD dwAttributes**. Specifies the attributes of the file.

- **PEGOID oidParent**. Specifies the object identifier of the parent directory.

- **WCHAR szFileName**. Specifies a null-terminated string that contains the name and path of the file.

- **FILETIME ftLastChanged**. Specifies a time stamp that indicates when the contents of the file were last changed.

- **DWORD dwLength**. Specifies the length, in bytes, of the file.

The PEGDIRINFO structure is defined as follows:

```
typedef struct _PEGDIRINFO {
        DWORD dwAttributes;
        PEGOID oidParent;
        WCHAR szDirName[MAX_PATH];
} PEGDIRINFO;
```

The PEGDIRINFO structure has the following members:

- **DWORD dwAttributes**. Specifies the attributes of the directory.

- **PEGOID oidParent**. Specifies the object identifier of the parent directory.

- **WCHAR szDirName**. Specifies a null-terminated string that contains the name and path of the directory.

The PEGRECORDINFO structure is defined as follows:

```
typedef struct _PEGRECORDINFO {
        PEGOID oidParent;
} PEGRECORDINFO;
```

The PEGRECORDINFO structure has one member: PEGOID oidParent, which specifies the object identifier of the parent database.

The PEGDBASEINFO structure is defined as follows:

```
typedef struct _PEGDBASEINFO {
        DWORD dwFlags;
        WCHAR szDbaseName[PEGDB_MAXDBASENAMELEN];
        DWORD dwDbaseType;
        WORD wNumRecords;
        WORD wNumSortOrder;
        DWORD dwSize;
        FILETIME ftLastModified;
        SORTORDERSPEC rgSortSpecs[PEGDB_MAXSORTORDER];
} PEGDBASEINFO;
```

The PEGDBASEINFO structure has the following members:

- **DWORD dwFlags**. Indicates the valid members of the structure. This parameter can be a combination of the following values:

PEGDBASEINFO Flag	Description
PEGDB_VALIDNAME	The szDbaseName member is valid and should be used.
PEGDB_VALIDTYPE	The dwDbaseType member is valid and should be used.
PEGDB_VALIDSORT SPEC	The rgSortSpecs member is valid and should be used.

- **WCHAR szDbaseName**. Specifies a null-terminated string that contains the name of the database. The string can have up to 32 characters, including the terminating NULL character.

- **DWORD dwDbaseType**. Specifies a type identifier for the database.

- **WORD wNumRecords**. Specifies the number of records in the database.

- **WORD wNumSortOrder**. Specifies the number of sort orders active in the database. Up to four sort orders can be active at a time.

- **DWORD dwSize**. Size, in bytes, that the database is using.

- **FILETIME ftLastModified**. Last time this database was modified.

- **SORTORDERSPEC rgSortSpecs**. Specifies the number of actual sort order descriptions. Only the first *n* array members are valid, where *n* is the value specified by the wNumSortOrder member.

Setting Database Information

Certain database information can be changed for an existing database. An application can change the database name, database type, and sort order descriptions for any database. The `PegSetDatabaseInfo` function is used to change database information. The following table lists `PegSetDatabaseInfo` parameters.

PegSetDatabaseInfo Parameter	Description
PEGOID oidDbase	Specifies the object identifier of the database for which parameters are to be set.
PEGDBASEINFO * pNewInfo	Points to a PEGDBASEINFO structure that contains new parameter information for the database. The wNumRecords member of the structure is not used.

An application specifies the database information to be changed by setting the appropriate fields in the PEGDBASEINFO structure. The PEGDBASEINFO structure is described in the "Retrieving Object Information" section of this chapter.

The return value from `PegSetDatabaseInfo` is TRUE if the function succeeds and FALSE otherwise. The `GetLastError` function can return the extended error codes listed in the following table.

Error Code	Description
ERROR_INVALID_ PARAMETER	A parameter was invalid.
ERROR_DISK_FULL	The object store is full, and any size changes required could not be accommodated. Changing sort orders can change the size of the stored records, though not by much.
ERROR_SHARING_ VIOLATION	The function tried to remove a sort order that is being used by a currently open database.

Handling Database Notification Messages

With no access control on the Windows CE database, multiple applications can have the database open at the same time. The Windows CE operating system does ensure the integrity of the database, in the event, for example, that one application is updating a record and another application is attempting to delete the record. The operating system also provides the capability for an application to know when a database that it has open has been changed by another application.

When an application opens a database with the `PegOpenDatabase` function, it can supply a window handle to receive notifications when another application makes changes to that database. Windows CE has added several new messages that are sent to the window to identify the type of change that has taken place in the database.

The window receives the DB_PEGOID_CREATED message, for example, when another application adds a new record to the open database. Table 10.3 lists the database notifications in Windows CE along with the wParam and lParam values for each message.

Table 10.3

Database Notifications

Notification Message	Description	WPARAM	LPARAM
DB_PEGOID_ CHANGED	Another thread modified an object in the object store	PEGOID: identifier of the modified object	PEGOID: identifier of the parent object
DB_PEGOID_ CREATED	Another thread created an object identifier in the object store	PEGOID: created object	PEGOID: identifier of the of the parent object
DB_PEGOID_ RECORD _DELETED	Another thread deleted a record	PEGOID: identifier of the deleted object	PEGOID: identifier of the parent object

Contacts Database

One of the standard applications included with Windows CE is the Contacts application. This application tracks such information as names, addresses, and phone numbers. The Contacts application stores all of the contact data in a Windows CE database—the Contacts database.

By storing data in a Windows CE database, the Contacts application makes its information available to other applications. If an application permits the user to enter a name, the application could then search the Contacts database for other relevant information about that name.

An application could use the standard database API functions, such as `PegOpenDatabase`, `PegReadRecordProps`, and so on, to retrieve information from the Contacts database. However, Windows CE also includes a special set of functions and structures that an application can use to query and manipulate the contents of the Contacts database. The Contact database API functions are listed in the Table 10.4.

Table 10.4

Contact APIs

Function	Description
AddAddressCard	Adds an address card to the Contacts database
CloseAddressBook	Closes the Contacts database
CreateAddressBook	Creates the Contacts database
DeleteAddressCard	Removes an address card from the Contacts database
FreeAddressCard	Frees memory allocated for an address card
GetAddressCardIndex	Retrieves the position index of an address card
GetAddressCardOid	Retrieves the object identifier of an address card
GetAddressCardProperties	Retrieves the properties of an address card
GetColumnProperties	Retrieves the property tags of columns that can be used to sort the Contacts database
GetMatchingEntry	Searches the name property of all address cards in the Contacts database for a name matching a specified string
GetNumberOfAddressCards	Returns the number of address cards in the Contacts database

continues

Table 10.4

Contact APIs, continued

Function	Description
GetPropertyDataStruct	Retrieves information about a property in the Contacts database
GetSortOrder	Retrieves the order in which the Contacts database is currently sorted
ModifyAddressCard	Modifies an address card in the Contacts database
OpenAddressBook	Opens the Contacts database
OpenAddressCard	Opens an address card and retrieves its properties
RecountCards	Recounts the number of address cards in the Contacts database
SetColumnProperties	Specifies the columns that can be used to sort the Contacts database
SetMask	Specifies which properties are present in an address card
SetSortOrder	Sets the sort order of the Contacts database

Address Cards

As with any Windows CE database, the Contacts database is comprised of a set of records. For the purposes of the Contacts database API functions, records in the Contacts database are referred to as *address cards*. Each address card contains a set of properties that define information about that particular entry.

All address cards contain the same set of predefined properties. The properties include addresses, phone numbers, and birthdays. Each address card property has an associated identifier called a *property tag*. The property tag requests specific address card information and identifies the information that is returned. The following list assembles the Contacts database property tag identifiers:

HHPR_ANNIVERSARY

HHPR_ASSISTANT_NAME

HHPR_ASSISTANT_TELEPHONE_NUMBER

HHPR_BIRTHDAY

HHPR_BUSINESS_FAX_NUMBER

HHPR_CAR_TELEPHONE_NUMBER

HHPR_CATEGORY

HHPR_CHILDREN_NAME

HHPR_COMPANY_NAME

HHPR_DEPARTMENT_NAME

HHPR_EMAIL1_EMAIL_ADDRESS

HHPR_EMAIL2_EMAIL_ADDRESS

HHPR_EMAIL3_EMAIL_ADDRESS

HHPR_GENERATION

HHPR_GIVEN_NAME

HHPR_HOME2_TELEPHONE_NUMBER

HHPR_HOME_ADDRESS_CITY

HHPR_HOME_ADDRESS_COUNTRY

HHPR_HOME_ADDRESS_POSTAL_CODE

HHPR_HOME_ADDRESS_STATE

HHPR_HOME_ADDRESS_STREET

HHPR_HOME_FAX_NUMBER

continues

HHPR_HOME_TELEPHONE_NUMBER

HHPR_MIDDLE_NAME

HHPR_MOBILE_TELEPHONE_NUMBER

HHPR_NAME_PREFIX

HHPR_NOTES

HHPR_OFFICE_ADDRESS_CITY

HHPR_OFFICE_ADDRESS_COUNTRY

HHPR_OFFICE_ADDRESS_POSTAL_CODE

HHPR_OFFICE_ADDRESS_STATE

HHPR_OFFICE_ADDRESS_STREET

HHPR_OFFICE_LOCATION

HHPR_OFFICE_TELEPHONE_NUMBER

HHPR_OFFICE2_TELEPHONE_NUMBER

HHPR_OTHER_ADDRESS_CITY

HHPR_OTHER_ADDRESS_COUNTRY

HHPR_OTHER_ADDRESS_POSTAL_CODE

HHPR_OTHER_ADDRESS_STATE

HHPR_OTHER_ADDRESS_STREET

HHPR_PAGER_NUMBER

HHPR_SPOUSE_NAME

HHPR_SURNAME

HHPR_TITLE

HHPR_WEB_PAGE

HHPR_LAST_FIRST_NAME

HHPR_FIRST_LAST_NAME

HHPR_HOME_ADDRESS

HHPR_OTHER_ADDRESS

HHPR_OFFICE_ADDRESS

HHPR_EMAIL_TYPE

HHPR_EMAIL_OR_PAGER_TYPE

Opening the Contacts Database

Before accessing information in the Contacts database, an application must first open the database. The OpenAddressBook function is used to open the Contacts database. As when opening other Windows CE databases, the OpenAddressBook function allows the application to specify a sort order and a window handle to receive notifications about changes made to the Contacts database.

Because the Contacts database is not created until the Contacts application is used, it is quite possible that the call to OpenAddressBook will fail. If the Contacts database does not yet exist and the application wants to add data to it, any application can create the Contacts database with the CreateAddressBook function. When creating the Contacts database, up to four sort orders can be specified. If an application does not specify sort order in the CreateAddressBook function, the system assigns the default sort order of HHPR_SURNAME, HHPR_COMPANY_NAME, HHPR_OFFICE_TELEPHONE_NUMBER, HHPR_HOME_TELEPHONE_NUMBER.

When an application is finished using the Contacts database, it must call the CloseAddressBook function.

Accessing Address Cards

In order to access the properties for an address card, it is necessary to have the object identifier of the desired address card. Each address card has a unique object identifier, which is assigned by the system when the address card is created. In addition to the object identifier, each address card has a position index. The position indices of the address cards are based on the current sort order of the database. The functions GetAddressCardOid and GetAddressCardIndex can be used to get the object identifier or the position index if an application has one of those values.

An application can search for an address card with the GetMatchingEntry function. This function searches for a given value in any one of the address card properties regardless of the current sort order for the database.

After an application obtains the object identifier for the desired address card, it can use the OpenAddressCard or GetAddressCardProperties function to retrieve the current properties for the address card. Both functions fill an AddressCard structure with the requested card's properties. Using the OpenAddressCard function retrieves all the properties for the address card, while using the GetAddressCardProperties retrieves only a specified set of properties. If only a few properties from the address card are needed, calling GetAddressCardProperties uses less memory than OpenAddressCard.

The AddressCard structure contains the values for the properties of the address card. The structure is defined as follows:

```
typedef struct _AddressCard {
        // System time members
        SYSTEMTIME stBirthday;
        SYSTEMTIME stAnniversary;

        // Business view fields
        TCHAR *pszBusinessFax;
        TCHAR *pszCompany;
        TCHAR *pszDepartment;
        TCHAR *pszEmail;
        TCHAR *pszMobilePhone;
```

```
TCHAR *pszOfficeLocation;
TCHAR *pszPager;
TCHAR *pszWorkPhone;
TCHAR *pszTitle;

// Personal view fields
TCHAR *pszHomePhone;
TCHAR *pszEmail2;
TCHAR *pszSpouse;

// Notes view fields
TCHAR *pszNotes;

// Other fields the user can select
TCHAR *pszEmail3;
TCHAR *pszHomePhone2;
TCHAR *pszHomeFax;
TCHAR *pszCarPhone;
TCHAR *pszAssistant;
TCHAR *pszAssistantPhone;
TCHAR *pszChildren;
TCHAR *pszCategory;
TCHAR *pszWebPage;
TCHAR *pszWorkPhone2;

// Name fields
TCHAR *pszNamePrefix;
TCHAR *pszGivenName;
TCHAR *pszMiddleName;
TCHAR *pszSurname;
TCHAR *pszGeneration;

// Address Fields
TCHAR *pszHomeAddrStreet;
TCHAR *pszHomeAddrCity;
TCHAR *pszHomeAddrState;
TCHAR *pszHomeAddrPostalCode;
TCHAR *pszHomeAddrCountry;

TCHAR *pszOtherAddrStreet;
TCHAR *pszOtherAddrCity;
```

```
        TCHAR *pszOtherAddrState;
        TCHAR *pszOtherAddrPostalCode;
        TCHAR *pszOtherAddrCountry;

        TCHAR *pszOfficeAddrStreet;
        TCHAR *pszOfficeAddrCity;
        TCHAR *pszOfficeAddrState;
        TCHAR *pszOfficeAddrPostalCode;
        TCHAR *pszOfficeAddrCountry;

        BYTE *rgbReserved[84]
} AddressCard;
```

When an application is finished using the data in the AddressCard structure, it must call the FreeAddressCard function to free the memory allocated in the system for the address card data. For every call to OpenAddressCard and GetAddressCardProperties, there must be a corresponding call to FreeAddressCard.

Adding or Modifying Address Cards

Address card data is added or modified with the same AddressCard structure used to retrieve data from an address card. To create a new address card, an application fills an AddressCard structure with the values for the card's properties. The application then calls the SetMask function for each of the properties that have valid data set in the AddressCard structure. Finally, the application calls the AddAddressCard function to create the new address card.

Modifying an existing address card uses a similar procedure. The application starts by filling an AddressCard structure with the current properties by using the GetAddressCardProperties or OpenAddressCard functions. It then modifies the desired properties and calls SetMask for each one. Finally, the application calls ModifyAddressCard to commit the address card changes to the database.

To completely remove an address card from the Contacts database, an application can use the DeleteAddressCard function.

TravelManager Database Use

A Windows CE database (or databases) is a likely location for most of the data that is displayed in the TravelManager application. The hard-coded data used in the previous chapters can now be retrieved from the TravelManager's database. The complete TravelManager's database is created in Chapter 14, "Remote API Functions."

Because each use of Windows CE database functionality in the TravelManager application would be very similar, only one use has been added for this chapter. The airline flights on the Air tab of the ItineraryView now are read from the TravelManager's database.

First, the ItineraryView::Create method was changed to remove the code that defined dummy data and then inserted it into the list view. The Create method now calls a new method, ItineraryView::ReadFromDatabase, to read airline flights from the database and insert them into the list view.

The ReadFromDatabase method first attempts to open the Windows CE database and proceeds only if it is successful. It then begins reading the set of seven properties that make up each record in the database, decoding each property, and then adding the information to the list view. The source code for the ReadFromDatabase method is listed as follows:

```
BOOL ItineraryView::ReadFromDatabase(HWND hwndLV)
{
  HANDLE      hDB;
  SYSTEMTIME  SystemTime;
  PEGOID           pegOid;
  PEGPROPID   pegpropid;
  TCHAR       szBuf[100];
  PEGOID           PegRecObj;
  PEGOID           PegOID = 0;
  DWORD       cbRecProps = 0;
  LPBYTE           lpRecProps = NULL;
  WORD        wNumRecProps = 0;
  WORD        i, row;
```

```
PPEGPROPVAL pPegPropVal;
LV_ITEM lvi;
lvi.mask = LVIF_TEXT;
lvi.iSubItem = 0;

// Find database to open by name
pegOid = 0;

// Use the date field for sort order
pegpropid = MAKELONG( PEGVT_FILETIME, 0);

hDB = PegOpenDatabase(&pegOid, TEXT("TravelManager Database"),
                      pegpropid, PEGDB_AUTOINCREMENT, NULL);
if ( hDB == INVALID_HANDLE_VALUE)
{
  // Could get extended error info with PegGetLastError
  return FALSE;
}

row = 0;
while ( (PegRecObj = PegReadRecordProps(hDB, PEGDB_ALLOWREALLOC,
             &wNumRecProps, NULL, &lpRecProps, &cbRecProps)) != 0)
{
  if ( lpRecProps )
  {
    if ( wNumRecProps )
    {
      pPegPropVal = (PPEGPROPVAL)lpRecProps;

      // add each property to the table
      for ( i= 0 ; i < wNumRecProps; i++)
      {
        switch (HIWORD(pPegPropVal[i].propid))
        {
          case 0:
            FileTimeToSystemTime(&(pPegPropVal[i].val.filetime),
&SystemTime);
            wsprintf(szBuf, TEXT("%d/%d"), SystemTime.wMonth,
SystemTime.wDay);
            lvi.iItem = row;
            lvi.pszText = szBuf;
```

```
            lvi.cchTextMax = 6;
            ListView_InsertItem(hwndLV, &lvi);
            break;
        case 1:
            wsprintf(szBuf, TEXT("%d"), pPegPropVal[i].val.uiVal);
            ListView_SetItemText(hwndLV, row, 1, szBuf);
            break;
        case 2:
            ListView_SetItemText(hwndLV, row, 2,
pPegPropVal[i].val.lpwstr);
            break;
        case 3:
            ListView_SetItemText(hwndLV, row, 3,
pPegPropVal[i].val.lpwstr);
            break;
        case 4:
            FileTimeToSystemTime(&(pPegPropVal[i].val.filetime),
&SystemTime);
            wsprintf(szBuf, TEXT("%d/%d"), SystemTime.wMonth,
SystemTime.wDay);
            ListView_SetItemText(hwndLV, row, 4, szBuf);
            break;
        case 5:
            FileTimeToSystemTime(&(pPegPropVal[i].val.filetime),
&SystemTime);
            wsprintf(szBuf, TEXT("%d/%d"), SystemTime.wMonth,
SystemTime.wDay);
            ListView_SetItemText(hwndLV, row, 5, szBuf);
            break;
        case 6:
            ListView_SetItemText(hwndLV, row, 6,
pPegPropVal[i].val.lpwstr);
            break;
      }
    }
  }
  LocalFree(lpRecProps);
}

// increase row and reset other parameters
row++;
cbRecProps = 0;
```

```
        lpRecProps = NULL;
        wNumRecProps = 0;
    }

    CloseHandle(hDB);

    return TRUE;
}
```

TravelManager Application—Windows CE Databases

In the interest of space, the entire TravelManager application is not re-listed here. However, you can find the full TravelManager application on the accompanying CD-ROM. See Appendix A, "Getting Started with the CD-ROM," for information on accessing the files on the accompanying CD-ROM.

11

Windows CE Help Files

Since the earliest versions, Windows has provided a standard mechanism for applications to add online help. Before Windows CE, the Windows help system was based on the WinHelp engine that was part of every Windows version. The early versions of WinHelp supported little more than an organized method of displaying simple text. By the Windows 95 version, however, WinHelp added support for full-text searching, graphics, and multimedia objects.

The extreme space limitations on Windows CE devices make the Windows WinHelp mechanism impractical. However, Windows CE does include its own help engine called *Pocket Help*. Instead of extending the method of building help files based on the WinHelp hypertext syntax to support Windows CE, Pocket Help files are authored in HyperText Markup Language (HTML). With the popularity of the Internet, HTML has become the standard display engine for presenting structurally hyperlinked data.

The Pocket Help engine does not support all the functionality of the previous WinHelp engine. Furthermore, Pocket Help does not support all the newest features in HTML. It does support, however, basic formatting, jumps, bitmaps, and table features. These should provide an application with enough functionality to develop an effective online help system while at the same time not using an abundance of memory resources.

With Windows 95, applications have routinely expanded their online help to include as much or even more information than any accompanying printed documentation. However, given the space considerations with Windows CE devices, providing endless online help is not realistic. Instead, the Windows CE Pocket Help file for your application probably should include only information on common tasks and key commands. More detailed information then can be included in another form of documentation.

Accessing Windows CE Pocket Help

Windows CE provides a variety of access methods to admit the user into the Windows CE help system. Users can access Pocket Help through the following methods:

- By selecting the Help command on the Start menu

- By pressing the Alt+H shortcut key

- By tapping the question mark button on a window (or a dialog box)

When the help system is accessed through the Start menu, the help file displayed is the standard system help file. The system help file provides tips for using Windows CE, information on changing system settings, and general troubleshooting advice. Figure 11.1 shows the Windows CE Pocket Help system displaying the system help file.

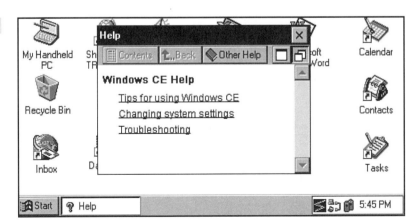

Figure 11.1

Windows CE Pocket Help.

When the help system is accessed through an application—either by tapping the question mark button in the command bar or by using the Alt+H shortcut key—the help file displayed is specified by the application.

A feature unique to the Windows CE help system is its ability to access other help files from any help topic. The Pocket Help display window provides an Other Help button that presents a list of all the help content files that exist in the Windows folder. Selecting a help file from the list opens that Pocket Help file. Figure 11.2 shows the Windows CE Pocket Help system listing the available help files displayed after the user selects the Other Help button.

Figure 11.2

Results of selecting the Other Help button.

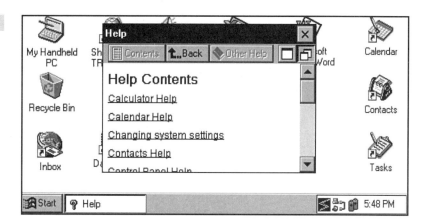

Navigating Pocket Help

Navigation through Windows CE Pocket Help files is very limited in order to keep it simple. Most navigation is handled through links, or jumps, within the help file. These links enable the help information to be structured in a meaningful way. For example, the Contents topic for the help file would be comprised of a set of links to the main topics of information in the help file. These links could lead to topics that display the information the user requested or topics that consist of other links.

In addition to links in the Pocket Help file, the help system provides some useful navigation mechanisms as well. These mechanisms are presented to the user through a set of navigation buttons at the top of the

Help window. The Contents button returns the display to the initial topic for the Pocket Help file. The Back button returns the display to the previous topic. The Other Help button displays a list of all Pocket Help files. The Standard View and Pop-Up View buttons size the Help window to a full-screen window or a floating pop-up window, respectively.

Pocket Help Components

Just as Windows WinHelp help files are built by combining multiple files of specific types, displaying help on Windows CE requires two different kinds of files.

The first type is the *contents file*, which has the extension .hpc. This file consists of the initial screen that provides links to other topics. The contents file should be placed in the Windows folder on the Windows CE device. The Windows folder is the only location searched when the user presses the Other Help button to see a list of other help files.

The second kind of file used with Pocket Help is the *topic file*, which has the .htp extension. The topic files typically contain the help information, although they also can contain links to other help topics. Each topic in Pocket Help is in a separate topic file, but these topic files need not be placed in the Windows folder. However, if the topic files are placed in a different folder, any location in which the files are referenced must contain a full path to the file.

Although they are not specific to Pocket Help, Windows CE *bitmap files* (.2bp) also can be part of the Pocket Help for an application. As with the topic files, the bitmap files are not required to be located in the Windows folder. Likewise, these files would require full paths if placed in another folder.

Both the contents file and topic file are authored using HTML, and Pocket Help supports a subset of the full list of HTML tags. A complete list of supported tags is provided in the Pocket Help HTML Tags section, which appears later in this chapter.

The Contents File

The contents file contains the list of topics for an application's help system. In other words, this file serves as the table of contents for the help file. Each of the items in the Contents list provides a link to a specified topic.

The contents file also is used to identify all help files on the Windows CE device. When the user chooses the Other Help button on the Help window, Pocket Help searches the Windows folder for all contents files (or files with the .htc extension). Pocket Help then displays a list of these files.

Based on a subset of HTML, the contents file is structured to have a head section and a body section. Each contents file must start with the <html> tag and end with the </html> tag.

The head section starts with the <head> tag and ends with the </head> tag. The head section should contain a <meta> tag that references the name of the contents file associated with this file. Unless help files are being nested, the value of this <meta> tag is usually blank.

The body section is defined by the <body> and </body> tags. This section typically contains a heading, which is marked with the <h1..6> tag. Following the body heading is the list of topics for the Pocket help file that is marked with the <menu> and </menu> tags. Each of the topics in the list is marked with the <li> tag and contains both the text to display and the associated file for the link.

The following example shows the HTML source for the standard Windows CE calculator's contents file:

```
<html>
<head>
<meta http-equiv=refer content="">
</head>
<body>
<h5>Calculator Help</h5>
<menu>

<li><a href="file:cc_basic.htp">Tips for using Calculator</a>
```

```
<li><a href="file:cc_paper.htp">Using the paper tape</a>

<li><a href="file:cc_pop.htp">Working in Pop-Up view</a>

</menu>
</body>
</html>
```

Figure 11.3 shows the Help window displayed when the Calculator help file is opened.

Figure 11.3

The Calculator contents file is displayed when the Calculator Help file is opened.

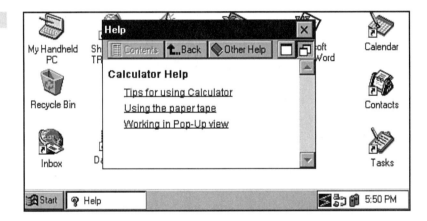

The Topic File

The topic file contains the information for a specific topic. This file can contain text, a bitmap, or a link to another topic file.

The format of the topic file is similar to the contents file. Each file is delimited by the <html> and </html> tags and contains a head section and a body section.

In the topic file, the <meta> tag in the head section refers to the contents file associated with this topic file. This entry is used to identify the contents file displayed when the user presses the Contents button on the Help window to extract a topic file.

The body section of a topic file displays the information relevant to the given topic. Generally, this includes paragraphs of text describing the help information.

In addition to plain text, the topic file also can include bitmap images and links to other contents or topic help files. The <IMG SRC> tag is used to include a bitmap in a Pocket Help file. The <a href> tag is used to specify a link and includes the file to link to and the text displayed for the link.

The following example illustrates the HTML source for the standard Windows CE calculator's Tips For Using Calculator topic file:

```
<html>
<head>
<meta http-equiv=refer content="file:Calculator Help.htc">
</head>
<body>
<h6>Tips for using Calculator</h6>

You can use Calculator in two different views: Standard view and
➥PopUp view.
<ul>

<li>In Standard view, Calculator uses on-screen buttons similar to
➥the Windows 95 Calculator and displays a <a
➥href="file:cc_paper.htp">paper tape</a> that retains the last 100
lines of calculations.

<li>In <a href="file:cc_pop.htp">Pop-Up view</a>, Calculator shows
➥only the entry box. To operate the Calculator from this view, use
the keyboard.
</ul>
<p>
</body>
</html>
```

Figure 11.4 shows the Help window displayed when the Calculator help file is opened and the Full Screen Mode button is selected.

Figure 11.4

Tips For Using
Calculator is
displayed in full-
screen mode.

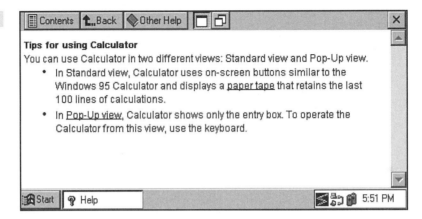

Displaying Pocket Help Programmatically

Although the user easily can display any Pocket Help file at any time by using the Other Help button, it is also useful for an application to be able to display help directly. The most important use of this is to enable an application to respond to the question mark help button or the Alt+H shortcut key.

When the user taps the question mark button or presses the Alt+H shortcut key, the system sends a WM_HELP message to the windows procedure or dialog procedure. It is the application's responsibility to respond appropriately to the WM_HELP message. Typically, the proper response involves invoking the Windows CE Pocket Help system with a topic or contents file that provides information on the current window or dialog box.

An application invokes the Windows CE Pocket Help system by running the PegHelp Windows CE application. (Although Windows 95 has an API function (WinHelp) that launches the WinHelp application, the Windows CE API does not contain such a function.) The CreateProcess function is used to start another application. The application to be started is PegHelp, and the command-line parameter is the name of the topic or contents file to be displayed. Consider the following examples, for instance:

```
CreateProcess(L"PegHelp", L"Calculator Help.htc",'...);
```

Or

```
CreateProcess(L"PegHelp", L"cc_basic.htp",'...);
```

Pocket Help HTML Tags

The format for Windows CE Pocket Help files is based on a subset of HTML syntax. The Pocket Help display engine supports most of the basic formatting tags from HTML, as well as tables and images. Pocket Help, however, does not support newer HTML features, such as frames. Table 11.1 lists the supported HTML tags in Pocket Help and offers a brief description of each tag.

Table 11.1

HTML Tags Supported in Pocket Help

HTML Tag	Description
<!--COMMENTS-->	Comment
<A>	Hypertext link
<ADDRESS>	Address (usually e-mail addresses)
<B>	Bold
<BASEFONT>	Base font
<BGSOUND>	Background sound
<BIG>	Big text
<BLINK>	Blink text
<BLOCKQUOTE>	Define quote
<BODY>	Document body
 	Line break
<CAPTION>	Table caption
<CENTER>	Center text
<CITE>	Citation
<CODE>	Source code

continues

Table 11.1

	HTML Tags Supported in Pocket Help, continued
HTML Tag	Description
<DD>	Definition description
<DFN>	Definition
<DIR>	Directory list
<DIV>	Division
<DL>	Definition list
<DT>	Definition term
<EM>	Emphasis
<FONT>	Font
<Hn>	Heading
<HEAD>	Document head
<HR>	Horizontal rule
<HTML>	HTML document
<I>	Italic text
<IMG>	Inline image
<KBD>	Keyboard
<LI>	List item
<LISTING>	Computer listing
<MENU>	Menu list
<META>	Meta
<NOBR>	No break
<OL>	Ordered list
<P>	Paragraph
<PLAINTEXT>	Plain text
<PRE>	Preformatted text
<S>	Strikethrough text

HTML Tag	Description
<SAMP>	Sample output
<SMALL>	Small text
<STRIKE>	Strikethrough text
<STRONG>	Strong emphasis
<SUB>	Subscript
<SUP>	Superscript
<TABLE>	Table
<TD>	Table data
<TH>	Table heading
<TITLE>	Document title
<TR>	Table row
<TT>	Teletype text
<U>	Underlined text
<UL>	Unordered list
<VAR>	Variable
<WBR>	Word break
<XMP>	Example

The following sections provide details on the HTML tags that are valid in Pocket Help files. The discussion of each tag includes a description of the tag, the attributes that the tag can accept, and a small example of using the tag.

<!--COMMENTS-->

This tag is used to add comments to the HTML document that will be ignored by the Pocket Help display engine. The text for the comments must be surrounded by the <!-- and the --> tags and cannot be nested, as shown in the following example:

```
<!-- this is a comment -->
```

<A>

The <A> tag designates an anchor element, which is a marked text that indicates the start and/or destination of a hypertext link. The following list details the attributes of this tag:

- **HREF**. Creates a hot-spot object that contains the HREF text from the anchor tag.

- **NAME**. Creates a markup header with the value of the name property as the text.

The following is an example of the <A> tag:

```
<P>Click on <A HREF="HTTP://www.microsoft.com>Microsoft</A> to go to
Microsoft web site.
```

<ADDRESS>

This tag displays text as italic, with a paragraph break before and after the text.

```
<ADDRESS>For more information, contact us at name@company.com
➥< ADDRESS>
```

<B>

This tag displays the text as bold.

```
This is <B>Bold</B> text.
```

<BASEFONT>

This tag defines the size of the font for the entire document, from the <BASEFONT> tag to the end.

The Size attribute sets the font size for which all sizes are based. This attribute has a valid range of 1–7.

The following is an example of the <BASEFONT> tag:

```
<BASEFONT SIZE=6>This would be size 6 text.
```

<BGSOUND>

This tag instructs the application to play a background sound. Its attributes include the following:

- **SRC**. Specifies URL of the sound.
- **LOOP**. Loops the sound played.

The following is an example of the <BGSOUND> tag:

```
<BGSOUND SRC="tada.wav">
```

<BIG>

The <BIG> tag displays text in a larger font than the base font.

```
This is <BIG>Big</BIG> text.
```

<BLINK>

This tag turns the display of a block of text on and off.

```
<BLINK>This text would be blinking</BLINK>
```

<BLOCKQUOTE>

This tag formats a quotation.

```
<P>Then he said:
<BLOCKQUOTE>Windows CE is cool.</BLOCKQUOTE>
```

\<BODY>

The \<BODY> tag indicates the start and end of the body, or the contents of the document immediately after the head.

See the contents and topic file examples at the beginning of this chapter for more information.

\

This tag starts a new line of text.

```
<P>Once upon a midnight dreary<BR>While I pondered weak and
➥weary<BR>Over many volumes of forgotten lore<BR>
```

\<CAPTION>

This tag adds a caption above or below a table. The \<CAPTION> tag should be used inside the \<TABLE> tag.

The ALIGN : top or bottom attribute enables the user to indicate placement of captions above or below a table.

```
<TABLE BORDER>
<CAPTION> Coordinates</CAPTION>
<TR><TH>X-Coordinate</TH><TH>Y-Coordinate</TH></TR>
<TR><TD>14</TD><TD>42</TD></TR>
</TABLE>
```

\<CENTER>

The \<CENTER> tag centers a line of text between the left margin and the right margin.

```
<CENTER>This line is centered.</CENTER>
```

<CITE>

This tag indicates a citation, such as a book or the name of an expert, by emphasizing it, usually with italics

```
This code is from <CITE>Windows CE Programming</CITE>
```

<CODE>

This tag applies a computer code font (monospace) to the specified text.

```
This is <CODE>computer code</CODE> text.
```

<DD>

This tag identifies a description in a definition list and is used in conjunction with the <DL> and <DT> tags. See the section on the <DL> tag for an example of this tag.

<DFN>

This tag identifies a definition term using emphasized text (italic).

```
The <DFN>DFN</DFN> tag identifies a defined term.
```

<DIR>

The <DIR> tag displays a short word list.

```
<DIR>
<LI>One
<LI>Two
<LI>Three
```

<DIV>

The <DIV> tag marks the beginning of a new division or section in a document.

The attribute for the <DIV> tag is ALIGN : left, right, or center.

For an example of this tag, refer to the section on the <P> tag.

<DL>

This tag defines a glossary or definition list that is an automatically format-ted two-column list with the terms on the left and their definitions on the right. See also the sections on <DT> and <DD> for related information.

```
<DL>
<DT>HTML<DD>The Hypertext Mark-Up Language.
<DT>HTTP<DD>The Hypertext Transport Protocol.
</DL>
```

<DT>

This tag names a term in a definition list.

For an example of this tag, see the section on the <DL> tag.

<EM>

The <EM> tag emphasizes the specified text, usually with italic.

```
This is text with some <EM>Emphasis</EM>
```

<FONT>

This tag changes the size or typeface of the selected font.

The <FONT> tag contains these attributes:

- **SIZE**. The size of the current font can range from one to seven. A +N or -N is relative to the BASEFONT, while N provides an absolute setting of the current font. (Note that a FONT SIZE=-n, always will be relative to BASEFONT, while operations such as <SUB>, <SMALL>, and <BIG> will modify the current font size value.)

- **FACE**. This attribute sets the face or type of text, such as <FONT FACE=Arial>. A list of font names can be specified, and if the first font is available on the system, it will be used. Otherwise, the second will be tried, and so on. If none are available, a default font will be used. The default font on the Pegasus is Arial.

The following is an example of the <FONT> tag:

```
<FONT FACE="Courier" SIZE=4>This text is in courier font.
```

<Hn>

This tag applies one of six heading characteristics to the specified text. The heading styles are defined as follows:

<H1> = Bold, Size = 6, flush left

<H2> = Bold, Size = 5, flush left

<H3> = Bold, Size = 4, flush left

<H4> = Bold, Size = 3, flush left

<H5> = Bold, Size = 2, flush left

<H6> = Plain, Size = 2, flush left

The <Hn> tag contains the ALIGN : center, right, or left attribute.

The following is an example of the <Hn> tag:

```
<H1>This is the Heading 1 style</H1>
```

<HEAD>

This tag begins (and ends) a part of the HTML document that refers to the document's usage context. The <TITLE> and <META> tags generally are enclosed in the <HEAD> tag.

```
<html>
<head>
<meta http-equiv=refer content="file:Calculator Help.htc">
</head>
```

<HR>

The <HR> tag inserts a horizontal rule line between the sections of a document. This tag contains the following attributes:

- **SIZE**. Indicates the height of the rule in pixels.

- **WIDTH**. Indicates the width of the rule in pixels, or percentage of the currently available page width. This can be reduced by images down the right and left sides of the page.

- **ALIGN**. Specifies left, right, or center positions.

- **NOSHADE**. Indicates that the rule should be drawn as a solid bar, not in 3-D.

The following is an example of the <HR> tag:

```
<HR WIDTH=400 ALIGN=LEFT>
```

<HTML>

This tag defines an HTML document.

For an example of this tag, see the examples on the contents and topic files at the beginning of this chapter.

<I>

The <I> tag applies italics to the specified text.

```
This is <I>italicized</I> text.
```

<IMG>

This tag inserts an inline image in the document. The <IMG> tag contains the following attributes:

- **SRC**. Specifies the URL of the image.

- **ALIGN**. Specifies whether the text that is inline with this image is located at the top, middle, or bottom of the page.

- **ALT**. Specifies an alternate name for the image.

- **ISMAP**. Specifies that the picture is a map that must be sent back to the server for processing. Image maps are graphics in which certain regions are mapped to URLs. By clicking different regions, different resources can be accessed from the same graphic.

- **VSPACE**. Sets the vertical space above and below the image in pixels.

- **HSPACE**. Sets the horizontal space to the left and right if an image is in pixels.

- **WIDTH**. Specifies the width (in pixels) of the graphic image.

- **HEIGHT**. Specifies the height (in pixels) of the graphic image.

- **BORDER**. Indicates the width of the border surrounding the graphic image.

The following is an example of the <IMG> tag:

```
<IMG SRC="picture.gif" ALIGN=top>
```

<KBD>

The <KBD> tag applies a keyboard input font (monospace) to the specified text.

```
This is <KBD>keyboard input</KBD> text.
```

<LI>

The <LI> tag lists items with an ordered <OL>, unordered <UL>, menu <MENU>, or directory <DIR> list. This tag contains the following attributes:

- **TYPE**. Indicates that a number or bullet style will be set in an ordered or unordered list, respectively.

- **VALUE**. Specifies a numeric starting value in an ordered list.

The following is an example of the <LI> tag:

```
<OL>
<LI>First
<LI>Second
<LI>Third
</OL>
```

<LISTING>

This tag applies a computer listing font (monospace) to the specified text.

```
<LISTING>This is text in the listing style</LISTING>
```

<MENU>

This tag displays a menu list of items and is used in the Contents page of a Pocket Help file.

```
<menu>
```

```
<li><a href="file:cc_basic.htp">Tips for using Calculator</a>
<li><a href="file:cc_paper.htp">Using the paper tape</a>
<li><a href="file:cc_pop.htp">Working in Pop-Up view</a>
</menu>
```

\<META\>

The \<META\> tag provides information about the current document and is used in Pocket Help topic files to specify the contents file for this help topic.

This tag contains the attribute HTTP-EQUIV, which specifies the referring contents file.

The following is an example of the \<META\> tag:

```
<meta http-equiv=refer content="file:Calculator Help.htc">
```

\<NOBR\>

The \<NOBR\> tag turns off the automatic word wrap and line breaks.

```
<NOBR>Word wrap and line breaks are turned off</NOBR>
```

\<OL\>

The \<OL\> tag starts an ordered (numbered) list. This tag contains the following attributes:

- **START**. Indicates a numeric starting value.

- **TYPE**. Indicates A (uppercase letters), a (lowercase letters), I (uppercase Roman numerals), i (lowercase Roman numerals), 1 (Arabic numbers).

The following is an example of the <OL> tag:

```
<OL>
<LI>Choice 1
<LI>Choice 2
<LI>Choice 3
</OL>
```

<P>

The <P> tag indicates the start of a new paragraph. It contains the ALIGN attribute, which specifies whether text should be positioned at center, left, or right.

```
<P>This starts a new paragraph.
```

<PLAINTEXT>

This tag applies a monospace font to the specified text.

```
<PLAINTEXT>This is plain text.</PLAINTEXT>
```

<PRE>

The <PRE> tag applies a monospace font to one or more lines of preformatted text and maintains the character and space formatting of the text. This tag contains the WIDTH attribute, which indicates the maximum line width.

The following is an example of the <PRE> tag:

```
<PRE>    This
        text
        is a
        column.</PRE>
```

<S>

The <S> tag is the same as the <STRIKE> tag. Refer to <STRIKE> in the following text for information.

<SAMP>

This tag applies a sample program output font (monospace) to the specified text.

```
This is <SAMP>sample output</SAMP> text.
```

<SMALL>

This tag displays text in a smaller font than the default starting font.

```
This is <SMALL>small</SMALL> text.
```

<STRIKE>

This tag strikes through the specified text.

```
This is <STRIKE>Strikeout</STRIKE>text.
```

<STRONG>

The <STRONG> tag is the same as the bold, <B> tag sequence. Refer to the <B> tag entry.

<SUB>

This tag moves the specified text below the base line on which the other text on the line sits. The <SUB> tag also applies a smaller font.

```
H<SUB>2</SUB>0
```

<SUP>

The <SUP> tag moves the specified text above the base line on which the other text on the line sits. This tag also applies a smaller font.

```
x<SUP>2</SUP> + y<SUP>2</SUP>
```

<TABLE>

This tag defines a table. It contains the following attributes:

- **BORDER.** Indicates whether the table has a border or not.

- **CELLSPACING=<value>.** Indicates the spacing, in pixels, between cells.

- **CELLPADDING=<value>.** Indicates the spacing, in pixels, between the contents of the cells and the cell borders.

- **WIDTH=<value_or_percent>.** Specifies the width, in pixels, or the percent of the entire width of the table.

The following is an example of the <TABLE> tag:

```
<TABLE BORDER>
<CAPTION> Coordinates</CAPTION>
<TR><TH>X-Coordinate</TH><TH>Y-Coordinate</TH></TR>
<TR><TD>14</TD><TD>42</TD></TR>
</TABLE>
```

<TD>

The <TD> tag defines the data in the table cell.

```
<TABLE BORDER>
<CAPTION> Coordinates</CAPTION>
<TR><TH>X-Coordinate</TH><TH>Y-Coordinate</TH></TR>
<TR><TD>14</TD><TD>42</TD></TR>
</TABLE>
```

<TH>

The <TH> tag defines a heading in a table cell and adds some emphasis (boldface).

```
<TABLE BORDER>
<CAPTION> Coordinates</CAPTION>
<TR><TH>X-Coordinate</TH><TH>Y-Coordinate</TH></TR>
<TR><TD>14</TD><TD>42</TD></TR>
</TABLE>
```

<TITLE>

This tag specifies a title for the document.

```
<TITLE>My Summer Vacation</TITLE>
```

<TR>

The <TR> tag defines a table row. This tag contains the following attributes:

- **ALIGN**. Specifies center, left, or right positioning.
- **VALIGN**. Specifies top, middle, or bottom positioning (the vertical alignment of the contents of the cells in the row).

The following is an example of the <TR> tag:

```
<TABLE BORDER>
<CAPTION> Coordinates</CAPTION>
<TR><TH>X-Coordinate</TH><TH>Y-Coordinate</TH></TR>
<TR><TD>14</TD><TD>42</TD></TR>
</TABLE>
```

<TT>

The <TT> tag applies a teletype font (monospace) to the specified text.

```
This is <TT>teletype</TT> text.
```

\<U\>

The \<U\> tag underlines the specified text.

```
This is <U>underlined</U> text.
```

\<UL\>

The \<UL\> tag starts an unordered (bulleted) list. This tag contains the following attributes:

- **TYPE**. Specifies the type of bullet to be used (disc, circle, or square).

- **COMPACT**. Suggests that the space between the bullet and the item be decreased.

The following is an example of the \<UL\> tag:

```
<UL>
<LI>Apple
<LI>Orange
<LI>Banana
</UL>
```

\<VAR\>

This tag indicates variable text by emphasizing it, usually with italic.

```
Use the <VAR>VAR</VAR> tag to highlight terms being introduced.
```

\<WBR\>

This tag inserts a line break within a no break \<NOBR\> line.

```
<NOBR>Some text<WBR>and some more text.</NOBR>
```

<XMP>

The <XMP> tag applies a monospace font to the specified text.

```
Here is an <XPM>example</XPM>
```

TravelManager Pocket Help Use

As an example of the structure of Windows CE help files, the Travel-Manager application includes a contents file and two topic files.

The contents file provides access to the topic files and contains examples of a menu list, heading styles, and a horizontal rule:

```
<html>
<head>
<meta http-equiv=refer content="">
</head>
<body>
<h5>TravelManager Help</h5>

<h6>Tap on a link below for more information on that topic:</h6>

<menu>

<li><a href="file:trvlmgr1.htp">Itinerary View</a>

<li><a href="file:trvlmgr2.htp">Expenses View</a>

</menu>

<HR WIDTH=400 ALIGN=LEFT>
The TravelManager application is a sample developed from
➡<CITE>Windows CE Programming</CITE>

</body>
</html>
```

The first topic file provides examples of using lists and tables:

```html
<html>
<head>
<meta http-equiv=refer content="file:trvlmgr.htc">
</head>
<body>
<h5>TravelManager's Itinerary View</h5>

The Itinerary View lists information for the current trip including:
<ul>

<li> Air: Information on airline and flight schedule

<li> Car: Information on automobile rental.

<li> Hotel: Information on hotel location and stay details.
</ul>

<HR WIDTH=400 ALIGN=LEFT>

<TABLE BORDER>
<CAPTION ALIGN=TOP> The following table describes the information
➥listed in the table on the Air tab of the Itinerary View.</CAPTION>
<TR>
<TH>Table Column</TH>
<TH>Description</TH>
</TR>
<TR>
<TD>Date</TD>
<TD>Date of flight</TD>
</TR>
<TR>
<TD>Flight</TD>
<TD>Flight number</TD>
</TR>
<TR>
<TD>From</TD>
<TD>Origination city</TD>
</TR>
<TR>
<TD>To</TD>
<TD>Destination city</TD>
```

```
</TR>
<TR>
<TD>Departs</TD>
<TD>Departure time</TD>
</TR>
<TR>
<TD>Arrives</TD>
<TD>Arrival time</TD>
</TR>
<TR>
<TD>Seat</TD>
<TD>Seat number</TD>
</TR>
</TABLE>
<p>
</body>
</html>
```

The other topic file provides an example of using a definition list:

```
<html>
<head>
<meta http-equiv=refer content="file:trvlmgr.htc">
</head>
<body>
<h5>TravelManager's Expenses View</h5>

The Expenses View lists provides functionality for tracking expenses:

<DL>
<DT>Expenses table<DD>Listing of all expenses that have been entered.
<DT>Today's Date<DD>The current date.
<DT>Add button<DD>Use to create a new expense entry.
<DT>Edit button<DD>Use to edit the selected expense entry.
<DT>Delete button<DD>use to remove the selected expense entry.
</DL>

<p>
</body>
</html>
```

CHAPTER 12

Windows CE Application Loader

A unique challenge in the development of Windows CE applications is the process of getting the application and associated files onto the Windows CE device. Fortunately, the Windows CE SDK provides functionality that can be used in conjunction with a setup program to install files onto the Windows CE device.

The installation process for a Windows CE application is unusual because the installation program actually is run from a desktop PC with a connection to the Handheld PC. After the setup program is finished installing files onto the desktop PC, it can use new functionality to copy components to the connected Windows CE machine.

The Windows CE SDK provides a dynamic-link library (DLL) called ppcload.dll that can be used by a setup program on the desktop PC to load a Windows CE application from a Windows-based personal computer to a Handheld personal computer. This DLL uses remote API function calls to communicate with the Windows CE device when installing an application's files.

In addition to simply copying files, the application-loading functionality with Windows CE enables an application to create directories, update the Windows CE registry, and create shortcuts. This functionality is driven by a simple script file that directs the operations to perform.

Application Loader Functions

The Windows CE application-loading functionality present in the ppcload.dll library is exposed through seven different functions, which are listed in Table 12.1.

Table 12.1

Application Loader Functions	
Load Function	Description
Load_AlreadyInstalled	Determines whether the application is already installed on the Handheld PC
Load_Exit	Terminates the application-loading process
Load_Init	Initializes the application-loading process
Load_PegCpuType	Determines the CPU type of the Handheld PC
Load_PegFreeSpace	Determines the amount of free memory in the Handheld PC's object store
Load_RegisterFileInfo	Registers file information with the Handheld PC Explorer
Load	Downloads applications to the Handheld PC and processes a supplied script file

Each of these application loader functions is detailed in the sections that follow.

Load_AlreadyInstalled

A setup application can use the Load_AlreadyInstalled function to determine if the specified application is already installed on the target Handheld PC. The syntax of the function is as follows:

```
BOOL bSuccess = Load_AlreadyInstalled( lpszAppName );
```

The lpszAppName in the preceding syntax is of type LPSTR and specifies the name of the application to look for on the Handheld PC.

The return value is a Boolean that indicates whether the application is already installed. A value of FALSE indicates that the specified application is not currently installed on the Handheld PC. A value of TRUE indicates that the application is currently installed, or that an error has occurred. A value of TRUE is returned for an error to prevent accidental overwriting of the application.

Load_Exit

Upon completion of the entire loading process, the setup application must call the Load_Exit function to end the loading process and stop the RPC service. The syntax of the function is as follows:

```
Load_Exit();
```

The Load_Exit function takes no parameters and has no return value.

Load_Init

The Load_Init function initiates the loading process and must be called before any other Load function. To communicate with the Handheld PC, the Load_Init function starts the Remote Procedure Call (RPC) service. The syntax of the function is as follows:

```
LOADERROR dwSuccess = Load_Init();
```

The Load_Init function takes no parameters and returns a LOADERROR. The return value can be either LOAD_SUCCESS or LOAD_FAILURE, which indicates whether the initialization has succeeded.

Load_PegCpuType

The Load_PegCpuType function can be used by the setup application to determine the CPU type of the target Handheld PC. This information might be necessary to decide which type of files to copy to the device. The syntax of the function is as follows:

```
char szCPUType[10];

BOOL bSuccess = Load_PegCpuType( &szCPUType );
```

The only parameter to the Load_PegCpuType function is a string buffer that is allocated and deallocated by the caller. If successful, the function places one of the following strings in the string buffer: either the SH3 string or the MIPS string.

The return value from Load_PegCpuType indicates whether the function is successful. A return value of TRUE indicates success, while FALSE indicates that an error occurred or that the CPU type of the device was unknown.

Note

For the Load_PegCpuType to be successful, the Handheld PC Explorer must have connected to the target device at least once prior to making the Load_PegCpuType function call.

Load_PegFreeSpace

The Load_PegFreeSpace function can be used to determine if enough free space exists on the target device for the installation to proceed. The syntax of the function is as follows:

```
DWORD dwFreeSpace = Load_PegFreeSpace();
```

The return value from the Load_PegFreeSpace function is the amount—in bytes—of memory remaining on the target Windows CE device.

Load_RegisterFileInfo

The Load_RegisterFileInfo function registers file information with Windows CE so that it can display the correct file type and icon associated with an application's files. The syntax of the function is as follows:

```
LOADERROR dwError = Load_RegisterFileInfo( szFileName, szIconFile,
➥szFileType, iIcon );
```

The parameters to the `Load_RegisterFileInfo` function are detailed in the following list:

- **LPSTR szFileName**. Application name with extension but without the path.

- **LPSTR szIconFile**. Full path to the file name that contains the icon.

- **LPSTR szFileType**. File type (currently not being used).

- **LPSTR iIcon**. Index to the icon.

`Load_RegisterFileInfo` can have one of the following return values:

- **LOAD_SUCCESS**. The process was successful.

- **LOAD_FAILED**. Generic load failure occurred.

- **LOAD_DISCONNECTED**. Communication to the device was disconnected.

- **LOAD_REG_ERROR**. Registry entry could not be created.

Load

The `Load` function is the main function for downloading an application from the desktop PC to the Windows CE device. In addition to loading application files, the `Load` function also adds application information to the Windows CE registry and automatically creates an unload script for the application. The `Load` function also can create a shortcut to the application and execute a program on the Windows CE device before the loading process completes.

The `Load` function has the following syntax:

```
LOADERROR dwError = Load( hWindow, szCommandLine );
```

The first parameter to the `Load` function is a window handle that is used as the parent for any windows created by the `Load` function. For instance, the window handle parameter is the parent of the window that indicates progress during the loading operation.

The second parameter to the Load function is the address of a buffer that contains a list of command-line arguments. These command-line arguments provide the information that ppcload.dll needs to load the application to the target device. The seven command-line arguments that must be included in the command-line string are detailed in the following list:

- **CPU type**. The type of CPU on the target Windows CE device. Currently, SH3 and MIPS are the only valid CPU types.

- **Application name**. The name of the application being installed.

- **Install directory**. The directory on the target Handheld PC where the application will be stored.

- **Total bytes to copy**. The number of bytes that will be copied to the Handheld PC.

- **User name**. The name of the person using the Windows CE device.

- **User company**. The name of the user's organization.

- **Load file**. The name of the load script file. Details of this file are covered later in this chapter.

The command-line arguments must be arranged in a given order and separated in the string buffer by spaces. If an argument must include a space, that argument can be delimited by quotation marks.

The return value of the Load function is of type LOADERROR. The possible values returned are detailed in the following list:

- **LOAD_SUCCESS**. The action was successful.

- **LOAD_OUTOFSTORAGE**. The device is out of memory.

- **LOAD_CANCELLEDBYUSER**. The user canceled the loading process.

- **LOAD_INVALID_PARAMETER**. The command line contains an invalid parameter.

- **LOAD_FAILED**. Generic load failure occurred.

- **LOAD_FAILEDCANTCLEANUP**. Load failure occurred, and the system cannot clean up what was done to the device.

- **LOAD_DISCONNECTED**. Communication to the device was disconnected.

- **LOAD_CANT_CREATE_DIR**. The destination directory could not be created.

- **LOAD_REG_ERROR**. The registry entry could not be created.

- **LOAD_ALREADY_LOADING**. Load( ) is already in progress.

The Load Script File

The final argument in the command-line parameter of the Load function is the fully qualified path of the load file. This load file is a text-based script file that contains a list of commands for the Load function to perform. Possible load file commands include creating directories on the Handheld PC, copying files, creating registry entries, executing programs on the Handheld PC, and adding items to the unload script.

In addition to load file commands, the load script file also can contain explanatory comments. The comments must begin with a double slash (//) and must start in the first column.

Each of the load file commands are detailed in the "Load File Commands" section later in this chapter.

The Unload Script

A feature introduced with Windows 95 that has carried forward to Windows CE is the capability to easily remove an installed application using the Control Panel. In order for the Remove Programs option in the Windows CE Control Panel to remove an application, the application must provide information about its components.

An application identifies the components to be removed through the unload script file. This script file is generated during the loading process and is used to remove all traces of the application from the Handheld PC, including all related files, registry entries, directories, and shortcuts. In addition, the loading process automatically runs the unload script if the load operation fails or is canceled by the user. This ensures that a partially installed application is not left on the Windows CE device.

Load File Commands

The commands listed in the load script file direct the operations to be performed during the loading process. Each command must start on its own line, and all of its arguments must be separated by spaces. If an argument includes spaces, the entire argument must be delimited by quotation marks. Some load file commands include optional arguments.

The available load file commands are listed and described in the following table and then detailed in the remainder of this chapter.

Load File Command	Description
appendToUnload	Adds a string to the end of the unload script.
copy	Copies a file from the desktop PC to the Handheld PC.
copyShared	Copies a shared file (such as a DLL) from PC to Handheld PC.
createShortcut	Creates a desktop shortcut on the Handheld PC.
execOnUnload	Adds the name of a program to be run into the unload script.
exit	Ends the processing of the load script file.

Load File Command	Description
mkdir	Creates a directory on the Handheld PC.
prependToUnload	Adds a string to the front of the unload script.
regInt	Writes an integer in the value field of a registry key.
regKeyCreate	Creates a registry key.
regString	Writes a string in the value field of a registry key.
regValueDelete	Deletes a value from the registry.
remoteExec	Runs a program on the Handheld PC.

Each of these functions is discussed in the following sections.

appendToUnload

The appendToUnload statement adds a string to the front of the unload script. Because all other load file statements automatically update the unload script, using this statement typically is not necessary. The syntax of the command is as follows:

```
appendToUnload   string
```

The argument of the appendToUnload command is string, which specifies the string to add to the unload script.

copy

The copy command copies a specified file from the desktop PC to the Windows CE device. The syntax of the command is as follows:

```
copy sourceDirectory destinationDirectory filename
```

The arguments of the copy command are detailed in the following list:

- **sourceDirectory**. Specifies the directory on the desktop PC that contains the files to be copied. The specified directory is relative to the install directory. This argument can be a period (.) to indicate that the source files are to be copied from the install directory on the desktop PC.

- **destinationDirectory**. Specifies the directory on the Handheld PC that receives the files being copied. This parameter can specify an absolute or a relative path.

  To specify an absolute path, this parameter must start with a backslash (\) to indicate the root directory followed by the complete path. This command will fail if the specified directory does not already exist on the Handheld PC.

  To specify a relative path, this parameter can be a period (.). This indicates the source files are to be copied to the load directory on the Handheld PC. The load directory is specified by the install directory argument of the Load function's command-line parameter.

- **filename**. Specifies the name of the file to copy.

When the copy command is used to copy .exe and .dll files from the desktop PC to the Handheld PC, the source file on the desktop PC should have the CPU type added as another extension to the filename. For instance, to copy a file named sample.exe to an SH3 device, the file on the desktop PC should be named sample.exe.sh3.

If the destination file already exists on the target device, the load process displays a message box asking the user whether to overwrite the file.

All files copied to the target device with the copy command automatically are added to the unload script for the application. These files then are removed from the device when the user removes the application, or if an error occurs during the loading process.

copyShared

The copyShared statement copies a shared file from the desktop PC to the Handheld PC. A shared file is typically a DLL that is used by one or more applications. The syntax of the command is as follows:

```
copyShared sourceDirectory destinationDirectory filename
```

The arguments of the copyShared command are detailed in the following list:

- **sourceDirectory**. Specifies the directory on the desktop PC that contains the files to be copied. The specified directory is relative to the install directory. This argument can be a period (.) to indicate that the source files are to be copied from the install directory on the desktop PC.

- **destinationDirectory**. Specifies the directory on the Handheld PC that receives the files being copied. This parameter can specify an absolute or a relative path.

  To specify an absolute path, this parameter must start with a backslash (\) to indicate the root directory followed by the complete path. This command will fail if the specified directory does not already exist on the Handheld PC.

  To specify a relative path, this parameter can be a period (.). This indicates that the source files are to be copied to the load directory on the Handheld PC. The load directory is specified by the install directory argument of the Load function's command-line parameter.

- **filename**. Specifies the name of the file to copy.

Unlike the copy command, the copyShared command does not prompt the user if the destination file already exists. Instead, if the destination directory already contains the file specified by the file parameter, the file's time-stamp is compared to that of the source file. The source file is copied only if it is newer than the destination file.

Windows CE tracks the use of shared files through a reference count in the Windows CE Registry. Every time the same shared file is copied to the target device, the reference count for that file is incremented.

All files copied to the target device with the copyShared command automatically are added to the unload script for the application. When an unload script that contains that shared file is run, the reference count is decremented. When the count reaches zero, the file is removed.

Windows CE does not support the concept of a working directory, so DLLs for all applications should be stored in the \Windows directory. If an application stores its DLLs in another directory, it must load them explicitly using the LoadLibrary API command.

createShortcut

The createShortcut statement creates a shortcut in the Windows CE shell on the Handheld PC and links the shortcut to an executable file. The syntax of the command is as follows:

```
createShortcut  directory  linkname  programDirectory  program
```

The arguments of the createShortcut command are detailed in the following list:

- **directory**. Specifies the directory in which the shortcut is to be created. This argument can be a period (.) to indicate that the shortcut is to be created in the load directory. The load directory is specified by the install directory argument of the Load function's command-line parameter.

- **linkname**. Specifies the name of the link file (for example, sample.lnk).

- **programDirectory**. Specifies the directory that contains the executable file to which the shortcut is to be linked. This argument can be a period (.) to indicate that the file is in the load directory on the Handheld PC.

- **program**. Specifies the name of the executable file.

Like the copied files, the shortcut information is added to the unload script for the application. When the application is removed, the shortcut also is removed from the Windows CE device.

execOnUnload

The execOnUnload statement adds the name of an executable file to the end of the unload script. The file is executed when the unload script is run on the Handheld PC. The syntax of the command is as follows:

```
execOnUnload   exefile
```

The argument of the execOnUnload command is exefile, which specifies the name of the executable file to be added to the unload script.

exit

The exit statement causes execution of statements in the load file to cease. The syntax of the command is as follows:

```
exit
```

No arguments to the exit command exist.

mkdir

The mkdir statement creates a directory in the Handheld PC file system. The syntax of the command is as follows:

```
mkdir   directory
```

The argument of the mkdir command is directory, which specifies the name of the directory to create. The directory can be an absolute path if the directory begins with a backslash (/). If the directory name does not begin with an absolute path, the new directory is created with the directory specified by the install directory argument of the Load function's command-line parameter.

prependToUnload

The prependToUnload statement adds a string to the front of the unload script. Because all other load file statements automatically update the unload script, using this statement generally is not necessary. The syntax of the command is as follows:

```
prependToUnload   string
```

The argument of the prependToUnload command is string, which specifies the string to add to the unload script.

regInt

The regInt statement writes an integer in the value field of a registry key. The syntax of the command is as follows:

```
regInt   key   subkey   bUninstall   value   integer
```

The arguments of the regInt command are detailed in the following list:

- **key**. Specifies the root key that contains the key to receive the integer. This argument can be the tilde character (~) to specify the "home" key (HKEY_LOCAL_MACHINE\SOFTWARE\ Apps\your_app_name), or it can be one of the following values: HKEY_CLASSES_ROOT, HKEY_CURRENT_USER, HKEY_LOCAL_MACHINE,or HKEY_USERS.

- **subkey**. Specifies the name of the key whose value field is to receive the integer.

- **bUninstall**. Specifies whether the value should be added to the list of items to be removed by the unload script. If this argument is set to one, the value will be removed by the unload script. If set to zero, the registry value will remain even after the application is uninstalled.

- **value**. Specifies the name of the value that is to receive the integer.

- **integer**. Specifies the integer.

The bUninstall argument is ignored unless the tilde (~) character is used to specify the home key in the key argument. This is to facilitate the anticipated future release of the Application Manager, which will use the registry values under the home key to determine user-defined preferences that should be saved if the program is uninstalled.

regKeyCreate

The regKeyCreate statement creates a key in the Handheld PC registry. The syntax of the command is as follows:

```
regKeyCreate  key  subkey  bUninstall
```

The arguments of the regKeyCreate command are detailed in the following list:

- **key**. Specifies the root key that contains the key to receive the integer. This argument can be the tilde character (~) to specify the "home" key (HKEY_LOCAL_MACHINE\SOFTWARE\ Apps\your_app_name), or it can be one of the following values: HKEY_CLASSES_ROOT, HKEY_CURRENT_USER, HKEY_LOCAL_MACHINE, or HKEY_USERS.

- **subkey**. Specifies the name of the key to create.

- **bUninstall**. Specifies whether the value should be added to the list of items to be removed by the unload script. If this argument is set to one, the value will be removed by the unload script. If set to zero, the registry value will remain even after the application is uninstalled.

The bUninstall argument is ignored unless the tilde (~) character is used to specify the home key in the key argument. This is to facilitate the anticipated future release of the Application Manager, which will use the registry values under the home key to determine user-defined preferences that should be saved if the program is uninstalled.

The setup program should create all possible registry keys and values for the application so they can be removed properly if the application is uninstalled.

regString

The regString statement writes a string in the value field of a registry key on the Windows CE device. The syntax of the command is as follows:

```
regString  key  subkey  bUninstall  value  string
```

The arguments of the regString command are detailed in the following list:

- **key**. Specifies the root key that contains the key to receive the integer. This argument can be the tilde character (~) to specify the "home" key (HKEY_LOCAL_MACHINE\SOFTWARE\ Apps\your_app_name), or it can be one of the following values: HKEY_CLASSES_ROOT, HKEY_CURRENT_USER, HKEY_LOCAL_MACHINE, or HKEY_USERS.

- **subkey**. Specifies the name of the key whose value field is to receive the string. This argument can be the tilde character (~) if the key argument is also a tilde. Using the tilde character specifies no subkey and that the value receiving the string is in the home key.

- **bUninstall**. Specifies whether the value should be added to the list of items to be removed by the unload script. If this argument is set to one, the value will be removed by the unload script. If set to zero, the registry value will remain even after the application is uninstalled.

- **value**. Specifies the name of the value that is to receive the string.

- **string**. Specifies the string. The characters %P are inserted in the string expand to be the installation path on the Handheld PC. If the characters "%P" are in the installation path itself, a LOAD_INVALID_PARAMETER error is returned to prevent infinite recursion.

The bUninstall argument is ignored unless the tilde (~) character is used to specify the home key in the key argument. This is to facilitate the anticipated future release of the Application Manager, which will use the registry values under the home key to determine user-defined preferences that should be saved if the program is uninstalled.

regValueDelete

The regValueDelete statement deletes a named value from a key in the Windows CE registry. Most setup applications do not use this statement. The syntax of the command is as follows:

```
regValueDelete  key  value
```

The arguments of the regValueDelete command are detailed in the following list:

- **key**. Specifies the root key that contains the key to receive the integer. This argument can be the tilde character (~) to specify the "home" key (HKEY_LOCAL_MACHINE\SOFTWARE\ Apps\your_app_name), or it can be one of the following values: HKEY_CLASSES_ROOT, HKEY_CURRENT_USER, HKEY_LOCAL_MACHINE, or HKEY_USERS.

- **value**. Specifies the name of the value to delete.

remoteExec

The remoteExec statement causes Windows CE to begin executing an application on the target device. The syntax of the command is as follows:

```
remoteExec  application  [args]
```

The arguments of the remoteExec command are detailed in the following list:

- **application**. Specifies the path and file name of the executable module that contains the application. The path is relative to the directory specified by the install directory command-line argument of the Load function. If this argument is NULL, the module name must be the first space-delimited token in the args string.

- **args**. Specifies the optional command-line arguments to pass to the application.

TravelManager Installation

The installation process for the TravelManager application is fairly simple because it has very few files to install. The steps needed in the installation process for TravelManager are as follows:

1. Create the TravelManager directory (handled in the call to the Load function).

2. Copy the executable file into that directory.

3. Create a shortcut on the desktop for TravelManager.

4. Copy the help files into the Windows directory.

The load script used to perform these actions is as follows:

```
// copy the files
copy . . trvlmgr.exe

// create a desktop shortcut
createShortcut \Windows\Desktop 'Trvlmgr.lnk' . trvlmgr.exe

// copy the help files
copy . \Windows 'TravelManager Help.htc'
copy . \Windows trvlmgr1.htp
copy . \Windows trvlmgr2.htp

exit
```

Another area that the installation process could handle is the creation of the registry keys and values that TravelManager uses. However, the application itself already does this (so that features developed in earlier chapters did not have to rely on this installation being performed first). Furthermore, although a Windows CE database for TravelManager does need to be created, it is accomplished with Windows CE Remote API functions, which are covered in Chapter 14, "Remote API Functions."

For a real application, the installation of components onto the Hand-held PC likely will be part of a full-fledged installation program that is beyond the scope of this book. To provide an example of the Application Loader functionality in Windows CE, the installation example contains a simple executable that merely calls the Application Loader with a load script file. See Appendix A, "Getting Started with the CD-ROM," for information on accessing this code from the accompanying CD-ROM.

CHAPTER 13

File Filters

O ne of the key features of Windows CE is the capability to transfer data between the Handheld PC and the desktop PC. The capability to share information between the desktop computer and the Handheld PC enables the Windows CE application to be much more than the applications found in traditional electronic organizers.

Many software applications designed for the Handheld PC are extensions of applications for the desktop PC. Typically, the Windows CE version of the application is a slimmed-down companion version of a full-featured Windows-based desktop application. The Handheld PC version of the application can be used for remote entry or viewing of data. This data can be shared and synchronized when the Handheld PC is connected to the desktop PC.

Windows CE supports multiple forms of desktop connectivity. The previous chapter presented functionality included with the Windows CE development environment for installing applications onto the Handheld PC. This chapter introduces another form of desktop connectivity—functionality.

Windows CE provides a mechanism for converting data when files are transferred from the desktop PC to the Handheld PC, or vice versa. The Handheld PC Explorer uses application-defined *file filters* to modify data as it is transferred. Microsoft Word documents, for example, are converted to a slightly different format when they are transferred to the Handheld PC. Objects and data not supported in Microsoft Pocket Word can be converted or stripped out as the file is transferred.

File Filter Overview

File filters provide the capability to modify a file's structure or data as it is being transferred from the desktop PC to the Handheld PC. A file filter is a dynamic-link library (DLL) that controls the transfer of files between the desktop PC and the Handheld PC.

The Handheld PC Explorer automatically adjusts file formats for some types of files. The file types that the Handheld PC Explorer will automatically convert include the following:

- Windows bitmap (.bmp) to Windows CE monochrome bitmap (.2bp)
- Word (.doc) to Pocket Word (.pwd)
- Pocket Word (.pwd) to Word (.doc)
- Excel (.xls) to Pocket Excel (.pxl)
- Pocket Excel (.pxl) to Excel (.xls)

A powerful feature of the Handheld PC is that applications can install their own file filters that the Handheld PC Explorer will use when transferring a file of the specified type. These application-defined file filters are installed on the desktop PC and used by the Handheld PC Explorer application when files are transferred to or from the Windows CE device.

Filter Direction

File filters can be used when transferring files to and from the Handheld PC. The terms *importing* and *exporting* are used to differentiate the direction and are relative to the Handheld PC. Importing a file involves transferring a file from the desktop PC to the Handheld PC. Likewise, exporting a file involves transferring a file from the Handheld PC to the desktop PC.

Fortunately, little difference exists between constructing a file filter for importing or constructing a file filter for exporting.

An application specifies whether a given file filter is used for importing or exporting through a registry setting. If the value named Import exists under the PegasusFilters key for the given filter's registry entry, that filter is used for importing files to the Handheld PC. See the following section for more information on the registry entries required for defining the file filters.

Registry Entries

The Handheld PC Explorer application on the desktop PC determines which file filter to use, if any, based on registry settings on the desktop PC. The file filter entries are queried in the registry based on the file extension of the file that is transferred with the Handheld PC Explorer. Therefore, it is important that each file filter is properly registered to be used as files are transferred.

Registering file filters involves adding entries into the Windows registry on the desktop PC. An extension key is added to define a new filter for a given file extension and a CLSID key is added to define the specifics of the filter.

Extension Key

One location where information must be set for a file filter is under the HKEY_LOCAL_MACHINE\SOFWARE\Microsoft\Pegasus\ Filters key. This information defines the extension of the file types that have available file filters.

Note

> Prior to the release of Windows CE, Microsoft used the code name Pegasus to identify the Windows CE project. The Pegasus key in the registry was set before the name Windows CE was chosen and apparently stuck—probably because many applications were already written to set and use that key.

The following listing shows the structure of the information under the .../Filters key:

```
HKEY_LOCAL_MACHINE\SOFTWARE\Microsoft\Pegasus\Filters
  \.<file extension>
    [DefaultImport = <Default import filter CLSID>]
    [DefaultExport = <Default export filter CLSID>]
    \InstalledFilters
      [<CLSID1> = ""]
      [<CLSID2> = ""]
      . . .
      [more CLSID's for this extension]
  . . .
  [more extensions]
```

Each key under the HKEY_LOCAL_MACHINE\SOFTWARE\ Microsoft\Pegasus\Filters is the name of a file extension, such as .bmp. These keys are called extension keys. Every extension key can have a DefaultImport named value and/or a DefaultExport named value, both of which identify the default file filter to use when importing or exporting files with the given extension.

In addition to listing the default file filter for the extension, each extension key has an InstalledFilters subkey that lists the possible file filters for that file type. This is because it is certainly possible to have multiple conversion options for a single file type. For instance, when Word documents are transferred, they could be converted to Pocket Word documents or to plain ASCII text documents. An interface in the Handheld PC Explorer application enables the user to set the conversion used for each file type.

The InstalledFilters keys must contain all possible file filters for that extension type. Therefore, even file filters specified in the DefaultImport or DefaultExport named values must also be listed in the Installed-Filters subkey.

File filters are specified and identified by the use of a unique class identifier (CLSID) data value. These class identifiers are universally unique identifiers that identify OLE Component Object Model (COM) objects. The CLSID identification is used with file filters because the filters are implemented as OLE COM objects.

CLSID Key

The other area where file filter information must be defined is under the HKEY_CLASSES_ROOT\CLSID key. This information defines the specific attributes and implementation details of the file filter. The following listing shows the structure of the information under the HKEY_CLASSES_ROOT\CLSID key:

```
HKEY_CLASSES_ROOT\CLSID

  \<CLSID>
    \(Default) = <Description listed in HPC Explorer>
    \DefaultIcon = <filename,index for the icon for this type>
    \InProcServer32 = <filename of the DLL that handles his type>
      ThreadingModel = "Apartment"
    \PegasusFilter
      [Import]
      [HasOptions]
      Description = <String to display in the conversion dialog>
      NewExtension = <extension of converted file>
  \. . . [more CLSIDs for filters]
```

Each key under the HKEY_CLASSES_ROOT\CLSID is the class identifier to an object. The CLSID is a series of hexadecimal numbers separated by dashes, such as DA01ED86-97E8-11CF-8011-00A0C90A8F78. An application defines its own class identifiers by using the GUID generator application, guidgen.exe. To a very high degree of certainty, this tool creates a unique CLSID—no other invocation on the same system or any other system should return the same value.

Under each individual CLSID is a set of values and keys that define the attributes of the object. The value for the CLSID key itself is the name of the file filter that is listed in the Handheld PC Explorer when it shows the available conversion filters.

The DefaultIcon subkey specifies the location of an icon to be associated with this file filter. The format of the value—*filename, index*—specifies the name of a file that contains icons, as well as the index for the appropriate icon.

The InProcServer32 subkey identifies the dynamic link library (DLL) that contains the implementation for this file filter. The value of this key is the name of the file filter plus the extension .dll. This key also has a subkey, ThreadingModel, whose value defines the Apartment model capabilities of the installed file filter. Generally, this value is set to "Apartment."

The PegasusFilter subkey defines information specific to file filters. This key can have the following named values:

- **Import**. If this named value exists, the conversion type is used for importing files to the Handheld PC. The absence of this value means that the conversion type is used for exporting files from the Handheld PC.

- **HasOptions**. If this named value exists, the file filter supports the FilterOptions method of the IpegasusFileFilter interface.

- **Description**. This named value is a line of text that describes the conversion that the Handheld PC Explorer displays in the conversion selection dialog box.

- **NewExtension**. This named value is the extension that is used for the destination file name.

Registry Entries Example

One way to visualize the set of necessary registration entries is to look at the Windows registry of a machine that has the Handheld PC Explorer installed. Another way is to look at a .reg file that can be used to add information to the registry. Following is a registration file that would add the entries necessary for the file filter to import bitmap files to the Handheld PC.

```
REGEDIT4

[HKEY_LOCAL_MACHINE\SOFTWARE\Microsoft\Pegasus\Filters\.bmp]
"DefaultImport"="{DA01ED80-97E8-11cf-8011-00A0C90A8F78}"

[HKEY_LOCAL_MACHINE\SOFTWARE\Microsoft\Pegasus\Filters\.bmp\InstalledFilters]
"{DA01ED80-97E8-11cf-8011-00A0C90A8F78}"=""

[HKEY_CLASSES_ROOT\CLSID\{DA01ED80-97E8-11cf-8011-00A0C90A8F78}]
@="H/PC Bitmap"

[HKEY_CLASSES_ROOT\CLSID\{DA01ED80-97E8-11cf-8011-
➥00A0C90A8F78}\DefaultIcon]
@="D:\\Handheld PC Explorer\\2bp.dll,-1000"

[HKEY_CLASSES_ROOT\CLSID\{DA01ED80-97E8-11cf-8011-
➥00A0C90A8F78}\InProcServer32]
@="D:\\Handheld PC Explorer\\2bp.dll"
"ThreadingModel"="Apartment"

[HKEY_CLASSES_ROOT\CLSID\{DA01ED80-97E8-11cf-8011-
➥00A0C90A8F78}\PegasusFilter]
"Import"=""
"Description"="H/PC Bitmap"
"NewExtension"="2bp"
```

Null File Filters

The presence of a file filter not only provides the capability to convert data as it is being transferred, but it also helps the user to see that the data is being changed into a format that will work on the Windows CE device. If a file is transferred and no file filter is registered for that file type, the Handheld PC Explorer displays a "No Converter Selected" warning, stating that the file will be transferred without conversion.

The solution to preventing this startling warning message is for an application to create a file filter for its file type. However, in some cases, the format does not need to change as the file is transferred.

Of course, it would be possible to create a real file filter that does no translation on data and merely passes the data on through. However, a much simpler method gives the appearance that a file filter is being used, but in actuality, no file filter is created.

Under this method, wave files (.wav), for instance, would maintain the same format on the desktop PC and the Handheld PC. The presence of a null file filter in the registry for the .wav file type would prompt no warning messages during the process of transferring .wav files.

The example registration file that follows (for the .wav file type) displays the registry entries necessary to create a null file filter:

```
REGEDIT4

[HKEY_LOCAL_MACHINE\SOFTWARE\Microsoft\Pegasus\Filters\.wav]
"DefaultExport"="Binary Copy"
"DefaultImport"="Binary Copy"

[HKEY_LOCAL_MACHINE\SOFTWARE\Microsoft\Pegasus\Filters\.wav\InstalledFilters]
```

Creating a null file filter requires adding the file type key under the ..\Pegasus\Filters key and setting the DefaultImport and DefaultExport values to "Binary Copy."

When a file with the given extension (.wav in this example) is transferred between the desktop PC and the Handheld PC, it appears as though a conversion process is taking place (because no warning message is displayed) even though no filter is being used.

File Filter Components

After the file filter is defined in the Windows registry, the Handheld PC Explorer then can invoke the file filter for the specified file type. The method for communication between the file filter and the Handheld PC Explorer is defined through the Component Object Model (COM).

COM is the fundamental underlying model that OLE is based upon, and it enables an application to expose its capabilities to other applications. COM stipulates that any component object must control its own life span and must be able to tell other objects about its capabilities in a strictly defined manner. These capabilities are grouped into logical sets called *interfaces*; each interface is a set of member functions necessary to support a certain capability.

COM and OLE are large topics, and the specific mechanisms of those technologies are beyond the scope of this book. The description of the file filter's implementation assumes some knowledge of COM. However, by adapting the file filter developed in this chapter (or the file filter example included with the Windows CE SDK), it is possible to implement a file filter without mastering all the details of COM.

This section describes the major components used when creating a file filter. Because much of the code used to build a file filter implements the standard infrastructure needed by COM, adapting components from sample file filters requires changes to only a few parts of the code.

IPegasusFileFilter Interface

The basic mechanism for implementing a file filter is to create a new class derived from the IPegasusFileFilter interface. IPegasusFileFilter defines the interface that a file filter must support to be invoked from the Handheld PC Explorer.

IPegasusFileFilter derives from IUnknown. The methods defined by IPegasusFileFilter include those inherited from IUnknown (Query-Interface, AddRef, and Release) and methods specific to file filters (NextConvertFile, FilterOptions, and FormatMessage). Table 13.1 describes the purpose of the methods defined by the IPegasusFileFilter interface.

Table 13.1

Methods Defined by IPegasusFileFilter

IpegasusFileFilter Method	Description
QueryInterface	Defined by COM. Returns pointers to supported interfaces.

continues

Table 13.1

Methods Defined by IPegasusFileFilter, continued	
IpegasusFileFilter Method	Description
AddRef	Defined by COM. Increments reference count.
Release	Defined by COM. Decrements reference count.
NextConvertFile	Called by the Handheld PC Explorer to convert a file type specified in the registry. This method is called repeatedly until the file filter DLL indicates that the file conversion is complete.
FilterOptions	Called by the Handheld PC Explorer to display a dialog box that directs the user to select from among the file-filtering options supported by a file filter. Not supported in Windows CE version 1.0.
FormatMessage	Called by the Handheld PC Explorer to format a message string.

Each of these methods is described in the following sections.

QueryInterface, AddRef, Release

These methods are defined by COM. The QueryInterface method allows the client to dynamically discover at runtime the interfaces supported by the object. The AddRef and Release methods are used for simple reference counting.

NextConvertFile

When the user transfers a file for which a file filter is defined, the Handheld PC Explorer calls the NextConvertFile method of the appropriate file filter DLL. Therefore, the NextConvertFile method should be overridden in the file filter's class derived from IPegasusFileFilter. The NextConvertFile method is defined as follows:

```
STDMETHOD(NextConvertFile) (THIS_
    int nConversion,
    PFF_CONVERTINFO* pci,
    PFF_SOURCEFILE* psf,
    PFF_DESTINATIONFILE* pdf,
    volatile BOOL *pbCancel,
    PF_ERROR *perr
} PURE;
```

The parameters of the NextConvertFile method are detailed in the following list:

- **int nConversion**. This counter is used to convert a single source file into multiple destination files. This parameter is zero the first time this function is called and is incremented for each successive call. A simple filter should return HRESULT_FROM_WIN32 (ERROR_NO_MORE_ITEMS) if this parameter is not zero.

- **PFF_CONVERTINFO * pci**. This parameter points to a PFF_CONVERTINFO structure that contains information about the conversion request and a pointer to an IPegasusFileFilterSite object.

- **PFF_SOURCEFILE * psf**. This parameter points to a PFF_SOURCEFILE structure that contains information about the source file.

- **PFF_DESTINATIONFILE * pdf**. This parameter points to a PFF_DESTINATIONFILE structure that contains information about the destination file.

- **BOOL * pbCancel**. This parameter is a pointer to a BOOL that signals when the user cancels the conversion process. This variable is updated asynchronously and can change at any time. The file filter should check this variable periodically during the file conversion and return ERROR_CANCELLED if it is ever set to TRUE.

- **PF_ERROR * perr**. This address of a filter-defined error code can be passed to the `IPegasusFileFilter::FormatMessage` member function. This error code will be ignored unless the return value from this function is E_FAIL.

The return value from NextConvertFile should be one of the following values:

- **NOERROR**. The subconversion was successful; proceed to the next subconversion.

- **HRESULT_FROM_WIN32 (ERROR_CANCELLED)**. The user canceled the conversion.

- **HRESULT_FROM_WIN32 (ERROR_NO_MORE_ITEMS)**. The conversion (or last subconversion) was successful. End calls to IPegasusFileFilter::NextConvertFile.

- **E_FAIL**. The perr parameter was filled with an error code that should be passed to IPegasusFileFilter::FormatMessage.

FormatMessage

This method is used to format message strings and requires a message definition as input. The message definition can come from a buffer passed into the function, or it can come from a message table resource in an already loaded module. The caller also can ask the function to search the system's message table resource(s) for the message definition.

The function finds the message definition in a message table resource based on a message identifier and a language identifier. The function copies the formatted message text to an output buffer, processing any embedded insert sequences if requested. The FormatMessage method also enables the filter to define message codes specific to the filter.

The FormatMessage method is defined as follows:

```
STDMETHOD(FormatMessage) (THIS_
    DWORD   dwFlags,
    DWORD   dwMessageId,
    DWORD   dwLanguageId,
    LPTSTR  lpBuffer,
    DWORD   nSize,
    va_list *  Arguments,
    DWORD   *pcb
) PURE;
```

The first parameter to the FormatMessage method is dwFlags, which is a DWORD containing a set of bit flags that specify aspects of the formatting process and tell how to interpret the lpSource parameter. The high-order byte can be a combination of the following bit flags:

- **FORMAT_MESSAGE_ALLOCATE_BUFFER.** Specifies that the lpBuffer parameter is a pointer to a PVOID pointer, and that the nSize parameter specifies the minimum number of bytes (ANSI version) or characters (Unicode version) to allocate for an output message buffer. The function allocates a buffer large enough to hold the formatted message and places a pointer to the allocated buffer at the address specified by lpBuffer. The caller should use the `LocalFree` function to free the buffer when it is no longer needed.

- **FORMAT_MESSAGE_IGNORE_INSERTS.** Specifies that insert sequences in the message definition are to be ignored and passed through to the output buffer unchanged. This flag is useful for fetching a message for later formatting. If this flag is set, the Arguments parameter is ignored.

- **FORMAT_MESSAGE_FROM_STRING.** Specifies that lpSource is a pointer to a null-terminated message definition. The message definition can contain insert sequences, just as the message text in a message table resource can. This bit flag cannot be used with FORMAT_MESSAGE_FROM_HMODULE or FORMAT_MESSAGE_FROM_SYSTEM.

- **FORMAT_MESSAGE_FROM_HMODULE.** Specifies that lpSource is a module handle containing the message-table resource(s) to search. If this lpSource handle is NULL, the current process's application image file will be searched. This bit flag cannot be used with FORMAT_MESSAGE_FROM_STRING.

- **FORMAT_MESSAGE_FROM_SYSTEM.** Specifies that the function should search the system message-table resource(s) for the requested message. If this flag is specified with FORMAT_MESSAGE_FROM_HMODULE, the function searches the system message table if the message is not found in the module specified by lpSource. This bit flag cannot be used with FORMAT_MESSAGE_FROM_STRING.

- **FORMAT_MESSAGE_ARGUMENT_ARRAY**. Specifies that the Arguments parameter is not a va_list structure but instead is just a pointer to an array of 32-bit values that represent the arguments.

The low-order byte of dwFlags can specify the maximum width of a formatted output line. The width can be any value between (and including) zero and FORMAT_MESSAGE_MAX_WIDTH_MASK.

The following is a list of the remaining parameters to the FormatMessage method:

- **DWORD dwMessageId**. Specifies the 32-bit message identifier for the requested message. This parameter is ignored if dwFlags includes FORMAT_MESSAGE_FROM_STRING.

- **DWORD dwLanguageId**. Specifies the 32-bit language identifier for the requested message. This parameter is ignored if dwFlags includes FORMAT_MESSAGE_FROM_STRING.

- **LPSTR lpBuffer**. Points to a buffer for the formatted (and NULL-terminated) message. If dwFlags includes FORMAT_MESSAGE_ALLOCATE_BUFFER, the function allocates a buffer by using the `LocalAlloc` function and places the address of the buffer at the address specified in lpBuffer.

- **DWORD nSize**. If the FORMAT_MESSAGE_ALLOCATE _BUFFER flag is not set, this parameter specifies the maximum number of bytes (ANSI version) or characters (Unicode version) that can be stored in the output buffer. If FORMAT_MESSAGE _ALLOCATE_BUFFER is set, this parameter specifies the minimum number of bytes or characters to allocate for an output buffer.

- **va_list * Arguments**. Points to an array of 32-bit values that are used as insert values in the formatted message: %1 in the format string indicates the first value in the Arguments array, %2 indicates the second argument, and so on.

- **DWORD * pcb**. Points to a DWORD that receives the length of the string returned by the function. If the FormatMessage function succeeds, pcb holds the number of bytes (ANSI version) or characters (Unicode version) stored in the output buffer, excluding the terminating NULL character.

IPegasusFileFilterSite Interface

The other major component used by the file filter is the IPegasusFile-FilterSite interface. The Handheld PC Explorer implements this interface, and a pointer to it is passed to some of the IPegasusFileFilter methods.

IPegasusFileFilterSite also derives from IUnknown. The methods defined by IPegasusFileFilterSite include those inherited from the file, as well as methods specific to the file. Table 13.2 describes the purpose of the methods defined by the IPegasusFileFilterSite interface.

Table 13.2

Methods Defined by IPegasusFileFilterSite	
IPegasusFileFilterSite Method	Description
QueryInterface	Defined by COM. Returns pointers to supported interfaces.
AddRef	Defined by COM. Increments reference count.
Release	Defined by COM. Decrements reference count.
OpenSourceFile	Called by a file filter to open a source file.

continues

Table 13.2

Methods Defined by IPegasusFileFilterSite, continued	
IPegasusFileFilterSite Method	Description
OpenDestinationFile	Called by a file filter to open a destination file.
CloseSourceFile	Called by a file filter to close a source file.
CloseDestinationFile	Called by a file filter to close a destination file.
ReportProgress	Called by a file filter to report the progress of a file conversion.
ReportLoss	Called by a file filter to report any data that it intentionally discarded during a file conversion.

QueryInterface, AddRef, Release

These methods are defined by the Component Object Model. The Query-Interface method allows the client to dynamically discover at runtime the interfaces supported by the object. The AddRef and Release methods are used for simple reference counting.

OpenSourceFile

This member function is used by a file filter to open a source file. The OpenSourceFile method is defined as follows:

```
STDMETHOD(OpenSourceFile) (THIS_
    int nHowToOpenFile,
    LPVOID *ppObj
) PURE;
```

The parameters to OpenSourceFile are detailed in the following list:

- **int nHowToOpenFile**. Specifies how the source file is to be opened. Currently, the only supported value is PF_OPENFLAT, which opens the file as a flat file.

- **LPVOID ppObj**. Specifies the address of an LPVOID variable that will receive an IStream pointer.

OpenDestinationFile

This member function is used by a file filter to open a destination file. The OpenDestinationFile method is defined as follows:

```
STDMETHOD(OpenDestinationFile) (THIS_
    int nHowToOpenFile,
    LPCSTR pszFullpath,
    LPVOID *ppObj
) PURE;
```

The parameters to OpenDestinationFile are detailed in the following list:

- **int nHowToOpenFile**. Specifies how the source file is to be opened. Currently, the only supported value is PF_OPENFLAT, which opens the file as a flat file.

- **LPCSTR pszFullpath**. Specifies the file name to open to override the default destination file name. If this parameter is NULL, the default destination file name is used.

- **LPVOID ppObj**. Specifies the address of an LPVOID variable that will receive an Istream pointer.

CloseSourceFile

This member function is used by a file filter to close a source file. This function is defined as follows:

```
STDMETHOD(CloseSourceFile) (THIS_
    LPUNKNOWN pObj
) PURE;
```

The parameter to CloseSourceFile is LPUNKNOWN pObj, which points to the IStream object returned from the IPegasusFileFilterSite ::OpenSourceFile method.

CloseDestinationFile

This member function is used by a file filter to close a destination file. The function is defined as follows:

```
STDMETHOD(CloseDestinationFile) (THIS_
    BOOL bKeepFile,
    LPUNKNOWN pObj
) PURE;
```

The parameters to CloseDestinationFile are detailed in the following list:

- **BOOL bKeepFile**. Indicates whether to keep or delete the destination file. A file filter should set this parameter to TRUE to keep the destination file, or FALSE to delete it.

- **LPUNKNOWN pObj**. Points to the IStream object returned from the IPegasusFileFilterSite::OpenDestinationFile method.

ReportProgress

This member function is used by a file filter to report the progress of a file conversion. The function is defined as follows:

```
STDMETHOD(ReportProgress) (THIS_
    UINT nPercent
) PURE;
```

The parameter to ReportProgress is UINT nPercent, which specifies the completed percentage of the operation. If, for example, the file filter has converted 25 percent of a file, this parameter should be set to 25.

ReportLoss

The ReportLoss member function is used by a file filter to report any information that it intentionally discarded during a file conversion. The file filter specifies a message that explains the data loss, and Handheld PC Explorer formats and displays the message in a message box when the file conversion is completed. The file filter can specify either the identifier of a message table resource or the address of a buffer that contains the message string.

The ReportLoss method is defined as follows:

```
STDMETHOD(ReportLoss) (THIS_
    DWORD dw,
    LPCTSTR psz,
    va_list args
) PURE;
```

The parameters to ReportLoss are detailed in the following list:

- **DWORD dw**. Specifies a 32-bit message identifier. The member function uses IPegasusFileFilter::FormatMessage to format the message. If the format fails (for example, the message identifier could not be recognized), then the system function FormatMessage is used.

- **LPCTSTR psz**. Points to the message string to display. This parameter should be NULL if the dw parameter is used.

- **va_list args**. Points to an array of 32-bit values that are used as insert values in the formatted message. %1 in the format string indicates the first value in the Arguments array, %2 indicates the second argument, and so on.

File Filter Structures

In addition to the interfaces that are implemented or used by a file filter, a number of file filter structures exist. These structures are passed to various filter methods and contain information about the conversion process.

The PFF_CONVERTINFO structure contains information that the IPegasusFileFilter::NextConvertFile method uses to perform file conversions. The members of this structure are detailed in the following list:

- **BOOL bImport**. Acts as a flag that is nonzero if the conversion is importing files to the Handheld PC. Otherwise, it is zero to indicate the conversion is exporting files from the Handheld PC.

- **HWND hwndParent**. Specifies the handle of the window that a file filter can use as the parent window for a dialog box.

- **BOOL bYesToAll**. Points to a flag that determines whether the Yes to All button is included in the Overwrite File? dialog box. This dialog box asks the user to verify that the destination file(s) should be overwritten. If there is more than one subconversion, the filter should set this member to TRUE to include the Yes to All button; otherwise, the filter should set this member to FALSE.

- **IPegasusFileFilterSite * pffs**. Points to an IPegasusFileFilterSite interface used for opening and closing files.

The PFF_DESTINATIONFILE structure contains information about a destination file. A pointer to this structure is passed in the call to the IPegasusFileFilter::NextConvertFile method. The members of this structure are detailed in the following list:

- **TCHAR szFullpath**. Specifies the default full path of the destination file.

- **TCHAR szPath**. Specifies the path of the directory where the destination file should be created.

- **TCHAR szFilename**. Specifies only the base name (no extension) of the destination file.

- **TCHAR szExtension**. Specifies the file name extension of the destination file.

The PFF_SOURCEFILE structure contains information about a source file. A pointer to this structure is passed in the call to the IPegasusFileFilter::NextConvertFile method. The members of this structure are detailed in the following list:

- **TCHAR szFullpath**. Specifies the fully qualified path of the source file.

- **TCHAR szPath**. Specifies the path of the directory containing the source file.

- **TCHAR szFilename**. Specifies only the base name (no extension) of the source file.

- **TCHAR szExtension**. Specifies the file name extension of the source file.

- **DWORD cbSize**. Specifies the size of the source file.

- **FILETIME ftCreated**. Specifies a FILETIME structure that indicates the time when the source file was created.

- **FILETIME ftModified**. Specifies a FILETIME structure that indicates the time when the file was last modified.

File Filter Process

The sequence of steps involved in file-conversion process with a file filter is defined and straightforward. The steps of the conversion process can be summarized as follows:

1. When requested to copy a file, the Handheld PC Explorer queries the registry for information on any file filter defined for that file type.

2. If a file filter is defined for that file type, the Handheld PC Explorer loads the specified filter DLL.

3. The Handheld PC Explorer calls the file filter's IPegasusFileFilter ::NextConvertFile method to perform the custom file conversion. The PFF_CONVERTINFO, PFF_DESTINATIONFILE, and PFF_SOURCEFILE structures are passed as parameters to provide information.

4. Inside the NextConvertFile method, the file filter begins the file conversion.

5. The source file is opened by using the IPegasusFileFilterSite ::OpenSourceFile method.

6. The destination file is opened by using the IPegasusFileFilterSite ::OpenDestinationFile method.

7. Data is read from the open source stream, converted, and written out to the open destination stream.

8. During the read-convert-write process, the file filter should call the IPegasusFileFilterSite::ReportProgress method to update a graphical display that shows the progress of the file conversion.

9. If the file filter DLL intentionally discards any of the file data, the filter can call the IPegasusFileFilterSite::ReportLoss method so that the Handheld PC Explorer can display a message when the file conversion is complete. This method can in turn call the filter's IPegasusFileFilter::FormatMessage method to properly format the message.

10. Steps 7-9 are repeated until all the data from the source file is read.

11. The source file is closed with the IPegasusFileFilterSite ::CloseSourceFile method.

12. The destination file is closed with the IPegasusFileFilterSite ::CloseDestinationFile method.

File Filter Example

The functionality of the TravelManager application does not require a specific file format, so no file filter is needed. However, to illustrate the file filter technique, a sample file filter has been created.

This sample file filter handles files on the desktop PC with the extension .lwr. When transferred to the Handheld PC, all characters in a .lwr file are converted to uppercase and are given the extension .upr.

The first step in defining a file filter is adding the proper entries to the registry on the desktop PC. An importable .reg file that configures the registry for the .lwr file is listed in the following code:

```
REGEDIT4

[HKEY_LOCAL_MACHINE\SOFTWARE\Microsoft\Pegasus\Filters\.lwr]
```

```
"DefaultImport"="{71eaa5b0-e920-11d0-9a30-204c4f4f5020}"

[HKEY_LOCAL_MACHINE\SOFTWARE\Microsoft\Pegasus\Filters\.lwr\InstalledFilters]
"{71eaa5b0-e920-11d0-9a30-204c4f4f5020}"=""

[HKEY_CLASSES_ROOT\CLSID\{71eaa5b0-e920-11d0-9a30-204c4f4f5020}]
@="File Filter Sample"

[HKEY_CLASSES_ROOT\CLSID\{71eaa5b0-e920-11d0-9a30-
204c4f4f5020}\DefaultIcon]
@="filter.dll,-102"

[HKEY_CLASSES_ROOT\CLSID\{71eaa5b0-e920-11d0-9a30-
➥204c4f4f5020}\InProcServer32]
@="e:\\wce\\code\\chap13\\release\\filter.dll"
"ThreadingModel"="Apartment"

[HKEY_CLASSES_ROOT\CLSID\{71eaa5b0-e920-11d0-9a30-
➥204c4f4f5020}\PegasusFilter]
"Import"=""
"Description"="FILTER: Copy a .lwr file converting to all uppercase."
"NewExtension"="upr"

[HKEY_CLASSES_ROOT\.lwr]
@="lwrfile"

[HKEY_CLASSES_ROOT\lwrfile]
@="FILTER: Lowercase File"

[HKEY_CLASSES_ROOT\lwrfile\DefaultIcon]
@="e:\\wce\\code\\chap13\\release\\filter.dll,-102"

[HKEY_CLASSES_ROOT\.upr]
@="uprfile"

[HKEY_CLASSES_ROOT\uprfile]
@="FILTER: Uppercase File"

[HKEY_CLASSES_ROOT\uprfile\DefaultIcon]
@="e:\\wce\\code\\chap13\\release\\filter.dll,-103"
```

After the registry is configured, the remaining step is to create the
fil-ter.dll that is used when a file of type .lwr is transferred to the

Handheld PC. In the interest of space, all the code required to create the filter.dll is not listed here. The companion CD-ROM contains the complete set of source code for the file filter. See Appendix A, "Getting Started with the CD-ROM," for information on accessing the code from the CD-ROM.

The most interesting part of the file filter source code is the ConvertFile function. This function performs the actual reading, converting, and writing of the file being transferred. If this file filter sample is used to create another file filter, this function is what must be changed to perform the proper conversion.

The ConvertFile function simply reads in a part of the file from the input stream, performs the conversion to lowercase, and writes the file back to the destination stream. ConvertFile continues this process until the entire file has been processed or it is signaled that the user has canceled the operation. The ConvertFile function is listed in the following code:

```
STDMETHODIMP ConvertFile (
    IStream *pstmSrc,                   // Stream to read from
    IStream *pstmDst,                   // Stream to write to
    IPegasusFileFilterSite *pffs,       // Site for reporting
➥progress and loss
    PFF_SOURCEFILE *psf,                // Source file information
    volatile BOOL *pbCancel,            // Will become true if
➥user cancels
    PF_ERROR *perr                      // Possible error message
)
{
    // Generic error code
    *perr = ERROR_ACCESS_DENIED;

    HRESULT hres;

    DWORD cb;
    DWORD cbProcessed = 0;
    BYTE buf[2048];

    for ( ; ; )
    {
```

```
        if (*pbCancel) return ERROR_CANCELLED;

        // read bytes from input stream

        hres = pstmSrc->Read((void*)buf, sizeof(buf)-1, &cb);
        if (!SUCCEEDED(hres) || 0==cb)
        {
            if (cbProcessed == psf->cbSize)
            {
                // We got to EOF
                // It is not clear what the return value will be when
the
                // end of the source is reached
                hres = NOERROR;
            }
            break;
        }

                if (*pbCancel) return ERROR_CANCELLED;

                //
                // Convert everything to uppercase
                buf[2047]='\0';
                strupr((char*)buf);

        //
        // write bytes to output stream

        hres = pstmDst->Write((void*)buf, cb, NULL);
        if (!SUCCEEDED(hres)) break;

                if (*pbCancel) return ERROR_CANCELLED;

        cbProcessed += cb;

        //
        // let the user know how we are progressing

        if (psf->cbSize)
        {
            pffs->ReportProgress((UINT)cbProcessed * 100 / psf
->cbSize);
```

```
        }
        else
        {
            pffs->ReportProgress(100);
        }

                if (*pbCancel) return ERROR_CANCELLED;
    }

    if (SUCCEEDED(hres) && 0==cbProcessed)
    {
        // Error message for a 0 byte file, just to demo error
➥reporting
        //
        *perr = ERROR_NOZEROBYTEFILES;
        hres = E_FAIL;
    }

    return(hres);
}
```

Remote API Functions

As discussed in previous chapters, Windows CE supports many forms of desktop connectivity. These include the capability to support the installation of applications onto the Windows CE device and the conversion of data as it is being copied to the device. Both of these are very powerful features.

Another powerful feature of the desktop connectivity of Windows CE is its capability to enable an application on the desktop PC to communicate directly with the Handheld PC. Windows CE supports a variety of remote API functions. These functions provide applications running on desktop PCs with the capability to invoke function calls on a Windows CE device. An application running on the desktop PC, for instance, can add, edit, or remove data from a Windows CE database on the Handheld PC.

Remote API Overview

Windows CE exposes a set of API functions that can be used by an application on the desktop PC to manipulate data on the Handheld PC while the device is connected to the desktop PC. These remote API (RAPI) functions give a RAPI client running on a desktop PC the capability to invoke function calls on a Windows CE device (the RAPI server).

Communication between the desktop PC and the Handheld PC takes place over the serial link utilizing Winsock. The function calls are synchronous and behave as much as possible like the equivalent Windows CE functions. For the most part, RAPI functions have the same syntax, argument list, and return values as the corresponding Windows CE versions. This also means that the RAPI functions expect strings in Unicode format, which means that if the desktop application is non-Unicode, it must use the appropriate conversion routines.

Using RAPI Functions

Although an application on the desktop PC can use the Windows CE remote API functions just like other Win32 API functions, the system first must be initialized. An application calls the `PegRapiInit` or `PegRapiInitEx` function to perform routine initialization and set up the communications link between the PC and the device. The only difference is that `PegRapiInit` is a synchronous operation, while `PegRapiInitEx` is not.

When an application is finished using the remote API functions, the `PegRapiUninit` function should be called to terminate the connection and perform any necessary cleanup. Creating and terminating connections are fairly expensive operations; whenever possible, an application should establish and terminate the link only once per session, not on a per-call basis.

PegRapiInit

The `PegRapiInit` function attempts to initialize the Windows CE Remote API. A call to `PegRapiInit` does not return until the connection is made, an error occurs, or another thread calls `PegRapiUninit`. The `PegRapiInit` function is defined as follows:

```
HRESULT PegRapiInit(void);
```

If this function succeeds, the return value is E_SUCCESS.

PegRapiInitEx

The `PegRapiInitEx` function also attempts to initialize the Windows CE Remote API. However, the `PegRapiInitEx` function is not synchronous and, therefore, returns immediately. The success or failure of the initialization is signaled through an event handle. An application uses the `WaitForSingleObject` function or `WaitForMultipleObjects` function to detect the completion of the connection (or an error). The syntax of the `PegRapiInitEx` function is as follows:

```
HRESULT PegRapiInitEx( RAPIINIT* pRapiInit );
```

The only parameter to the `PegRapiInitEx` function is a pointer to a RAPIINIT structure. The RAPIINIT structure has the following members:

- **DWORD cbSize**. Specifies the size of the RAPIINIT structure being passed.

- **HANDLE heRapiInit**. Specifies a handle to an event. The event is set when the RAPI connection is made or when an error occurs.

- **HANDLE hrRapiInit**. Specifies the results—success or failure—of the RAPI connection.

An application uses the heRapiInit handle to determine when the RAPI connection is initialized or that an error has occurred. Once the event handle is signaled, the hrRapiInit member specifies the success (E_SUCCESS) or failure (E_FAIL) of the connection.

PegRapiUninit

The PegRapiUninit function uninitializes the Windows CE Remote API and gracefully closes down the connection to the Handheld PC. The PegRapiUninit function should be called when the application has completed its use of the remote API services. If called when not in an initialized state, this function returns E_FAIL. The syntax of the function is as follows:

```
STDAPI PegRapiUninit(void);
```

Available RAPI Functions

The set of remote API functions available to a desktop PC application encompasses many different areas of Windows CE. The list of supported remote API functions can be grouped into the following areas:

- **RAPI support functions**. Functions needed for the initialization and usage of the remote API system.

- **Object store functions**. Functions to access the Windows CE file system and object store.

- **Database functions**. Functions to manipulate Windows CE databases.

- **Registry functions**. Functions to manipulate the Windows CE registry.

- **Window functions**. Functions to access current windows on the Windows CE device.

- **System functions**. Functions to access device and system information.

The following sections detail the specific remote API functions for each of these groups. In most cases, the syntax of the function (such as parameters and return values) is identical to the regular Windows CE version of the function. For this reason, the syntax of the RAPI functions will not be re-listed here unless the syntax is different or the function is not found elsewhere in this book.

RAPI Support Functions

Table 14.1 lists the RAPI functions that are used for initialization and support of the RAPI process.

Table 14.1

RAPI Initialization and Support Functions

Function	Description
GetRapiError	Returns the last RAPI error value.
PegGetLastError	Returns the calling thread's last-error value; equivalent to calling GetLastError on the device.
PegRapiInit	Initializes the Windows CE Remote API asynchronously.
PegRapiInitEx	Attempts to initialize the Windows CE Remote API asynchronously.
PegRapiUninit	Uninitializes the Windows CE Remote API.
RapiFreeBuffer	Frees the memory on the desktop PC allocated by a call to PegFindAllDatabase, PegFindAllFiles, or PegReadRecordProps.

Each of these functions is discussed in the following sections.

GetRapiError

The GetRapiError function can be used to determine whether a call failed due to an internal failure within the Remote API. GetRapiError is a host-side RAPI function. The syntax of the function is as follows:

```
HRESULT GetRapiError(void);
```

The return value is the last RAPI error-code value.

PegGetLastError

The function `PegGetLastError` returns the calling thread's last error code. This is the RAPI version of the function `GetLastError`. The syntax of the function is as follows:

```
DWORD PegGetLastError(void);
```

The return value is the calling thread's last error code.

PegRapiInit

Syntax for this function is listed in the "Using RAPI Functions," section later in this chapter.

PegRapiInitEx

Syntax for this function is listed in the "Using RAPI Functions," section later in this chapter.

PegRapiUninit

Syntax for this function is listed in the "Using RAPI Functions," section later in this chapter.

RapiFreeBuffer

The `RapiFreeBuffer` function frees the memory on the desktop PC allocated by a call to `PegFindAllDatabases`, `PegFindAllFiles`, or `PegReadRecordProps`. Any RAPI function that allocates memory on the desktop PC on the user's behalf must be freed by calling the `RapiFreeBuffer` function. The syntax of the function is as follows:

```
STDAPI RapiFreeBuffer( LPVOID Buffer );
```

Object Store Functions

Table 14.2 lists the RAPI functions that enable an application to access the Windows CE object store.

Table 14.2

RAPI Object Store Functions

Function	Description
PegCloseHandle	Closes an open object handle.
PegCopyFile	Copies an existing file to a new file.
PegCreateDirectory	Creates a new directory.
PegCreateFile	Creates, opens, or truncates a file, pipe, communications resource, disk device, or console.
PegDeleteFile	Deletes an existing file.
PegFindAllFiles	Retrieves information about all files in a given path.
PegFindClose	Closes a search handle.
PegFindFirstFile	Searches a directory for a file.
PegFindNextFile	Continues a file search from a previous call to the PegFindFirstFile function.
PegGetFileAttributes	Returns the attributes of a file or directory.
PegGetFileSize	Retrieves the size, in bytes, of a file.
PegGetFileTime	Retrieves the date and time that a file was created, last accessed, and last modified.
PegGetStoreInformation	Gets the size of the object store and the amount of free space currently in it.
PegMoveFile	Renames an existing file or a directory (including all its children).
PegOidGetInfo	Retrieves information about an object in the object store.
PegReadFile	Reads data from a file.
PegRemoveDirectory	Deletes an existing empty directory.
PegSetEndOfFile	Moves the end-of-file position to the current position of the file pointer.

continues

Table 14.2

RAPI Object Store Functions, continued	
Function	Description
PegSetFileAttributes	Sets a file's attributes.
PegSetFilePointer	Moves the file pointer of an open file.
PegSetFileTime	Sets the date and time that a file was created, last accessed, or last modified.
PegWriteFile	Writes data to a file.

Most of the object store functions are identical to the Windows CE object store functions, which are presented elsewhere in this book. The functions PegFindAllFiles and PegGetStoreInformation are described in the following sections.

PegFindAllFiles

The PegFindAllFiles function retrieves information about all files and directories in the given directory of the Windows CE object store. The function copies information to an array of PEG_FIND_DATA structures. The syntax of the function is as follows:

```
BOOL PegFindAllFiles(
    LPCWSTR szPath,
    DWORD dwFlags,
    LPDWORD lpdwFoundCount,
    LPLPPEG_FIND_DATA ppFindDataArray
);
```

The parameters to PegFindAllFiles are defined in the following list:

- **LPCWSTR szPath**. Pointer to the name of the path in which to search for files.

- **DWORD dwFlags**. A combination of filter and retrieval flags. The filter flags specify what kinds of files to document, and the retrieval flags specify which members of the structure PEG_FIND_DATA to retrieve. The filter and retrieval flags can be a combination of the values in Table 14.3.

- **LPDWORD lpdwFoundCount**. Pointer to a variable that receives a count of the items found.

- **LPLPPEG_FIND_DATA ppFindDataArray**. Pointer to the address of an array of PEG_FIND_DATA structures that receive information about the found items. It is the application's responsibility to free the memory used by the array. To free the memory, you must call `RapiFreeBuffer`.

Table 14.3

Filter and Retrieval Flags

Filter or Retrieval Flag	Description
FAF_ATTRIB_NO_HIDDEN	Does not retrieve information for files or directories that have the hidden attribute set.
FAF_FOLDERS_ONLY	Only retrieves information for directories.
FAF_NO_HIDDEN_SYS_ROMMODULES	Does not retrieve information for files or directories that have the hidden, system, or inrom attributes set.
FAF_ATTRIB_CHILDREN	Retrieves the FILE_ATTRIBUTE_HAS_CHILDREN file attribute and copies it to the dwFileAttributes member.
FAF_ATTRIBUTES	Retrieves the file attributes and copies them to the dwFileAttributes member.
FAF_CREATION_TIME	Retrieves the file creation time and copies it to the ftCreationTime member.

continues

Table 14.3

Filter and Retrieval Flags, continued	
Filter or Retrieval Flag	Description
FAF_LASTACCESS_TIME	Retrieves the time the file was last accessed and copies it to the ftLastAccessTime member.
FAF_LASTWRITE_TIME	Retrieves the time the file was last written to and copies it to the ftLastWriteTime member.
FAF_SIZE_HIGH	Retrieves the high-order DWORD value of the file size and copies it to the nFileSizeHigh member.
FAF_SIZE_LOW	Retrieves the low-order DWORD value of the file size and copies it to the nFileSizeLow member.
FAF_OID	Retrieves the object identifier of the file and copies it to the dwOID member.
FAF_NAME	Retrieves the file name and copies it to the cFileName member.

PegGetStoreInformation

The PegGetStoreInformation function fills in a STORE_INFORMATION structure with the size of the object store and the amount of free space currently in the object store. This is the RAPI version of GetStoreInformation. The syntax of the function is as follows:

```
BOOL PegGetStoreInformation( LPSTORE_INFORMATION lpsi );
```

The lpsi parameter is a pointer to a STORE_INFORMATION structure to be filled by this function. The STORE_INFORMATION structure has two DWORD members—dwStoreSize and dwFreeSize—that specify the size (in bytes) of the object store and the amount of free space (in bytes) in the object store, respectively.

Database Functions

Table 14.4 lists the RAPI functions used to manipulate Windows CE database from an application running on the desktop PC.

Table 14.4

RAPI Database Functions

Function	Description
PegCreateDatabase	Creates a new database.
PegDeleteDatabase	Removes a database from the object store.
PegDeleteRecord	Deletes a record from a database.
PegFindAllDatabases	Retrieves information about all databases of a given type residing on the device.
PegFindFirstDatabase	Opens an enumeration context for all databases in the system.
PegFindNextDatabase	Retrieves the next database in an enumeration context.
PegOpenDatabase	Opens an existing database.
PegReadRecordProps	Reads properties from the current record.
PegSeekDatabase	Seeks a record in an open database.
PegSetDatabaseInfo	Sets various database parameters.
PegWriteRecordProps	Writes a set of properties to a single record.

Most of the remote database functions are identical in syntax to the Windows CE database functions, with the exception of the PegFindAllDatabases function.

PegFindAllDatabases

The PegFindAllDatabases function is a RAPI function that retrieves information about all databases of a given type that reside on the Handheld PC. This function copies information to an array of PEGDB_FIND_DATA structures. The syntax of the function is as follows:

```
BOOL PegFindAllDatabases(
    DWORD dwDbaseType,
    WORD wFlags,
    LPWORD cFindData,
    LPLPPEGDB_FIND_DATA ppFindData
);
```

The parameters to PegFindAllDatabases are detailed in the following list:

- **DWORD dwDbaseType**. Type identifier of the databases to seek.

- **WORD wFlags**. Members of the PEGDB_FIND_DATA structure that are to be retrieved. This parameter can be a combination of the following values:

  FAD_OID. Retrieves the OidDb member.

  FAD_FLAGS. Retrieves the DbInfo.dwFlags member.

  FAD_NAME. Retrieves the DbInfo.szDbaseName member.

  FAD_TYPE. Retrieves the DbInfo.dwDbaseType member.

  FAD_NUM_RECORDS. Retrieves the DbInfo.dwNumRecords member.

  FAD_NUM_SORT_ORDER. Retrieves the DbInfo.dwNumSortOrder member.

FAD_SORT_SPECS. Retrieves the DbInfo.rgSortSpecs member.

- **LPWORD cFindData**. Pointer to a variable that receives a count of the items found.

- **LPLPPEGDB_FIND_DATA ppFindData**. Pointer to the address of an array of PEGDB_FIND_DATA structures that receives information about the found items. It is the application's responsibility to free the memory used by the array. To free the memory, the application must call RapiFreeBuffer.

The members of the PEGDB_FIND_DATA are detailed in the following list:

- **PEGOID OidDb**. Specifies the object identifier of a database in the Windows CE object store.

- **PEGDBASEINFO DbInfo**. Specifies a PEGDBASEINFO structure that contains information about a database.

Registry Functions

Table 14.5 lists the RAPI functions that are used to access the Windows CE registry on the Handheld PC.

Table 14.5

RAPI Registry Functions

Function	Description
PegRegCloseKey	Releases a key handle.
PegRegCreateKeyEx	Creates a key.
PegRegDeleteKey	Deletes a key and all its descendants.
PegRegDeleteValue	Deletes a value from a key.
PegRegEnumKeyEx	Enumerates the subkeys of an open key.
PegRegEnumValue	Enumerates the values of an open key.

continues

Table 14.5

RAPI Registry Functions, continued

Function	Description
PegRegOpenKeyEx	Opens a key.
PegRegQueryInfoKey	Retrieves information about a key.
PegRegQueryValueEx	Retrieves the type and data for a value name associated with an open key.
PegRegSetValueEx	Stores data in the value field of an open key.

All the remote registry functions have the same syntax as the Windows CE Registry functions, which are described in Chapter 9, "Registry and File System."

Window Management Functions

The RAPI functions used to perform simple window management are listed in Table 14.6.

Table 14.6

RAPI Window Management Functions

Function	Description
PegGetClassName	Retrieves the name of a window's class.
PegGetWindow	Retrieves a window handle.
PegGetWindowLong	Retrieves information about a window.
PegGetWindowText	Gets the text of a window's title bar, if it has one.

System Functions

Table 14.7 lists the RAPI functions that grant system access to the Windows CE device.

Table 14.7

RAPI System Access Functions

Function	Description
PegCheckPassword	Compares a string to the system password.
PegCreateProcess	Creates a new process and its primary thread.
PegGetDesktopDeviceCaps	Retrieves device-specific information.
PegGetSystemInfo	Returns information about the current system.
PegGetSystemMetrics	Retrieves the system-configuration settings and the dimensions of display elements.
PegGetSystemPowerStatusEx	Retrieves the system power status.
PegGetVersionEx	Obtains extended information about the currently running version of the operating system.
PegGlobalMemoryStatus	Gets information on the physical and virtual memory of the system.
PegSHCreateShortcut	Creates a shortcut.
PegSHGetShortcutTarget	Retrieves the path to which a shortcut points.

Each of these functions is discussed in the following sections.

PegCheckPassword

The PegCheckPassword function compares a specified string to the system password. This function is the RAPI version of the Windows CE CheckPassword function. The syntax of the function is as follows:

```
BOOL PegCheckPassword( LPWSTR lpszPassword );
```

The lpszPassword parameter is a pointer to a wide character string to compare with the system password. The function returns TRUE if lpszPassword matches the system password or FALSE if it doesn't match.

PegGetDesktopDeviceCaps

The `PegGetDesktopDeviceCaps` function retrieves device-specific information about a specified device. This is the remote API version of the `GetDeviceCaps` function. The syntax of the function is as follows:

```
INT PegGetDesktopDeviceCaps( INT nIndex );
```

The nIndex parameter specifies the information to return. This parameter can be one of the following values listed in Table 14.8.

Table 14.8

PegGetDesktopDeviceCaps Information

Function	Description
DRIVERVERSION	The device driver version.
TECHNOLOGY	Device technology. The return value could be DT_PLOTTER, DT_RASDISPLAY, or DT_RASPRINTER.
HORZSIZE	Width, in millimeters, of the physical screen.
VERTSIZE	Height, in millimeters, of the physical screen.
HORZRES	Width, in pixels, of the screen.
VERTRES	Height, in raster lines, of the screen.
LOGPIXELSX	Number of pixels per logical inch along the screen width.
LOGPIXELSY	Number of pixels per logical inch along the screen height.
BITSPIXEL	Number of adjacent color bits for each pixel.
PLANES	Number of color planes.
NUMBRUSHES	Number of device-specific brushes.
NUMPENS	Number of device-specific pens.
NUMFONTS	Number of device-specific fonts.
NUMCOLORS	Number of entries in the device's color table, if the device has a color depth of no more than 8 bits per pixel. For devices with greater color depths, −1 is returned.

Function	Description
ASPECTX	Relative width of a device pixel used for line drawing.
ASPECTY	Relative height of a device pixel used for line drawing.
ASPECTXY	Diagonal width of the device pixel used for line drawing.
CLIPCAPS	Flag that indicates the clipping capabilities of the device. If the device can clip to a rectangle, it is 1. Otherwise, it is 0.
SIZEPALETTE	Number of entries in the system palette. This index is valid only if the device driver sets the RC_PALETTE bit in the RASTERCAPS.
NUMRESERVED	Number of reserved entries in the system palette. This index is valid only if the device driver sets the RC_PALETTE bit in the RASTERCAPS index and is available only if the driver is compatible with Windows version 3.0 or later.
COLORRES	Actual color resolution of the device, in bits per pixel. This index is valid only if the device driver sets the RC_PALETTE bit in the RASTERCAPS index and is available only if the driver is compatible with Windows version 3.0 or later.
RASTERCAPS	Value that indicates the raster capabilities of the device. The return value is RC_BITBLT, RC_PALETTE, or RC_STRETCHBLT.
CURVECAPS	Value that indicates the curve capabilities of the device.
LINECAPS	Value that indicates the line capabilities of the device. The return value is LC_POLYLINE, LC_WIDE, or LC_STYLED.
POLYGONALCAPS	Value that indicates the polygon capabilities of the device. The return value is PC_POLYGON, PC_RECTANGLE, PC_WIDE, or PC_STYLED.
TEXTCAPS	Value that indicates the text capabilities of the device.

Each of these functions is discussed in the following sections.

PegGetSystemInfo

The PegGetSystemInfo function returns information about the current system. This is the RAPI version of the GetSystemInfo function. The syntax of the function is as follows:

```
void PegGetSystemInfo( LPSYSTEM_INFO lpSystemInfo );
```

The lpSystemInfo parameter is a pointer to a SYSTEM_INFO structure to be filled in by this function. The SYSTEM_INFO structure has the following members:

- **DWORD dwOemId**. Always set to zero.

- **DWORD dwPageSize**. Returns the page size and specifies the granularity of page protection and commitment.

- **LPVOID lpMinimumApplicationAddress**. Returns the lowest memory address accessible to applications and dynamic-link libraries (DLLs).

- **LPVOID lpMaximumApplicationAddress**. Returns the highest memory address accessible to applications and DLLs.

- **DWORD dwActiveProcessorMask**. Returns a mask representing the set of processors configured into the system. Bit zero is processor zero; bit 31 is processor 31.

- **DWORD dwNumberOfProcessors**. Returns the number of processors in the system.

- **DWORD dwProcessorType**. Returns the processor type, which can be one of the following values:

    PROCESSOR_INTEL_386

    PROCESSOR_INTEL_486

    PROCESSOR_INTEL_PENTIUM

    PROCESSOR_MIPS_R2000

    PROCESSOR_MIPS_R3000

PROCESSOR_MIPS_R4000

PROCESSOR_HITACHI_SH3

PROCESSOR_ALPHA_21064

- **DWORD dwAllocationGranularity**. Returns the allocation granularity in which memory will be allocated. This value was hard-coded as 64K in the past, but other hardware architectures might require different values.

- **DWORD dwReserved**. Is reserved and not used.

PegGetSystemPowerStatusEx

The `PegGetSystemPowerStatusEx` function retrieves the power status of the system. This status indicates whether the system is running on AC or DC power and whether or not the batteries are currently charging. The power status also returns the remaining life of main and backup batteries. The `PegGetSystemPowerStatusEx` function is the RAPI version of the `GetSystemPowerStatusEx` function. The syntax of the function is as follows:

```
BOOL PegGetSystemPowerStatusEx(
    PSYSTEM_POWER_STATUS_EX pstatus,
    BOOL fUpdate
);
```

The fUpdate parameter specifies where to get the requested power information. If this parameter is set to TRUE, `PegGetSystemPowerStatusEx` gets the latest information from the device driver. Otherwise, the function retrieves cached information that could be out of date by several seconds.

The pstatus parameter is a pointer to the SYSTEM_POWER_STATUS_EX structure receiving the power status information. This structure has the following members:

- **BYTE ACLineStatus**. AC power status. This parameter can be a value of 0 for offline, 1 for online, or 255 for unknown status.

- **BYTE BatteryFlag**. Battery charge status. This parameter can be a value of 1 for high, 2 for low, 4 for critical, 8 for charging, 128 for no system battery, or 255 for unknown status.

- **BYTE BatteryLifePercent**. Percentage of full battery charge remaining. This member can be a value in the range 0 to 100, or 255 if status is unknown. All other values are reserved.

- **DWORD BatteryLifeTime**. Number of seconds of battery life remaining, or 0xFFFFFFFF if remaining seconds are unknown.

- **DWORD BatteryFullLifeTime**. Number of seconds of battery life when at full charge, or 0xFFFFFFFF if full lifetime is unknown.

- **BYTE BackupBatteryFlag**. Backup battery charge status, which must be one of the following:

    BATTERY_FLAG_HIGH

    BATTERY_FLAG_CRITICAL

    BATTERY_FLAG_CHARGING

    BATTERY_FLAG_NO_BATTERY

    BATTERY_FLAG_UNKNOWN

    BATTERY_FLAG_LOW

- **BYTE BackupBatteryLifePercent**. Percentage of full backup battery charge remaining. Must be in the range 0 to 100, or BATTERY_PERCENTAGE_UNKNOWN.

- **DWORD BackupBatteryLifeTime**. Number of seconds of backup battery life remaining, or BATTERY_LIFE_UNKNOWN if remaining seconds are unknown.

- **DWORD BackupBatteryFullLifeTime**. Number of seconds of backup battery life when at full charge, or BATTERY_LIFE_UNKNOWN if full lifetime is unknown.

PegSHCreateShortcut

The PegSHCreateShortcut function creates a shortcut. This is the RAPI version of the SHCreateShortcut function. The syntax of the function is as follows:

```
DWORD PegSHCreateShortcut( LPWSTR lpszShortcut, LPWSTR lpszTarget );
```

The szShortcut parameter is a pointer to a buffer that contains the name of the shortcut to create. Passing a NULL value for this parameter will cause an exception.

The szTarget parameter is a pointer to a buffer that contains the target path of the shortcut.

PegSHGetShortcutTarget

The PegSHGetShortcutTarget function retrieves the path to which the shortcut points. This is the RAPI version of the SHGetShortcutTarget function. The syntax of the function is as follows:

```
BOOL PegSHGetShortcutTarget(
    LPWSTR lpszShortcut,
    LPWSTR lpszTarget,
    int cbMax
);
```

The parameters to the PegSHGetShortcutTarget function are detailed in the following list:

- **LPWSTR szShortcut**. Pointer to a buffer that contains the name of the shortcut to retrieve.

- **LPWSTR szTarget**. Pointer to a buffer that gets the target path of the shortcut.

- **int cbMax**. Maximum number of characters to copy (size of szTarget buffer).

RAPI Example

An example of the Windows CE Remote API functionality can be seen in the example program used to create and populate the TravelManager's Windows CE database. This RAPI application creates the data for TravelManager that was retrieved and displayed with the changes from Chapter 10, "Windows CE Databases."

The RAPI example performs the following steps:

1. Initializes the RAPI connection.

2. Creates the TravelManager database with the `CreateDatabase` function.

3. Inserts some records into the database with the `InsertData` function.

4. Disconnects from the device.

The source code for this RAPI example follows and also can be found on the companion CD-ROM. See Appendix A, "Getting Started with the CD-ROM," for information on using the CD-ROM.

```
//--------------------------------------------------------
//
// Sample application from Windows CE Programming
//
// Description: This console application uses RAPI to
//              create a Windows CE database on the H/PC
//              and insert some records into the
//              database.
//
//--------------------------------------------------------


#include <windows.h>
#include <tchar.h>
#include <stdio.h>
#include <rapi.h>
```

```
// Function prototypes
PEGOID CreateDatabase();
BOOL InsertData(PEGOID PegOid);

int main( int argc, char *argv[])
{
        HRESULT hRapiResult;
        PEGOID PegOid;

        tprintf(TEXT("Initializing RAPI Connection..."));

        hRapiResult = PegRapiInit();

        if (FAILED(hRapiResult))
        {
                tprintf(TEXT("FAILED.\n"));
                return -1;
        }
        else
        {
                tprintf(TEXT("Success.\n"));
        }

                tprintf(TEXT("Creating TravelManager database..."));

        if ((PegOid = CreateDatabase()) == (PEGOID)NULL)
          {
                tprintf(TEXT("FAILED.\n"));
                return -1;
          }
        else
          {
                tprintf(TEXT("Success.\n"));
          }

          tprintf(TEXT("Inserting records..."));

      if (InsertData(PegOid) == FALSE)
          {
                tprintf(TEXT("FAILED.\n"));
                        return -1;
          }
          else
```

```
                  {
                          _tprintf(TEXT("Success.\n"));
                  }

              _tprintf(TEXT("Disconnecting from device.\n"));

      PegRapiUninit();

              _tprintf(TEXT("Database installation complete..\n"));
}

PEGOID CreateDatabase()
{
        PEGOID PegOid;
        TCHAR szDBName[PEGDB_MAXDBASENAMELEN];
        DWORD dwDBType;
              SORTORDERSPEC sortorders[1];

        tcscpy(szDBName, TEXT("TravelManager Database"));
        dwDBType = 123456;

        sortorders[0].propid = MAKELONG( PEGVT_FILETIME, 0);

        PegOid = PegCreateDatabase(szDBName, dwDBType, 1,
➥sortorders);

        if (PegOid == (PEGOID)NULL)
        {
                // Could get extended error info with
➥PegGetLastError
                        return (PEGOID)NULL;
        }

        return PegOid;
}

BOOL InsertData(PEGOID PegOid)
{
        HANDLE     hDB;
        PEGPROPVAL Properties[7];
        FILETIME   FileTime;
        SYSTEMTIME SystemTime;
        LPVOID     lpStr1, lpStr2, lpStr3;
        PEGOID pegoidRecord;
```

```
        hDB = PegOpenDatabase(&PegOid, NULL, 0, 0, NULL);
        if ( hDB == INVALID_HANDLE_VALUE)
        {
                // Could get extended error info with
➡PegGetLastError
                return FALSE;
        }

        // Insert record #1

        //Date - FILETIME type
        SystemTime.wYear = 1997;
        SystemTime.wMonth = 6;
            SystemTime.wDayOfWeek = 6;
        SystemTime.wDay = 14;
        SystemTime.wHour = 0;
        SystemTime.wMinute = 0;
        SystemTime.wSecond = 0;
        SystemTime.wMilliseconds = 0;

        SystemTimeToFileTime(&SystemTime,&FileTime);
        Properties[0].propid = MAKELONG( PEGVT_FILETIME, 0);
        Properties[0].wLenData = 0;
        Properties[0].wFlags = 0;
        Properties[0].val.filetime = FileTime;

        //Flight - USHORT type
        Properties[1].propid = MAKELONG( PEGVT_UI2, 1);
        Properties[1].wLenData = 0;
        Properties[1].wFlags = 0;
        Properties[1].val.uiVal = 1412;

        //From - LPWSTR type
        lpStr1 = LocalAlloc(LMEM_FIXED, 50 * sizeof(TCHAR));
        tcscpy(lpStr1, TEXT("Indianapolis"));

        Properties[2].propid = MAKELONG(PEGVT_LPWSTR, 2);
        Properties[2].wLenData = 0;
        Properties[2].wFlags = 0;
        Properties[2].val.lpwstr = lpStr1;

        //To - LPWSTR type
        lpStr2 = LocalAlloc(LMEM_FIXED, 50 * sizeof(TCHAR));
        tcscpy(lpStr2, TEXT("Seattle"));
```

```
Properties[3].propid = MAKELONG(PEGVT_LPWSTR, 3);
Properties[3].wLenData = 0;
Properties[3].wFlags = 0;
Properties[3].val.lpwstr = lpStr2;

//Departs - FILETIME type
SystemTime.wYear = 1997;
SystemTime.wMonth = 6;
SystemTime.wDayOfWeek = 6;
SystemTime.wDay = 14;
SystemTime.wHour = 8;
SystemTime.wMinute = 20;
SystemTime.wSecond = 0;
SystemTime.wMilliseconds = 0;

SystemTimeToFileTime(&SystemTime,&FileTime);
Properties[4].propid = MAKELONG( PEGVT_FILETIME, 4);
Properties[4].wLenData = 0;
Properties[4].wFlags = 0;
Properties[4].val.filetime = FileTime;

//Arrives - FILETIME type
SystemTime.wYear = 1997;
SystemTime.wMonth = 6;
SystemTime.wDayOfWeek = 6;
SystemTime.wDay = 14;
SystemTime.wHour = 11;
SystemTime.wMinute = 45;
SystemTime.wSecond = 0;
SystemTime.wMilliseconds = 0;

SystemTimeToFileTime(&SystemTime,&FileTime);
Properties[5].propid = MAKELONG( PEGVT_FILETIME, 5);
Properties[5].wLenData = 0;
Properties[5].wFlags = 0;
Properties[5].val.filetime = FileTime;

//Seat - LPWSTR type
lpStr3 = LocalAlloc(LMEM_FIXED, 50 * sizeof(TCHAR));
tcscpy(lpStr3, TEXT("11A"));

Properties[6].propid = MAKELONG(PEGVT_LPWSTR, 6);
Properties[6].wLenData = 0;
```

```
Properties[6].wFlags = 0;
Properties[6].val.lpwstr = lpStr3;

if (!PegWriteRecordProps(hDB, 0, 7, Properties))
{
        if( lpStr1 )
                LocalFree(lpStr1);
        if( lpStr2 )
                LocalFree(lpStr2);
        if( lpStr3 )
                LocalFree(lpStr3);

        CloseHandle(hDB);

        return FALSE;
}

// Insert record #2

//Date - FILETIME type
SystemTime.wYear = 1997;
SystemTime.wMonth = 6;
SystemTime.wDayOfWeek = 6;
SystemTime.wDay = 21;
SystemTime.wHour = 0;
SystemTime.wMinute = 0;
SystemTime.wSecond = 0;
SystemTime.wMilliseconds = 0;

SystemTimeToFileTime(&SystemTime,&FileTime);
Properties[0].propid = MAKELONG( PEGVT_FILETIME, 0);
Properties[0].wLenData = 0;
Properties[0].wFlags = 0;
Properties[0].val.filetime = FileTime;

//Flight - USHORT type
Properties[1].propid = MAKELONG( PEGVT_UI2, 1);
Properties[1].wLenData = 0;
Properties[1].wFlags = 0;
Properties[1].val.uiVal = 682;

//From - LPWSTR type
_tcscpy(lpStr1, TEXT("Seattle"));
```

```
Properties[2].propid = MAKELONG(PEGVT_LPWSTR, 2);
Properties[2].wLenData = 0;
Properties[2].wFlags = 0;
Properties[2].val.lpwstr = lpStr1;

//To - LPWSTR type
_tcscpy(lpStr2, TEXT("Indianapolis"));

Properties[3].propid = MAKELONG(PEGVT_LPWSTR, 3);
Properties[3].wLenData = 0;
Properties[3].wFlags = 0;
Properties[3].val.lpwstr = lpStr2;

//Departs - FILETIME type
SystemTime.wYear = 1997;
SystemTime.wMonth = 6;
SystemTime.wDayOfWeek = 6;
SystemTime.wDay = 21;
SystemTime.wHour = 14;
SystemTime.wMinute = 5;
SystemTime.wSecond = 0;
SystemTime.wMilliseconds = 0;

SystemTimeToFileTime(&SystemTime,&FileTime);
Properties[4].propid = MAKELONG( PEGVT_FILETIME, 4);
Properties[4].wLenData = 0;
Properties[4].wFlags = 0;
Properties[4].val.filetime = FileTime;

//Arrives - FILETIME type
SystemTime.wYear = 1997;
SystemTime.wMonth = 6;
SystemTime.wDayOfWeek = 6;
SystemTime.wDay = 21;
SystemTime.wHour = 21;
SystemTime.wMinute = 50;
SystemTime.wSecond = 0;
SystemTime.wMilliseconds = 0;

SystemTimeToFileTime(&SystemTime,&FileTime);
Properties[5].propid = MAKELONG( PEGVT_FILETIME, 5);
Properties[5].wLenData = 0;
Properties[5].wFlags = 0;
```

```
Properties[5].val.filetime = FileTime;

//Seat - LPWSTR type
_tcscpy(lpStr3, TEXT("8D"));

Properties[6].propid = MAKELONG(PEGVT_LPWSTR, 6);
Properties[6].wLenData = 0;
Properties[6].wFlags = 0;
Properties[6].val.lpwstr = lpStr3;

pegoidRecord = PegWriteRecordProps(hDB, 0, 7, Properties);

if( lpStr1 )
        LocalFree(lpStr1);
if( lpStr2 )
        LocalFree(lpStr2);
if( lpStr3 )
        LocalFree(lpStr3);

CloseHandle(hDB);

if (pegoidRecord == 0)
{
        return FALSE;
}
else
{
        return TRUE;
}


}
```

A

Getting Started with the CD-ROM

The companion CD-ROM contains the sample source code and executable files for the examples presented in this book.

The sample code is organized according to chapter; for each chapter of the book (starting with Chapter 5), a corresponding directory on the CD-ROM contains the sample code or application for that chapter. The TRVLMGR directory on the CD-ROM contains the final version of the TravelManager application developed throughout the book.

The source code on the CD-ROM may be freely copied and used in the development of your own Windows CE programming projects.

Installation

The source code for each chapter is organized in a Visual C++ 5.0 project workspace. Each project has been built for all the supported project configurations—the proper executable can be copied directly to the emulation environment or Windows CE device.

If you would like to modify or extend a particular project, follow these steps:

1. Create a directory on your PC, for instance:

   c:\wceprog\trvlmgr

2. Copy the contents of the desired directory from the CD-ROM to the directory on the PC:

   copy f:\trvlmgr*.* c:\wceprog\trvlmgr

3. Open the project workspace file from the new directory in Visual C++ 5.0.

4. Modify and rebuild the project as desired.

Technical Support

If you cannot get the CD to install properly or you need assistance with a particular situation in the book, please feel free to check out the Knowledge Base on our Web site at http://www.superlibrary.com/ general/support. We have answers to our most Frequently Asked Questions listed there. If you do not find your specific question answered, please contact Macmillan Technical Support at 317-581-3833. We can also be reached by e-mail at support@mcp.com.

Index

M